Icelandic Constitutional Reform

People, Processes, Politics

Edited by Ágúst Þór Árnason and Catherine Dupré

Routledge
Taylor & Francis Group
LONDON AND NEW YORK

First published 2021
by Routledge
2 Park Square, Milton Park, Abingdon, Oxon OX14 4RN

and by Routledge
605 Third Avenue, New York, NY 10017

First issued in paperback 2022

Routledge is an imprint of the Taylor & Francis Group, an informa business

British Library Cataloguing-in-Publication Data
A catalogue record for this book is available from the British Library

Library of Congress Cataloging-in-Publication Data
A catalog record for this book has been requested

ISBN 13: 978-0-367-55708-9 (pbk)
ISBN 13: 978-1-138-49185-4 (hbk)
ISBN 13: 978-1-351-03190-5 (ebk)

DOI: 10.4324/9781351031905

Typeset in Times New Roman
by Apex CoVantage, LLC

This collection is dedicated to
Elín Gudbjörg Sveinsdóttir, Gudjona Gudjonsdóttir,
Jóhann Hjaltason, and Þórarinn Auðunsson
For conversations about life, politics, and religion
From as far back as my memory goes

and to
Ágúst Þór Árnason
who taught me so much.

Contents

Preface

Ágúst Þór Árnason died on 11 April 2019, and when we discussed our work on this collection shortly before his death, there was no doubt in our minds that he should remain a full co-editor. By the time of my last visit to him in April 2019, we had closely reviewed all the chapters but one, finalised the core contents of the introduction, and clarified all outstanding editorial issues. We had worked closely together on this project since organising the 2016 conference in Akureyri and discussing the book proposal in 2017. In 2018, our work intensified as most of the chapters were delivered in that year and we finished editing the presidential address. We jointly interviewed the Prime Minister in September 2018 and decided on how best to edit her contribution. We also started discussing Ágúst Þór's chapter from an editorial perspective. However, he did not have time to complete his own chapter, so we agreed that I would write it up for him. We were grateful to the publisher for accommodating this change of plan and accepting a slightly different presentation for his chapter.

Few have understood Icelandic constitutionalism and the constitutional reform process like Ágúst Þór did, and I have completed this collection drawing on our discussions. For their invaluable assistance in providing information about Ágúst Þór's work, I wish to thank Guðmundur Alfreðsson and Sigríður Vilhjálmsdóttir, Project Manager at the Library of the University of Akureyri. I am also grateful to all contributors for their support with the final stage of editing, especially to Skúli Magnússon.

Catherine Dupré
Truro, 9 April 2020

Acknowledgements

Rooted in years of reflection and close observation, this collection is the result of three eventful years between 2016 and 2019. In spring 2016, the Panama Papers scandal led to the resignation of the Prime Minister, and it became obvious that political changes were afoot. This meant that completing the revision of the 1944 Constitution was unlikely to happen within that parliamentary term as had been intended. After so much work on the constitutional reform by so many since 2009, disappointment was bitter, and a sense of failure was widely shared. The reform process that was originally designed to unite Icelanders had generated deep disagreement and resentment that divided families and friends, MPs and voters, lay drafters and experts. Ágúst Þór and I decided that it was time to take stock of the reform process and to try to understand it in its entirety, focussing on what might have been achieved and seeking to identify what lessons might be learned from this unprecedented experience so as to take the discussion forward. This edited collection arose out of a conference entitled 'The Icelandic Constitutional Reform: People, Principles, Processes' that we jointly convened at the University of Akureyri (UNAK). It was held on 23–24 September 2016 ahead of the anticipated general election of 29 October 2016. We are grateful to the Prime Minister's Office and the parliamentary Constitutional Committee who sponsored the conference and agreed to share their reflections and experience. We are also grateful to Guðni Th. Jóhannesson, the President of the Republic, for accepting to deliver the opening address, which has become the first chapter in this collection.

The conference discussions encouraged us to pursue this project as an edited collection. Contributors and topics were carefully selected so as to construct an overview of the whole reform process considered in its wider context, and providing a unique first-hand account of drafters, together with critical and theoretical reflections. We wish to thank warmly all contributors who engaged so constructively and patiently with the peer review and editing processes, making this collection – we hope – much more than the sum of its parts. We are particularly grateful to Katrín Jakobsdóttir for maintaining her contribution after she became the Prime Minister in November 2017 and for agreeing to give us an interview to replace the chapter that she no longer had time to write. Garrett Barden, Catherine Caine, Günter Frankenberg, Hans Petter Graver, Mike Karlsson, James May, Jakob Th. Möller, Alex Prichard, and Cheryl Saunders provided valuable feedback on draft chapters and shared their expertise on specific issues discussed in this collection. Stephen Skinner's generous linguistic assistance was essential for polishing some chapters. Last but not least, we are grateful to the Routledge editorial team, especially Alison Kirk and Emily Summers for their understanding and support with the various changes we had to make as the project developed.

Finally, we wish to express our deep gratitude to the family of Ágúst Þór Árnason and to all friends who supported us in so many wonderful and generous ways towards the end.

Ágúst Þór Árnason and Catherine Dupré
Akureyri, 9 April 2019

In Memoriam[1]: Ágúst Þór Árnason

26 May 1954–11 April 2019

Ágúst Þór Árnason was involved in the constitutional reform process from the start when he was selected by the parliament to sit on the Constitutional Commission (2010–2011) along with six other experts. He was a very active member of the Commission whose task was inter alia to organise the National Forum of 950 citizens and to provide the Constitutional Assembly (which became the Constitutional Council) with materials and ideas for a future Constitution of Iceland. Ágúst Þór distinguished himself by continuing to be involved in the reform process after the Commission had fulfilled its mission and by providing advice formally and informally. Although his contributions were sometimes critical, he always endeavoured to unlock difficult situations and to move the reform forward. For instance, together with Skúli Magnússon, he published a series of articles and gave talks on the unfolding process in order to promote better understanding of it amongst the public.

Ágúst Þór believed in people's ability to mature and prosper, and he considered the constitutional reform as a means to enhance the quality of democracy and make Iceland a better place to live for everyone. A tireless and enthusiastic activist, he was unhindered by disciplinary boundaries or professional identities. He worked as a journalist for the Icelandic State Radio when living in Berlin, where he covered the collapse of communism and the first free elections in (former) East Germany. Back in Iceland, he maintained his involvement in journalism and his interest in democracy throughout his life, while especially focussing on promoting human rights. Among many undertakings, this led him to become one of the co-founders – and for years director – of the Icelandic Center for Human Rights in Reykjavik and of the Reykjavik Academy for independent scholars of the humanities. Education was another long-standing commitment of his, and he became a

1 This concise biography is intended to convey a sense of who Ágúst Þór Árnason was and to record some of the ways in which he contributed to a better understanding and practice of law, human rights, philosophy and politics, in Iceland and beyond. It was co-written by Guðmundur Alfreðsson and Catherine Dupré, with our thanks to Margrét Heinreksdóttir and Skúli Magnússon for their comments on earlier drafts.

core member of the team setting up the Law School at the University of Akureyri (UNAK) under the leadership of Professor Mike Karlsson. They favoured a cross-disciplinary approach to law teaching, actively combining the appreciation and understanding of current law with legal history, philosophy, political science, and comparative law. Trained in political philosophy and legal theory at Berlin Free University and Frankfurt University in the 1980s and 1990s, Ágúst Þór developed and taught many courses at UNAK, including comparative constitutional law, constitutional theory, sociology of law, and theory of rights. He followed closely the constitutional developments in the Faroe Islands and in Greenland and became one of the co-founders of the Polar Law Program at UNAK, where, amongst other activities, he was in charge of overseeing student exchanges with Greenland. He also established the Polar Law Institute (www.polarlaw.is) in co-operation with Guðmundur Alfreðsson and Arngrímur B. Jóhannsson. His educational endeavour was not confined to the university classroom, and he developed human rights projects involving local school children. In Akureyri, he also founded a series of philosophical discussions on wide-ranging current issues, known as the 'philosophy café,' held at the Bláa Kannan café, which celebrated its tenth anniversary in November 2018.

Ágúst Þór had a deep understanding of Icelandic constitutionalism and unique knowledge of its complexity, historical roots, and human dimensions. His involvement in the constitutional reform process was the culmination of lifelong dedication to greater freedom and democracy. He was a loyal friend and a constant source of inspiration and unfailing support and motivation. His love for Iceland was combined with a commitment to international cooperation, and he always sought to put Iceland on the world map while bringing back new ideas and people in the pursuit of mutual learning and friendships. He was determined to make the constitutional revision happen; discussing it with friends and contributors brought him special happiness in the last days of his life.

Contributors and editors

Ágúst Þór Árnason (1954–2019) taught constitutional law, legal theory, and sociology of law at the University of Akureyri. He sat on the Constitutional Commission (2010–2011) in charge of organising the 2010 National Forum and preparing the work of the Constitutional Assembly/Council. See also the *In Memoriam*.

Catherine Dupré is Associate Professor of Comparative Constitutional Law at the University of Exeter. She has studied processes of constitutional change and reform in Hungary (post-communism and since 2010) and in the UK since 1998. Her main focus in recent years has been the connections between the concept of human dignity as a foundation of human rights and the development of constitutional democracy in Europe. She is the author of *Importing the Law in Post-Communist Transitions: The Hungarian Constitutional Court and the Right to Human Dignity* (Hart Publishing 2003) and of *The Age of Dignity: Human Rights and Constitutionalism in Europe* (Hart Publishing 2015). She has been following the Icelandic constitutional changes since 2008, when she first visited the University of Akureyri as a guest lecturer.

Thorvaldur Gylfason is Professor of Economics at the University of Iceland. He has contributed regularly to Icelandic media since the mid-1980s, writing a weekly column for *Fréttablaðið*, Iceland's largest daily newspaper (2003–2019), and for *Stundin* since 2019. He was critical of Iceland's economic path leading to the 2008 financial crash, put his name forward in the Constitutional Assembly election in 2010, and was elected. In his writings, he has consistently advocated for national ownership of natural resources, electoral reform through equal apportionment of seats in Parliament, and increased transparency in public affairs, three hallmarks of the 2011 Constitutional Council Proposal. Since then, he has published several scholarly articles on Iceland and its constitution in English as well as in Icelandic.

Kristrún Heimisdóttir was a Member of Parliament between 2003 and 2009 for the Social Democratic Alliance. She was on the front line of the management of the financial crisis that hit Iceland in 2008 during which she served as the political advisor of the Foreign Minister (2007–2009). As the political advisor of the

Minister of Social Affairs (2009–2010), she worked on the ground-breaking bill on debt restructuring as part of a cross-party cooperation, and she also served as political advisor to the Minister of Economics (2010–2011). Between 2013 and 2015, she was the director of the Chamber of Industry. She also held various academic positions in Iceland, in particular as Associate Professor at the University of Akureyri (2011–2013). She is currently registered as a PhD student with a thesis on the financial crisis using legal theory of finance at Colombia University (NYC).

Katrín Jakobsdóttir is an Icelandic politician serving as the twenty-eighth Prime Minister of Iceland since 30 November 2017. She has been a member of the Alþing (the Icelandic Parliament) for the Reykjavík North constituency since 2007. She became deputy chairperson of the Left-Green Movement in 2003 and has been their chairperson since 2013. Katrín Jakobsdóttir was Iceland's Minister for Education, Science and Culture and of Nordic Co-Operation from 1 February 2009 to 23 May 2013. She was a member of the Constitutional Committee between 2013 and 2016, and she is now leading the work on constitutional revision in Iceland's Parliament.

Guðni Th. Jóhannesson is the President of the Republic of Iceland, elected in June 2016 and re-elected in June 2020, and formerly Professor of History at the University of Iceland. He studied at Oxford University and graduated with an MSt degree in history in 1999. In 2003, he completed his PhD in history from Queen Mary, University of London. He authored a number of books on the lives of some of the presidents of the Republic and articles on the role and status of the president of the Republic. Guðni Th. Jóhannesson was also active as a political commentator on the role and the status of the president of the Icelandic Republic. He is the author of *The Collapse: Iceland on the Verge of Bankruptcy and Dissolution* (JPV, Reykjavík, 2009).

Aðalheiður Jóhannsdóttir is Professor of Environmental Law in the Faculty of Law at the University of Iceland. She was involved as an expert adviser on environmental law issues in several stages of the constitutional reform process. She wrote expert opinions on questions of environmental law for the Constitutional Council (2011) and the parliamentary Constitutional Committee (2013–2016).

Skúli Magnússon became Cand. Jur. (University of Iceland) in 1995 and Mag. Jur. (University of Oxford) in 1998. He is at present Judge at Reykjavik District Court and Associate Professor at the University of Iceland, as well as ad hoc judge for the European Court of Human Rights. He was elected by the Alþing to be a member of the Constitutional Commission of 2010–2011 and later appointed by the Prime Minister to the 2013–2016 Constitutional Committee, where he sat until 2014. He is the author of a number of publications in the field of legal theory, constitutional law, and European law.

Salvör Nordal has a PhD in philosophy and was Director of the Centre for Ethics and Assistant Professor at the University of Iceland until 2017 when she became the Ombudsman for Children in Iceland. She was a member of the Working Group on Ethics, which formed part of a Special Investigation Commission set up by the Icelandic Parliament, 2009–2010, to investigate the fall of the Icelandic banks. She was elected to the Constitutional Assembly in 2010 and chaired the Constitutional Council in 2011. Salvör Nordal has been active in academic discussion on the Icelandic constitution experiment and written several papers on the current situation in Iceland.

Jón Ólafsson is Professor of Comparative Cultural Studies at the University of Iceland and holds a PhD in philosophy from Columbia University. He has published widely on the constitutional reform and has edited *Lýdraedistilraunir* (*Democratic Experiments*, 2014), which discusses democratic innovation in Iceland following the financial crisis. He has a special interest in direct participation and has taken part in arranging public discussion on the constitution in a form similar to that of the National Forum in November 2010. Together with 521 candidates, Jón Ólafsson ran for office as a member of the Constitutional Council (originally called the Constitutional Assembly), but he was not elected.

Páll Þórhallsson is currently Director of the Department of Legislative Affairs at the Prime Minister's Office. He was Chairman of the Constitutional Committee (2014–2016), which drafted the three constitutional proposals in 2016. He also chaired the expert group, which advised Parliament on the 2012 Constitutional Bill based on the 2011 Proposal for a New Constitution delivered by the Constitutional Council to Parliament on 29 July 2011. He also sat on the Preparatory Committee established by Act 90/2010.

Ragnheiður Elfa Þorsteinsdóttir is Lecturer in Law at the University of Akureyri, specialising in public international law, European law, and environmental law, which she has taught as part of the Polar Law Program. She served as Head of the Faculty of Law (2015–2016, and in 2019) and was previously Director of the Natural Resources and Environment Department at the Ministry for Foreign Affairs (2009–2013). In that role, she participated in international negotiations on climate change and in the 2012 UN Conference on sustainable development, and her responsibilites included fisheries resources, energy, and other environmental matters. Ragnheiður Elfa Þorsteinsdóttir also worked as the chief lawyer at the Ministry for the Environment between 1995 and 1998.

Björg Thorarensen is Professor of Constitutional Law, International Human Rights Law, and Data Protection Law at the University of Iceland and the chairperson of the board of the Icelandic Data Protection Authority. She has actively participated in repeated revision processes of the Icelandic Constitution since 2005. This includes membership of committees appointed by the government to revise certain parts of the 1944 Constitution: one operating between 2005 and 2007 and another advisory working group appointed by the Prime Minister in February 2009, which submitted a bill to amend the Constitution in March 2009. She furthermore advised on the drafting of the bill on the Constitutional

Assembly, which became Act 90/2010. She was appointed by the Alþing to the 2010–2011 Constitutional Commission. More recently, she has also advised the current committee of chairmen of all the political parties in the Alþing appointed by the Prime Minister, Katrín Jakobsdóttir, in the spring of 2018, on the revision of selected parts of the constitution.

The constitutional reform at a glance[1]

Translating is an essential part of any engagement with comparative law. In the absence of a uniform translation of phrases referring to key stages, institutions and documents in the constitutional reform process, editorial choices are set out and explained here.

Icelandic uses two special characters (in addition to accented vowels), that are sometimes anglicised: e.g. Guðni/Gudni and Þór/Thór.

Framework of the constitutional reform process (chronological order)

Act 90/2010 on the Constitutional Assembly: www.thjodfundur2010.is/other_files/2010/doc/Act-on-a-Constitutional-Assembly.pdf

Althing resolution (Um skipan Stjórnlagaráðs) *19/139 of 24 March 2011 appointing the Constitutional Council members:* www.althingi.is/altext/139/s/1120.html

Act 31/2011 repealing Act 90/2010 with immediate effect: www.althingi.is/altext/139/s/1280.html

Constitutional Act 91/2013 on the interim constitutional revision procedure: www.althingi.is/altext/142/s/0088.html

End of the constitutional reform process: 30 April 2017 as per Act 91/2013: www.althingi.is/altext/142/s/0088.html

Bodies involved in the constitutional reform (chronological order)

- *Alþingi (Althingi or Althing): the Icelandic mono-cameral Parliament:* www.althingi.is/english
- *2010–2011 Constitutional Commission (Stjórnlaganefnd) chaired by Guðrún Pétursdóttir*

  As it was designed to prepare the work of the Constitutional Assembly, it is sometimes referred to as 'preparatory Constitutional Commission.' The seven Commission members were directly elected by the Parliament.

1 With thanks to Björg Thorarensen and Skúli Magnússon.

Established under Act 90/2010, the Commission was designed to 'work independently' (interim provision of Act 90/2010). Information about the Constitutional Commission was included on the website of the Constitutional Council indicated below.

- *2010 National Forum (Þjóðfundur):* www.thjodfundur2010.is/english/

  To be distinguished from the 2009 National Gathering convened by the Anthill (Mauraþúfan) organisation (www.thjodfundur2009.is/thjodfundur/maurathufan/). The Icelandic language uses the same word for what is translated here as 'gathering' to refer to the 2009 meeting held *outside* the constitutional reform framework, and as 'forum' to refer to the 2010 meeting that was part of the constitutional reform process (see National Forum website above).

- *2011 Constitutional Council (Stjornlagarad), chaired by Salvör Nordal:* http://stjornlagarad.is/english/

  Body of 25 members originally elected to form the consultative Constitutional Assembly (Stjórnlagaþing) but eventually appointed by the parliament after the Supreme Court invalidated the election on technical grounds.

- *2013–2017 Constitutional Committee (Stjórnarskrárnefnd), chaired by Páll Þórhallsson:* www.stjornarradid.is/verkefni/stjornskipan-og-thjodartakn/stjornarskrain/stjornarskrarnefnd-2013-2017/.

  This Committee was set up by the Prime Minister on the basis of nominations from political parties, i.e. the majority parties nominated two members each, and the minority parties one each. Its members, however, were not necessarily members of the Parliament. It has to be distinguished from the 2010–2011 Constitutional Commission (see preceding entry) and the standing Constitutional and Supervisory Committee (see next entry).

- *Constitutional and Supervisory Committee (Stjórnskipunar – og eftirlitsnefnd): standing committee in the Althing in charge of constitutional issues:* www.althingi.is/english/members-of-parliament/standing-committees-/

Key documents and constitutional bills

- *The 2011 two-volume Report of the Constitutional Commission.*

  Volume I: www.stjornlagarad.is/other_files/stjornlagarad/skyrsla-stjornlaganefndar/skyrsla_stjornlaganefndar_fyrra_bindi.pdf-
  Volume II: www.stjornlagarad.is/other_files/stjornlagarad/skyrsla-stjornlaganefndar/skyrsla_stjornlaganefndar_seinna_bindi.pdf

- *The Proposal for a New Constitution with a Commentary (Frumvarp til stjórnarskipunarlaga ásamt skýringum) of 29 July 2011:* www.stjornlagarad.is/other_files/stjornlagarad/Frumvarp-enska.pdf

- *The 2012 Constitutional Bill (Frumvarp til stjórnarskipunarlaga):* www.althingi.is/altext/141/s/0510.html

  Based on the text of the 2011 Proposal (see above entry) after some revision made by the Constitutional and Supervisory Committee. Presented to the parliament on 16 November 2012, it was ultimately not voted on by the Althing before the general election in April 2013.

- *The 2016 Constitutional Bill (Frumvarp til stjórnarskipunarlaga), including three draft constitutional provisions: articles 79, 80, and 81:* www.althingi.is/altext/145/s/1577.html

  This was to be added to the 1944 Constitution if approved under the Article 79 of the Constitution procedure. It was presented to the Althing by Prime Minister Sigurður Ingi Jóhannsson on 25 August 2016. The Althing did not get to the final round of discussion, nor was the bill voted on by the parliament before it was dissolved ahead of the early election of 29 October 2016.

1 Introduction

Making sense of the Icelandic constitutional reform[1]

Catherine Dupré

The key features of the Icelandic constitutional reform are apparently well known: it arose in the context of total collapse of the banking system in October 2008, with demands for a new constitution being made in a revolution during which, in the coldest and darkest months of the year, Icelanders took to the streets and surrounded Parliament (Althing), equipped with no more than pots and pans, to demand justice and a new government.[2] Outside Iceland, the most often acclaimed feature of the reform is the unprecedented involvement of ordinary Icelanders through a so-called crowdsourcing process, which resulted in a proposal for a brand-new constitution at the end of July 2011.[3] In contrast, the reform's most frequently deplored feature is no doubt its inability to produce any constitutional revision at all by the time it came to a formal end on 30 April 2017. For some, this apparent failure proves the parliament's unwillingness to adopt a new constitution presented as having been mostly drafted by the people. For others, it testifies to the resilience of the 1944 Constitution, which might need some specific amendments but does not need to be replaced by a brand-new text. A sense of anticlimax is shared by many if not all.

1 This introduction is based on the detailed outline that Ágúst Þór and I discussed and developed together, but he had no time to write it up with me. With thanks to Günter Frankenberg for his comments on an earlier version of this text.

2 Jérôme Skalski, *La révolution des casseroles: Chronique d'une nouvelle constitution pour l'Islande* (La Contre Allée 2012); Árni Daníel Júlíusson and Magnús Sveinn Helgasson, 'The Roots of the Saucepan Revolution in Iceland' in Christina Flesher Fominaya and Laurence Cox (eds), *Understanding European Movements: New Social Movements, Global Justice Struggles, Anti-Austerity Protest* (Routledge 2013) 189; Jón Gunnar Bernburg, *Economic Crisis and Mass Protest: The Pots and Pans Revolution in Iceland* (Routledge 2016).

3 Hélène Landemore, 'Inclusive Constitution-Making: The Icelandic Experiment' (2015) 23 *The Journal of Political Philosophy* 166 and 'What Is a Good Constitution? Assessing the Constitutional Proposal in the Icelandic Experiment' in Tom Ginsburg and Aziz Huq (eds), *Assessing Constitutional Performance* (Cambridge University Press 2016) 71; Anne Meuwese, 'Popular Constitution-Making: The Case of Iceland' in Dennis J Galligan and Mila Versteeg (eds), *The Social and Political Foundations of Constitutions* (Cambridge University Press 2013) 469, 481–485; and Alexander Hudson, 'When Does Public Participation Make a Difference? Evidence from Iceland's Crowdsourced Constitution' (2017) *Policy and the Internet* 185.

Has nothing happened, and were all these years of hard work and intense discussions ultimately a pointless experience, a waste of time, and a missed opportunity? Of course not. While there may be something of a paradox in dedicating a whole volume to a constitutional reform that ultimately introduced no change at all to the constitution in force, our starting point is that this apparently fruitless or failed reform was an incredibly rich and innovative process that deserves closer intellectual engagement and comprehensive recording. Despite the fact that no new constitution was adopted, these years of discussion and work have arguably transformed the ways in which the Icelandic Constitution is perceived, shedding new light on the 1944 text.[4] In Iceland, this might hopefully be informative for future reform of the Constitution.[5] Seen in its wider European perspective, this was the first (and so far only) reform process of this magnitude to take place in a democratic context and manner in the twenty-first century.[6] Its many innovations have triggered complex theoretical questions about the nature of constitutions, their purposes and contents, as well as about the best ways of adopting and reforming them. As a result, while it might be tempting to fit the Icelandic reform into existing theoretical frameworks, the methodology underpinning this collection does not try to do so. Instead, the volume aims to understand, as far as possible, the reform *as it was* before attempting to make sense of it from an (a priori) theoretical perspective. If anything, our hypothesis is that the reform does not prove any legal or political theory (or political agenda for that matter) right or wrong, but rather that it challenges scholars, politicians, and activists to rethink assumptions and to revisit what we thought we knew about constitutions, their drafting and adoption processes. The first step towards this is to seek to form a comprehensive picture of what happened during the long reform process and to document its key stages and issues.

Aims and scope of the collection

Against this background, this collection has three principal aims. The first aim is to position the reform process in its wider context and to seek to nuance two frequent assumptions. Firstly, while the financial crisis undeniably played a key role in

4 Baldvin Thor Bergsson, 'The Constitution as a Political Tool in Iceland: From the Periphery to the Center of the Political Debate' in Paul Blokker (ed), *Constitutional Acceleration within the European Union and Beyond* (Routledge 2018) 156.

5 The Prime Minister's plan is to undertake the reform over the next two parliamentary terms (2018–2025), on a cross-party basis. In terms of substance, the first term (2018–2021) focusses on natural resources, protection of the environment, direct democracy, constitutional amendments, status of the Icelandic language, and finally the chapter on the Executive (President, Cabinet of Ministers and Ministers); see: official website. www.stjornarradid.is/verkefni/stjornskipan-og-thjodartakn/stjornarskrain/stjornarskrarendurskodun-2018-2025/

6 Contrast with Hungary in 2010–2011: Gábor Attila Tóth (ed), *Constitution for a Disunited Nation: On Hungary's 2011 Fundamental Law* (Central European University Press 2012). More generally, see: Xenophon Contiades (ed), *Constitutions in the Global Financial Crisis: A Comparative Analysis* (Ashgate 2013).

triggering demands for constitutional reform, the causal link between the two cannot be presumed: the consequences of the banking collapse were tackled through a different route,[7] and none of the revision proposals (or bills) was designed to address the complex relationship between constitutionalism and financial capitalism. Similarly, the so-called 'pots and pans revolution' was a unique moment of popular uprising;[8] however, whether it justified engaging a constitutional reform outside the framework provided by the 1944 Constitution is another question. This approach, which was chosen by Social Democrat Prime Minister Jóhanna Sigurðardóttir in 2009, has variously been understood as a positive and necessary innovation attempting to address people's lack of trust in politicians, as a constitutional revolution calling for a brand-new constitution or as questioning the 1944 constitutional framework perceived as making it impossible to adopt any changes. The collection brings to light older calls for a new constitution, which according to some go as far back as the adoption of the current Constitution in 1944,[9] as well as more recent projects to reform some aspects of the Constitution, which had not been brought to fruition by 2009 and which, following the Icelandic procedure (set out later) of constitutional reform, tended to simply disappear. Finally, it is important to note that the reform at the heart of this collection was preceded by seven successful reforms of the 1944 Constitution on a range of specific issues.[10]

The collection's second aim is to document and analyse the constitutional reform considered in its entirety from 2009 to 2017, including the drafting process as well as its substantive outcomes. In terms of time frame, the collection spans the events between the early days of 2009, when the first calls for a constitutional revision were heard in the media, and 30 April 2017, when the period attributed by the interim revision procedure under Constitutional Act 91/2013 elapsed.[11] This encompasses four main stages in terms of drafting (and preparation towards it) and four bodies: (1) the 2010–2011 Constitutional Commission of seven members, (2) the 2010 National Forum of 950 Icelanders, randomly selected on the basis of the National Population Register and held on 6 November 2010, which was designed to identify the peoples' values and views on constitutional issues, (3) the Constitutional Council (2011) originally called the Constitutional Assembly, and (4) the Constitutional Committee (2013–2017). This collection does not single out the so-called crowdsourcing involved in the drafting of the 2011 Proposal for a New Constitution as a separate process. This is partly because it has been the most visible dimension (certainly to outsiders) of the constitutional reform and partly

7 Valur Ingimundarson, Philippe Urfalino, and Irma Erlingsdóttir (eds), *Iceland's Financial Crisis: The Politics of Blame, Protest, and Reconstruction* (Routledge 2016).

8 Bernburg (n 2).

9 Notably, this was the view of Sveinn Björnsson, the Governor of Iceland (1941–1944) and its first president in 1944.

10 Ágúst Þór Árnason and Martin Scheinin, 'Republic of Iceland' in Gisbert H. Flanz (ed), *Constitutions of the Countries of the World*, Release 99–1 (Oceana Publications 1999) ix.

11 The text is available on www.althingi.is/altext/142/s/0088.html

because this topic, including the use of the term 'crowdsourcing' deserves a fuller investigation than could be undertaken here.[12]

The collection also discusses, albeit in different degrees of depth, all the constitutional proposals that were produced as part of the reform process. In chronological order, these are (1) the two-volume Report that the Constitutional Commission delivered to the Constitutional Council on 6 April 2011, which, while not intended to be a draft constitution as such, offered two versions of possible (re)formulation of some constitutional provisions; (2) the 2011 Proposal for a New Constitution delivered by the Constitutional Council to the parliament on 29 July 2011; (3) the 2012 Constitutional Bill introduced in parliament on 16 November 2012 (largely based on a slightly revised version of the 2011 Proposal) but not voted on before the 2013 general election; and finally (4) the 2016 Constitutional Bill bringing together three different provisions (Articles 79, 80, and 81) presented to parliament by interim Prime Minister Sigurður Ingi Jóhannsson (Progressive Party) on 25 August before the early election of 29 October 2016 but not voted on in parliament before its dissolution.

The collection's third aim is to start reflecting on the significance of the Icelandic constitutional reform. The end date of the period under scrutiny in this collection, 2017, might be seen as a turning point for Iceland in many respects. That year was when the constitutional reform process, started in 2009, came to its formal end on 30 April; it was also when Icelandic politics returned to some sort of 'normality' (if there is such a thing) with the end of unstable coalition governments that had characterised the period from spring 2016 to November 2017, and when Katrín Jakobsdóttir was appointed Prime Minister (Left-Green Movement). Moreover, the Icelandic economy seemed to have recovered, and Icelanders seemed to have moved on, with their feelings about the constitutional reform apparently no longer running so high. In the autumn of 2016, when Ágúst Þór and I discussed how we might move forward the work of our conference on the constitutional reform, we felt this was a good time to start reflecting on the journey travelled. The elapsed 30 April 2017 deadline gave us a meaningful closing point for our project. We wanted to start recording events and issues while they were still fresh in people's minds, especially on those who had been directly involved in this unprecedented process and whom we invited to contribute to this collection.

Issues of method

Since the constitutional reform process had not been documented and studied as a whole, we were keen to include first-hand accounts from some of the key actors in this process. This seemed an appropriate way of compensating for the dearth of secondary accounts and analysis of the reform. In addition, we wanted to include those first-hand accounts without seeking to fit them, or assessment of them, into a pre-existing interpretative framework. Comparative law tends to involve a third

12 E.g.: Bjarki Valtysson, 'Democracy in Disguise: The Use of Social Media in Reviewing the Icelandic Constitution' (2014) 36 (1) *Media, Culture and Society* 52.

party, namely the comparatist, who is usually a foreigner or outsider to the system he endeavours to present to his own audience,[13] often through the oversimplified prism of families, systems, or traditions.[14] It is only quite recently that comparative law has started to involve academic study of a legal system primarily produced by scholars inside that system but aimed at a foreign (or international) audience and written in English, which has become the lingua franca of Western scholarship.[15] Our comparative and editorial methodology has endeavoured to take this logic further as we chose to focus on first-hand accounts of the reform process,[16] written both for international and Icelandic audiences.

First-hand accounts of key actors presented in context

The story of the unprecedented Icelandic constitutional reform needs to be told by those who made it happen. We were particularly (but not exclusively) interested in giving drafters a voice as, too often, they tend to be absorbed into the collective identity of the 'founding fathers' (sic), with some of them acquiring a kind of mythical status over time and others disappearing altogether from history and constitutional law scholarship. Our overarching criterion for selecting contributors was their direct and sustained involvement in the reform either as drafter, commentator, or advisor. Despite the relatively small pool of people directly involved in the process, this collection could not include all of them,[17] so a complete and systematic recording of this will need to wait for another project, towards which this collection might be a first step. In Iceland, roles and professional identities often overlap as one person may be called upon to play several roles at once; in the case of our contributors, holding an academic position is perhaps their most common denominator.

Our selection of the contributors was guided by a flexible combination of criteria, such as the degree of their involvement in the process, the need to document the constitutional reform from beginning to end, including both processes and outcomes, as well as to represent a diversity of opinions and perspectives. Some contributors chose to write in the first person, others not. Regardless of styles, readers will no doubt note the strength of opinion and the depth of feelings that

13 Catherine Dupré 'The Perspective of Law Importation, the Hungarian Experience' in Andrew Harding and Esin Örücü (eds), *Comparative Law in the 21st Century* (Kluwer Academic Publishers 2002), 267–281; Günter Frankenberg, *Comparative Law as Critique* (Edward Elgar 2016).

14 Frankenberg (n 13) 47–52.

15 See e.g.: Helle Krunke and Björg Thorarensen (eds), *The Nordic Constitutions: A Comparative and Contextual Study* (Hart 2019).

16 Despite the attraction that Icelandic constitutional reform has had on foreign (mainly U.S.-based) scholars, our decision not to include international analyses of and commentary on the reform was deliberate. This, we thought, might be pursued in a second volume or in a different format.

17 See in particular the Constitutional Society, which 'was founded in the summer of 2010. Its objective was to support the drafting of a new Constitution by the people of Iceland, to be put to a referendum.': https://stjornarskrarfelagid.is/?page_id=2598 (accessed 2 June 2020).

animate the chapters without having to read too much between the lines. Accounts presented in this collection are not, however, purely subjective reminiscences as chapters contain an extensive body of footnotes documenting the developments and setting out the wider legal parameters in which these accounts unfold. This is further complemented by chapters specifically designed to embed the recollection and analysis of the reform in the wider historical, economic, and theoretical contexts of Icelandic constitutionalism, which are set out at the start of the collection. Finally, while an appendix with the full text of the key proposals would have usefully complemented the chapters, we chose to refer instead to the existing online materials, in English, whenever possible and in Icelandic when not.

Editors as comparatists: teamwork

While this collection focusses solely on Icelandic constitutionalism, with its contributors being exclusively Icelanders, it is no doubt a comparative project in its endeavour to present these Icelandic developments to a non-Icelandic readership. As comparatists, we made up a complementary team. Ágúst Þór Árnason was a deeply committed participant to the reform and a panoramic observer with a long memory of constitutional developments during his lifetime and a deep knowledge of Icelandic history, constitutionalism, politics, and society.[18] By contrast, Icelandic constitutionalism was a new territory for me,[19] so my role was that of the foreigner and outsider, who has followed from a distance the constitutional reform process since its beginning in 2009.[20] Like many international observers, the 2008–2009 events drew my attention, and, like many constitutional law scholars, I became curious about the unprecedented constitutional revision process, especially because it contrasted so drastically with the Hungarian developments that I was closely following at the time.[21] The Icelandic constitutional reform has been an easy victim of what Günter Frankenberg calls 'exoticisation,'[22] which has undoubtedly been compounded by the smallness of Iceland and perhaps to some extent by its increasing popularity as a tourist destination. As will be discussed, Icelandic constitutionalism is not well known outside Iceland, and the 'exoticisation' of its constitutional reform by some international commentators has, to some extent, also been belittling, most certainly with the best intentions of providing good advice. As editors, we were keen to let the actors in the constitutional process speak for themselves.

18 See: 'In Memoriam' at the beginning of this collection.

19 Catherine Dupré, *Importing the Law in Post-Communist Transitions: The Hungarian Constitutional Court and the Right to Human Dignity* (Hart Publishing 2003); and *The Age of Dignity: Human Rights and Constitutionalism in Europe* (Hart 2015).

20 This changed after April 2019 as I had to write Ágúst Þór's chapter and reconstruct his analysis of the constitutional reform.

21 Catherine Dupré, 'Human Dignity: Rhetoric, Protection, Instrumentalisation' in Gábor Attila Tóth (ed), *Constitution for a Disunited Nation: Hungary's 2011 New Fundamental Law* (Central European University Press 2012) 143–170.

22 Frankenberg (n 13) 107.

Orality played an important part in drawing ideas and experience together, ultimately producing the knowledge presented here. This started with the conference that we convened at the University of Akureyri in September 2016, opened by the address of the (then) newly elected President of Iceland, which has become the first chapter in this collection. This continued with close editorial discussions with most of the contributors over 2017–2020, either face to face in Reykjavik or Akureyri or through videoconference. The highest level of orality was no doubt generated by the interview with the Prime Minister in September 2018. Katrín Jakobsdóttir had initially agreed to contribute a chapter on the 2013–2016 Constitutional Committee on which she sat as the leader of the Left-Green Movement. When she became Prime Minister in November 2017, she maintained her commitment to contribute to the collection, and we suggested to her that she might do so in the format of an edited interview rather than a substantive book chapter. Considering her new position and her unique trajectory in the reform process, first as an MP; as Minister of Education, Science and Culture and of Nordic Co-Operation (2009–2013); as the Leader of the Left-Green Movement since 2013; and eventually as the Prime Minister formally in charge of constitutional revision (since 2017), her contribution acquired a more panoramic scope than initially envisaged. The importance of orality was a spontaneous feature of our comparative endeavour and development of our editorial work. Icelanders might be well known for their storytelling skills, but the significance of orality for this collection goes well beyond its Icelandic scope. As we sometimes felt that we were trespassing into the territory of oral history, we realised that comparative law, both as a discipline and a method, has yet to fully reflect on its approaches to gathering and constructing knowledge of foreign law and on the role that orality plays in this process.

Linguistic issues and translation choices

While the study of a foreign system very often implies a foreign language too, linguistic issues are, in most cases, not discussed at all in comparative law studies and methodology.[23] In putting this collection together, we greatly benefitted from the high quality of English spoken and written by Icelanders in general and by contributors in particular. We also benefitted from the existence of a number of English translations (with various degrees of authenticity): these included the 90/2010 Act setting up the Constitutional Assembly, the 2011 Proposal for a New Constitution of the Constitutional Council, and the 2016 Constitutional Bill. Moreover, official websites of the bodies involved in the constitutional reform contained some information in English, especially those of the Constitutional Council and the National Forum.[24] While providing non-Icelandic readers with valuable information, due

23 Vivian Grosswald Curran, 'Difference and Categories in U.S. Comparative Law' (1998) 46 *The American Journal of Comparative Law* 43.

24 National Forum's website www.thjodfundur2010.is/english/. Constitutional Council's website http://stjornlagarad.is/english/

to the lack of uniformity, these translations also triggered some confusion, in particular regarding the phrases used to refer to the various institutions involved in the reform process.

Clarifying our choice of translation was therefore a priority from the outset of this project.[25] A key criterion in this process was to give each institution a distinctive name in English that could not be mixed up with that of another institution also involved in the reform. While our choices might not always be the most felicitous from an Icelandic perspective, at least they set up a consistent semantic framework within which we could operate and communicate. We have also sought to explain and make our choices transparent by indicating the original Icelandic phrase wherever relevant. Transparency is an essential requirement of academic rigour, and it was also important to us that Icelandic readers could recognise their institutions despite the mediation of the foreign language. In addition, we were mindful of the fact that translating is rarely an innocent or neutral operation. For instance, the term 'frumvarp' can mean both 'bill' (the text put forward in Parliament at the start of the formal law-making process), as in 'frumvarp til stjórnarskipunarlagaand' ('a bill for a statute on constitutional matters'), and 'proposal.' We chose 'proposal' for the 2011 text because the proposed constitution drafted by the Constitutional Council was not part of the formal law-making parliamentary procedure, and, on the contrary, it had been explicitly and deliberately delegated to a body cut off from Parliament. It is also the translation adopted by the official website of the Constitutional Council.[26]

Icelandic constitutionalism in a nutshell

Possibly due to Iceland's small size and, generally for most of its history, unproblematic constitutional developments, publications in English on this topic are few. Icelandic constitutionalism is, as a result, little known outside Iceland and not easy to locate on the wider map of legal systems. It has been variously positioned as Scandinavian,[27] Nordic,[28] West Nordic,[29] or even North American.[30] In recent years, Iceland seems to be increasingly seen in terms of its arctic location.[31] These

25 These are set out at the front of this volume, under the 'The Constitutional Reform at a Glance' section.

26 www.stjornlagarad.is/other_files/stjornlagarad/Frumvarp-enska.pdf

27 Peter Wahlgren (ed), *What Is Scandinavian Law? Social Private Law* (Stockholm Institute for Scandinavian Law 2007).

28 Krunke and Thorarensen (n 15).

29 Kàri à Rògvi, *West-Nordic Constitutional Judicial Review* (Djof Publishing 2013).

30 'When we look at a map of Europe, we see that Iceland is an island which lies far to the north west of the other European countries. Although Icelandic society is rooted in Medieval European culture, it has a number of North American characteristics': Ágúst Þór Árnason, 'The European Union Seen from the Top: The View from an Inside-Outsider' in Joakim Nergelius (ed), *Nordic and Other Constitutional Traditions* (Brill 2006) 27.

31 Jensen Leif Christian (ed), *Handbook of the Politics of the Arctic* (Edward Elgar 2015).

categorisations might be of little help because, as Helle Krunke and Björg Thorarensen perceptively observe in their recent book, 'viewed from the outside – a European or global perspective – the Nordic constitutional systems share some common features [. . .]. However, viewed from a closer Nordic perspective, differences appear in the aforementioned general pattern.'[32] For the purpose of understanding the 2009–2017 constitutional reform, the key features of Icelandic constitutionalism can be identified as follows.[33]

Firstly, Iceland has an ancient practice of what might nowadays be called direct democracy, and its Parliament – the Althing – is known for being one of the oldest law-making assemblies in the world. In addition, with 63 members, its only chamber (since the 1991 constitutional reform) makes it possibly one of the smallest parliaments within a broadly European perimeter. An important feature of the Icelandic law-making process is its routine consultation of the public, a feature that has perhaps led to overstating the significance or originality of the Constitutional Council's transparent and consultative approach to drafting its 2011 Proposal.[34] Secondly, Iceland is a republic, which gained its full independence from the Danish King in 1944, when the current Constitution was adopted after being submitted to a referendum in 1944 with a turnout of 98,61%.[35] The resulting text of the Constitution has often been criticised for merely endorsing the previous Constitution that had been 'given' to Icelanders by the Danish monarch.[36] However, an essential change was the creation of a President of the Republic as the new Head of State, replacing the King. Directly elected by all Icelanders, the new Head of State was given the power to call a referendum under Article 26, which was used for the first time in April 2010 in relation to the Icesave legislation and the related dispute with the Netherlands and the United Kingdom.[37] Thirdly, Iceland joined the Council of Europe in 1950 and ratified the European Convention on Human Rights in 1953,[38] eventually amending the Constitution in 1995 to reflect these

32 Krunke and Thorarensen (n 15) 2.

33 Árnason and Scheinin (n 10) and Ágúst Þór Árnason, 'Iceland' in Gerhard Robbers (ed), *Encyclopedia of World Constitutions*, Volume II (Facts on File 2007) 93.

34 Bergsson (n 4) 161.

35 The referendum was based on a specially adopted Constitutional Act 97/1942. Ágúst Þór Árnason, 'The Constitutionalism of the Republic of Iceland and the Role and Status of the President' in Asbjørn Eide, Jakob Th Möller, and Ineta Ziemele (eds), *Making People Heard: Essays on Human Rights in Honour of Gudmundur Alfredsson* (Martin Nijhoff 2011) 589.

36 Ágúst Þór Árnason, 'The History of the Icelandic Constitution and Some Economic Issues' in L Lyck (ed), *Constitutional and Economic Space of Small Nordic Jurisdictions: The Aaland Islands, the Faroe Islands, Greenland, Iceland* (NordREFO 1997), 48–73.

37 Finnur Magnússon, 'Opening Pandora's Box: The Refusal of a President to Sign a Bill' (2010) 2 *Zeitschrift für öffentliches Recht* 203; and Ørebech, Peter, 'The Icesave Bank of Iceland; From Rock-Solid to Volcano Hot: Is the EU Deposit Guarantee Scheme Resisting Financial Meltdown?' (2010) 6 *Croatian Yearbook of European Law and Policy* 127.

38 Gudrun Gauksdóttir, 'Iceland' in Robert Blackburn and Jörg Polakiewicz (eds), *Fundamental Rights in Europe: The ECHR and Its Member States, 1950–2000* (OUP 2001) 399.

developments. It also joined the European Economic Area in 1993.[39] Its relationship with the European Union (EU) is more complex and has come under greater scrutiny in recent years.[40] An application for EU membership was initiated under the premiership of Jóhanna Sigurðardóttir and was swiftly retracted after the 2013 election, apparently without much explication.[41] Although the issue of EU membership as such was not part of the constitutional reform process, the question of delegation of sovereignty to international organisations acquired prominence in these discussions. It was included in the 2011 Proposal for a New Constitution, featured in one of the 2012 referendum questions, and was also selected by the 2013–2016 Constitutional Committee before being promptly abandoned. Fourthly, with Iceland, size matters and 'the acquaintance and informality factor pervasive in a small society' shapes human relationships.[42] This has arguably also influenced the practice of parliamentary democracy, as well as possibly Icelanders' expectations for greater involvement in decision-making and constitutional revision processes. Moreover, this has influenced the constitutional reform as the pool of possible drafters, advisors, and commentators is quite small, which has sometimes meant that a given person has played several roles throughout the whole process.[43] Finally and perhaps above all, Icelanders form a tightly knit community, and this affects interpersonal relationships and politics in ways that are hard to fathom from the outside.[44] For instance, when your mother was the physical education teacher of the Prime Minister, or your father was involved in the design of the 1944 Constitution, the constitution is literally close to home. In these situations, it can be difficult to disentangle the personal from the political or the political from the constitutional. While this is not an aspect addressed in this collection, understanding the deeper personal and family connections might be necessary to make fuller sense of some of the underlying logics at work in the reform process and of their constitution's significance for Icelanders. Overall and seen from the outside, Icelandic constitutionalism has engendered social peace

39 Stefan Már Stefánsson, *The EEA Agreement and Its Adoption in Icelandic Law* (Scandinavian University Press 1997).

40 Árnason, 'The European Union Seen from the Top' (n 30) 27–45; Aðalheiður Jóhannsdóttir, 'The European Union and the Arctic: Could Iceland's Accession to the EU Change the EU's Influence in the Arctic?' (2011) 54 *German Yearbook of International Law* 351; Baldur Thorhallsson, 'Iceland: A Reluctant European' in Erik O Eriksen, John Erik Fossum (eds), *European Union's Non-Members: Independence under Hegemony?* (Routledge 2015) 118.

41 Gunnar Helgi Kristínsson, 'Iceland the European Union: Non-Decision on Membership' in Lee Miles (ed), *The European Union and the Nordic Countries* (Routledge 1996) 150; and Piotr Kobza, 'Accession of Iceland to the European Union: A Failure beyond Repair?' (2017) 22 *European Foreign Affairs Review* 129.

42 Vilhjálmur Árnason, 'Democratic Practices, Governance, and the Financial Crash' in Ingimundarson, Urfalino, and Erlingsdóttir (eds) (n 7) 127. Generally see: Lise Lyck (ed), *Constitutional and Economic Space of Small Nordic Jurisdictions: The Aaland Islands, the Faroe Islands, Greenland, Iceland* (NordREFO 1997).

43 See the contributors' concise biographies at the front of the collection.

44 Mark S Weiner, *The Rule of the Clan* (Picador 2014).

and political stability since 1944, two features that were badly affected in the years during which the reform took place.

Overview of the constitutional reform: 2009–2017

In 2009, the idea of reforming the Constitution was nothing new. Two projects for a full reform of the Constitution had been considered and then dropped, one almost as soon as the 1944 Constitution was adopted, and the other later in 1983 when Prime Minister Gunnar Thoroddsen (Independence Party) submitted his own proposal but lost the subsequent general election.[45] By contrast, partial reforms of the 1944 Constitution had successfully been undertaken seven times since its adoption.[46] In particular, the voting system was altered twice in 1959 and 1991, the second chamber of Parliament was abolished in 1991, and Parliament strengthened vis-à-vis the government, and the human rights section was revised in 1995 (mostly but not only) to bring it into line with Iceland's commitment to international law.[47] The procedure for reforming the Constitution under Article 79(1) does not seem to have raised major issues and reads:

> Proposals to amend or supplement this Constitution may be introduced at regular as well as extraodinary sessions of Althingi. If the proposal is adopted, Althingi shall immediately be dissolved and a general election held. If Althingi then passes the resolution unchanged, it shall be confirmed by the President of the Republic and come into force as constitutional law.

Comparatively, this is not an unusual approach to revising a constitution.[48] While this procedure gives a key role to Parliament, the requirement of a general election ensures that the people are also involved. Moreover, and importantly, there is a distinction between the parliament proposing a reform of the Constitution and the new parliament adopting it. Finally, in a parallel to the ordinary law-making procedure, the President of the Republic has to give the proposed change(s) the final seal of approval.[49] As a result, the Icelandic constitution-making procedure follows ordinary law-making procedure, while giving it an additional layer with the

45 Árnason, 'The History of the Icelandic Constitution' (n 36) 58–62.

46 Árnason (n 10) ix–xvii. See also: Aðalheidur Ámundadóttir, 'Samantekt tillagna um breytingar á stjórnarskrá frá lýðveldisstofnun til 2010' [Summary of Proposals on Amendments of the Constitution from the Foundation of the Republic until 2010] in *Skýrsla Stjórnlaganefndar*, 2. bindi [Report of the Constitutional Commission, Vol. 2] 227–300.

47 Tuomas Ojanen, 'Human Rights in the Nordic Constitutions' in Krunke and Thorarensen (n 15) 141.

48 Stefan Voigt (ed), *Design of Constitutions* (Edward Elgar 2013); Cheryl Saunders, 'Constitution-Making in the 21st Century' (2012) 4 *International Review of Law* 1.

49 Björg Thorarensen, 'The People's Contribution to Constitutional Changes: Writing, Advising or Approving?' in Xenophon Contiades and Alkmene Fodiadou (eds), *Participatory Constitutional Change: The People as Amenders of the Constitution* (Routledge 2017) 103, 115–116.

requirement of confirmation by the newly elected parliament. As a result, constitutional reform is part of normal political discussion in Iceland. For instance, the codification of a basic framework on natural resources within the Constitution was being considered in 2009 as part of an ongoing discussion on this issue.[50]

Three factors contributed to making the 2009–2017 reform process unusual, triggering an unprecedentedly complicated constitutional configuration. The first and best-known factor was the exceptional situation of crisis in which the reform of the constitution took place. The collapse of the whole banking sector in October 2008 has been well documented.[51] The so-called 'pots and pans revolution' was definitely an expression of Icelanders' anger and sense of injustice against those in power. Inside parliament, calls for a constitutional reform came from the opposition. The new Prime Minister, Social-Democrat Jóhanna Sigurðardóttir, went ahead with the project of reforming the Constitution, which unfolded (albeit in a different fashion from what she had initially envisaged) throughout her time in government between 2009 and 2013. This was also a time during which the top priority was to rescue the Icelandic banking sector and to shelter people from the worst of its consequences.[52]

The second factor creating unprecedented complications was parliament's decision to bypass Article 79(1) of the Constitution and to establish instead a specially created framework under Act 90/2010 adopted on 16 June 2010. This statute provided for the election of a consultative Constitutional Assembly of 25 ordinary citizens[53] asked to 'review [sic] the constitution.'[54] As discussed in some chapters in this volume, the exact scope of revision was left open,[55] thus giving the Constitutional Assembly a wide discretion in interpreting its own task but little time for completing it. While this might not necessarily have been a bad way of seeking to rebuild trust between the people and the politicians, this process suffered one major design flaw. That is, having provided a framework for constitutional reform outside the Article 79(1) procedure, Act 90/2010 did not provide a way back into the normal framework for reforming the Constitution, an omission that raised numerous questions about the constitutional, moral, and political status of the

50 See Chapter 10 in this collection by Ragnheiður Elfa Thorsteinsdóttir.

51 E.g.: Roger Z Aliber and Zoeda Gylfi (eds), *Preludes to the Icelandic Financial Crisis* (Palgrave Macmillan 2011); Eiríkur Bergmann, *Iceland and the International Financial Crisis: Boom, Bust and Recovery* (Palgrave Macmillan 2014).

52 The EFTA Court ruling of 28 January 2013 cleared Iceland of all charges and is considered as marking the end of its dispute with the Netherlands and United Kingdom: *EFTA Surveillance Authority v Iceland*, 28 January 2013, Case E-16/11.

53 Article 6 of 90/2010 Act explicitly excludes MPs: 'Persons who qualify to stand for election to the Althing may stand for election to the Constitutional Assembly. However, the President of the Republic of Iceland, members of parliament, their alternates, cabinet ministers and members of the Constitutional Commission and the Organising Committee are not eligible to stand for the election.' See: www.thjodfundur2010.is/other_files/2010/doc/Act-on-a-Constitutional-Assembly.pdf

54 Article 1 of 90/2010 Act.

55 Article 3 of 90/2010 Act lists eight issues that the Assembly has to 'address specifically' and states that it 'may decide to address additional matters.'

Proposal for a New Constitution presented to the Althing on 29 July 2011 by the Constitutional Council (Assembly). The Althing sought to address this by deciding, in May 2012,[56] to organise an advisory referendum about the 2011 Proposal to be held on 20 October 2012. However, the referendum failed to provide both the necessary clarification about the substance of the constitutional changes that were expected or required and the political impetus for doing so. As a result, by the end of its term, Althing did not complete the reform process that it had set in motion four years earlier. It did, however, manage to agree on an interim revision procedure by adopting Constitutional Act 91/2013, designed to expire on 30 April 2017, that is, by the expected end of the following parliament.[57]

The third complicating factor relates to unprecedented political turbulences that characterised the 2009–2017 period, during which the reform took place. At the start, Iceland's apparent political and social stability was shattered by the financial crisis, the shock waves of which continued to be felt long after, particularly in 2013 with the emergence of new political parties, fragmenting the political visions about how best to continue with the constitutional reform. Carried over into the next parliament under Constitutional Act 91/2013, the reform process was hit by the Panama Papers crisis three years later. The Prime Minister was forced to step down in April 2016, and he eventually called for an early election held on 29 October 2016. Without this untimely interruption, the more optimistic observers note that the 2013–2016 Constitutional Committee's work might have come to fruition with a constitutional bill being adopted by the end of the 2013–2017 parliament as envisaged by Constitutional Act 91/2013. This, in turn, might have made it possible both to reach the end of the interim reform procedure time frame (30 April 2017) and to allow for the constitutional reform process to be reabsorbed into the constitutional framework of Article 79(1). However, this was not to be, and the early election led to a fragile coalition government, which collapsed in September 2017, when the Bright Future Party decided to withdraw from it.[58] While this crisis was perhaps of smaller political magnitude, it did prompt a second early election within one year of the first. This brought to power a new coalition government with the Independence Party and the Progressive Party under the premiership of Katrín Jakobsdóttir (Left-Green Movement), marking the end of the constitutional reform cycle started in the early weeks of 2009.

Fourthly and finally, while any full revision of a constitution is a momentous project requiring at least a solid procedural framework and a clear overall aim, it is fair to say that the Icelandic process faced exceptional adversity in the unfolding of that unprecedented framework. The 2009–2013 parliament sought to address political and financial crises head-on by exploring a new route to revise the 1944

56 See: Resolution of 24 May 2012 and the debates in Althingi: www.althingi.is/thingstorf/thingmalalistar-eftir-thingum/ferill/?ltg=140&mnr=636

57 Constitutional Act 91/2013 adopted before the 2013 election was confirmed on 5 July 2013 (after the election): www.althingi.is/altext/141/s/0510.html

58 *The Economist*, 15 September 2017: http://country.eiu.com/article.aspx?articleid=95891993

Constitution. This new process, designed at the time of the worst crisis Iceland ever had to face was perhaps overly complicated with numerous ad hoc bodies, ambitious and well-meaning involvement of both experts and lay people, making it particularly vulnerable. One such unfortunate and unpredictable development was the invalidation of the election of the Constitutional Assembly by the Supreme Court on 25 January 2011, which weakened its perceived legitimacy as the main drafting body, originally designed precisely to address the Althing's legitimacy tainted by the collapse of the financial sector. In response to the Supreme Court's ruling, parliament formally appointed 24 out of the 25 originally elected members of the Constitutional Assembly, which was renamed Constitutional Council by a resolution of 24 March 2011.[59] However, the principal drafting body arguably never fully recovered, despite managing to deliver its Proposal for a New Constitution within the allocated time. Finally, fatigue set in affecting all involved: the 2009–2013 parliament, which had had to firefight a financial collapse of unprecedented magnitude, reached the end of its term in a state of almost total exhaustion. The Icelandic people, who had attracted worldwide attention in the winter of 2008–2009 with their pots and pans, appeared to have a waning interest in reforming the constitution as indicated by the turnout of just above 48% in the 2012 referendum. The 2013 election:

> proved to be historical in many ways. The total collapse of the two government parties was unprecedented in Iceland's history, the fragmentation of the electorate was evident through the number of parties running, and more people than ever voted for parties that did not cross the 5 per cent threshold needed to gain seats.[60]

The constitutional reform issue divided political candidates, including the former members of the Constitutional Council.[61]

Chapters outline

The chapters are grouped according to four broad themes: the volume's first part discusses the overall context and background of the constitutional reform; the second part focusses on the drafters and drafting bodies; the third part concentrates on the substance of the constitutional reform; and the fourth and final part offers

59 Resolution 19/139: www.althingi.is/altext/139/s/1120.html. Act 90/2010 was repealed by Act 31/2011 of 12 April 2011.

60 Bergsson (n 4) 165.

61 Bergsson (n 4) 165: 'While some members of the Constitutional Council joined [a new list] Dawn, others created a new party called the Democracy Watch, led by Þorvaldur Gylfason. Another Council member founded a third party, called The Party of the Households. Many found it odd that the three parties did not join forces since they shared many of the same values and campaigned on similar grounds. Personal issues seem to have played a role and on some issues, such as the indexation of mortgages, which is an important issue in Iceland, the parties did not agree.'

a reflective overview of the reform. While the chapters were carefully designed to ensure a fluid narrative of events in a broadly chronological order, they do not all strictly start where the previous one finishes; as editors, we felt it necessary to allow each chapter to tell the story from its own starting point. These connections between chapters are complemented by editorial cross-referencing throughout the collection.

Three chapters stand out for their slightly unusual style. Chapter 2 is the edited opening address that the President of the Republic gave at the 2016 conference in which this collection is rooted. Ágúst Þór Árnason and I decided to retain its rhetorical style and edited it only to provide some references and essential background information in footnotes. The next chapter, by Ágúst Þór Árnason, due to his untimely death, is a posthumous chapter which I wrote up at his request. The third chapter with an unusual style (Chapter 13) is that of Prime Minister Katrín Jakobsdóttir, which, as previously explained, is an edited version of the interview she gave us on 25 September 2018.

Part I ('Contexts') starts by setting out the wider context in which the reform took place. Guðni Th. Jóhannesson, the then newly elected President of Iceland and historian, outlines the evolving views and involvement of Icelandic presidents in constitutional matters since the Constitution came into force in 1944. Unlike the Prime Minister, the President plays no formal role in triggering or steering constitutional reform. However, as Guðni Th. Jóhannesson shows, Icelandic presidents have demonstrated a keen interest in constitutional matters, including the scope of their own constitutional role and constitutional reform. The current president is no exception: he sees his role as promoting consensus and encourages compromises necessary to complete the constitutional revision.

Next, Ágúst Þór Árnason's chapter positions the reform in the wider framework of Icelandic constitutionalism. Reflecting on the reasons why a reform of the Constitution was needed, he questioned the decision to opt for a total revision of the 1944 text, which in his view did not have any flaws so substantial that they could not be addressed through partial revision, as had been the case until 2009. Instead, this chapter brings to light the impact that the 2010 Icesave referendum had on the 1944 Constitution. It argues that, by confirming the full exercise of the president's power under Article 26 of the Constitution, this referendum completed the construction of the institution of the Head of State (the main innovation in 1944) and thus of Iceland's constitutional identity as a republic.

In Chapter 4, Kristrún Heimisdóttir recalls the unprecedented magnitude of the collapse of the Icelandic banking and financial sector, known as 'a near-death experience.' She discusses how Iceland, against the odds, managed to come back from this abyss and to reclaim its financial and political sovereignty via the ordinary law-making process – admittedly by taking quite exceptional decisions in substance – all the time remaining within the framework of the 1944 Constitution. She highlights Icelanders' key role in this process, notably through the two Icesave referendums of 2010 and 2011. Therefore, as she argues, the 1944 Constitution demonstrated its capacity to evolve and overcome this unprecedented crisis. By contrast, the project to adopt a brand-new constitution to bring a New Republic or New Iceland into existence was not completed, leading to the 'pots and pans revolution' to abort.

The collection's second part ('Drafters and Drafting Processes') focusses on two key stages in the revision process. Björg Thorarensen discusses the role played by the Constitutional Commission (2010–2011), on which she sat, in preparing the 2010 National Forum and producing a detailed Report designed to facilitate the work of the 2011 Constitutional Assembly/Council. Her chapter provides a unique insight into this Report, which is not available in English. The two-volume Report collates the wishes and ideas for the constitutional reform resulting from the National Forum held on 6 November 2010, and it outlines two possible sets of formulations for core constitutional provisions to be amended according to Article 3 of Act 90/2010. In addition, the 2011 Report includes twelve studies on specific constitutional issues, mostly but not exclusively written by the members of the Constitutional Commission. Reflecting on the Report's ultimate influence on the actual drafting of the 2011 Proposal for a New Constitution by the Constitutional Council, the author observes that the Council's decision to go for a total revision meant that the 2011 Report could not be as useful as originally intended.

Salvör Nordal reflects on her experience as the chairperson of the Constitutional Council and explains how the Council organised its work and drafted the 2011 Proposal for a New Constitution. In so doing, she paints a more nuanced picture of the Council's drafting process that included but was not limited to reliance on public consultation, often described as 'crowdsourcing.' While it was admittedly no small achievement to produce a full draft for a new constitution in such little time, her own assessment of the 2011 Proposal is more cautious, due to the substance of the text itself and to the weak framework within which the Constitutional Council operated.

Jón Ólafsson, who had run unsuccessfully for election to the Constitutional Assembly, maintained a keen interest in the drafting process. In Chapter 7, he focusses on the Icelandic constitutional revision's perhaps most innovative feature, namely the involvement of lay drafters, especially the work of the Council. Noting, as many observers have done, that the Council had been given an unclear mission by parliament, he reflects on the resulting ambiguous status of 2011 Proposal of the Constitutional Council. Amongst the reasons why it was ultimately not taken forward by the Althing, Jón Ólafsson discusses the tension between the so-called lay drafters and the community of academic experts who put up 'a formidable resistance' against the Proposal. He further reflects on parliament's absence of preparation to receive the 2011 Proposal and to act on it before the 2013 election.

The third part ('Constitutional Proposals and Bills') seeks to provide a sense of what the constitutional reform involved in substance, a dimension of the reform that could, however, not be addressed comprehensively. This part opens with an analysis of the 2011 Proposal for a New Constitution by Skúli Magnússon, who sat on the 2010–2011 Constitutional Commission and briefly on the 2013–2016 Constitutional Committee. Drawing on the Commentary on the 2011 Proposal drafted the Constitutional Council and not available in English, the author illuminates the Council's decision to opt for a full revision of the 1944 Constitution by reference to the ideal of New Iceland that emerged in the winter of 2008–2009 following the collapse of the financial sector. The chapter focusses on the key features of the 2011 Proposal and discusses them against the 1944 Constitution, as well as in their interrelations in consideration of their workability. These include the quality of parliamentarianism, the role of the President of the Republic, the redesign of the executive branch, the implications for direct democracy, the rule of law framework, and the reformulation of fundamental rights.

Páll Þórhallsson, the chairman of the Constitutional Committee (2013–2016), appointed by the Prime Minister to continue the constitutional reform after the 2013 election, discusses the proposals produced by that Committee. They were delivered to interim Prime Minister Sigurður Ingi Jóhannsson on 1 July 2016 and presented by the Prime Minister to the Althing in the form of a single constitutional bill on 25 August 2016. At the start of its work, the Committee identified four priority issues, namely referendums requested by voters, transfer of state sovereignty to international organisations, national ownership of natural resources, and environmental protection. The Committee had to drop the issue of transfer of sovereignty due to serious reservations among the two coalition parties on this. Reflecting on this apparent 'modest result' considering the time available to the Council and compared with the 2011 Proposal of the Constitutional Council, Páll Þórhallsson notes the difficulties in finding political agreement on each of these highly sensitive issues.

Ragnheiður Elfa Þorsteinsdóttir, who was Director of the Natural Resources and Environment Department at the Ministry for Foreign Affairs between 2009 and 2013, discusses the issue of natural resources, including fish and other marine resources. Not regulated under the 1944 Constitution, natural resources featured prominently throughout the constitutional reform process, being identified, both by people (at the National Forum) and all drafters, as requiring constitutional codification to ensure better use and protection. The chapter outlines previous unsuccessful attempts to amend the 1944 Constitution in this respect, including a proposal put forward by the Prime Minister in March 2009. Against this background, Ragnheiður Elfa Þorsteinsdóttir focusses on the two constitutional provisions on natural resources, namely Article 34 of the 2011 Proposal for a New Constitution and Article 80 of the 2016 Constitutional Bill. While the author analyses the controversial question of ownership, she also seeks to move the discussion towards the issue of natural resources use, that is, the sustainability of their uses and management – with corresponding obligations for owners, be they private or public – regardless of type of ownership. Noting the special significance of natural resources for a small island like Iceland, she reflects on the best ways to secure protection through constitutional codification, while giving the law-maker sufficient flexibility.

The following chapter, focussed on protection of the environment, is written by Aðalheiður Jóhannsdóttir, who advised both the 2010–2011 Constitutional Council and the 2013–2016 Constitutional Committee on these issues. She notes that, compared to other Nordic states, Iceland has been slow in developing environmental protection through its Constitution, despite an attempt to do so as early as in 1983, and that this reluctance is still visible in the 2011, 2012, and 2016 proposed provisions on this matter. The author focusses on the last proposal of the reform period, i.e. Article 79 included under the 2016 Constitutional Bill, which she analyses with reference to earlier versions (both the 2011 Proposal and the 2012 Constitutional Bill) and to similar developments in Nordic states. Observing the broad similarity of wording across these various drafts, she suggests that the proposal to codify a right to a healthy environment under (a revised) Article 79 might not have generated new guarantees beyond those already existing under Article 71 of the 1944 Constitution combined with Article 2 (right to life) and Article 8 (right to private and family life) of the European Convention on Human Rights. By contrast, the codification of the right to roam (almannaréttur), so close to Icelanders' hearts, would have represented a real innovation, even if the detail of its substance and exercise was left to the law-maker.

The fourth part of the volume ('Reflections') brings together two different perspectives on the overall reform. Thorvaldur Gylfason, a member of the Constitutional Council and very prolific commentator on the reform, expresses his concerns about what he sees as the failure of parliament to 'ratify the Constitutional Bill supported by 2/3 of the voters in the 2012 advisory referendum' before the 2013 election and ever since then. He is particularly concerned with what he sees as this failure's negative impact on Icelandic democracy, i.e. that parliament did not comply with the advisory referendum results according to which 67% of the voters expressed their support for using the 2011 Proposal as a basis for the new constitution, in addition to supporting other individual provisions, especially those concerning the equal vote principle and ownership of natural resources. An ardent supporter of the 2011 Proposal, which he was involved in drafting, he argues that it is 'never too late to do the right thing' and calls for parliament to adopt it.

Katrín Jakobsdóttir's edited interview (Chapter 13) provides both a unique insider's view into the reform in which she was involved in a range of capacities, including as Prime Minister since November 2017, and a longer-term perspective on the reform process. The interview draws on her recollection of events, both as an observer and an active participant, as well as her own political agenda as the Prime Minister formally in charge of taking the 2009–2017 reform process forward and committed to completing it. As a politician, her approach to the constitutional revision is more pragmatic. Reflecting on the failure to completely revise the 1944 Constitution and on her experience as a member of the 2013–2016 Constitutional Committee, she is pursuing a more gradual approach. As the new Prime Minister, she secured a cross-party agreement and intends to focus on one set of issues at a time, using the 2016 Constitutional Bill as a basis, and starting with natural resources. Inspired by the Norwegian experience, this new stage of the constitutional reform is designed to be completed within the next two parliamentary terms in compliance with Article 79(1) of the 1944 Constitution.

The conclusion, written by the editor, suggests that while no change was made to the 1944 Constitution, its reform process has transformed how it is perceived and has given Icelanders the opportunity to take ownership of it by subjecting it to sustained critical discussion in almost all its aspects. Icelanders' new identity as constitution-makers has raised the key – and as yet unanswered – question of how best to equip people so that they can play a democratically meaningful role in reforming their constitution or adopting a new one. Ultimately, at the heart of reforming a constitution lies the question of a people's sovereignty and how it can or must be reimagined in a democratic context in response to new challenges.

Part I

Contexts

2 The President and the Constitution[1]

Guðni Th. Jóhannesson

From the outset, the President of Iceland has taken an interest in constitutional matters, the position of the Head of State in the constitutional structure, and the possible need to revise the Constitution, not least the section dealing with the presidency, its powers, and its responsibilities.

Before we consider the situation as it is today, I think it is appropriate to say a few words about the position adopted by our earlier presidents and their involvement in these issues. Sveinn Björnsson became Governor of Iceland in spring 1941.[2] While in that position, he did not consider it proper for him to comment publicly on the proposals for a new constitution that were then being made in the Alþing. Behind the scenes, however, he spoke about 'attempts to grab as much power as possible for parliament'[3] and said he would hardly be prepared to occupy the position of Head of State under the drastic terms that were in the offing.[4]

1 Editors' note: this text is a minimally edited version of the President's opening address to the international conference on 'Icelandic Constitutional Reform: People, Principles, Processes' held at the University of Akureyri, 23–24 September 2016. In order to keep the style of the presidential address, editing has been mainly about adding essential contextual information (e.g. dates of the various presidencies), updating the time frame of the opening address, and providing sources in footnotes. Most materials referred to here are letters and diaries of the former presidents Sveinn Björnsson, Ásgeir Ásgeirsson, Kristján Eldjárn, and Vigdís Finnbogadóttir. They are located in the Archives of Alþing, the National Archives of Iceland, the National and University Libraries of Iceland, the National Archives of the UK in London, and the Danish Rigsarkivet in Copenhagen. In the case of Ásgeir Ásgeirsson (the second president of the Republic of Iceland), they are still within his family. Much of this information can also be found in Guðni Th. Jóhannesson, *Fyrstu forsetarnir – Embætti þjóðhöfðingja Íslands á 20. Öld* [The First Presidents: The Office of the Head of State of Iceland in the 20th Century] (Sögufélag 2016). All translations are the author's.

2 Sveinn Björnsson became Governor (or Regent) of Iceland in spring 1941. Following the Nazi German occupation of Denmark, on 9 April 1940 the government of Iceland assumed all the prerogatives in Icelandic affairs that were previously held by the King of Iceland and Denmark, Christian X. The Parliament of Iceland, Alþing, elected Sveinn Björnsson, the then Icelandic ambassador to Denmark, as Regent of Iceland on 17 June 1941, and handed those prerogatives over to him. Björnsson was re-elected by the Parliament as Regent of Iceland in 1942 and 1943. On 17 June 1944, he was elected by the Parliament as the first president of the Republic of Iceland.

3 Jóhannesson, *The First Presidents* (n 1) 55, footnote nr. 185. Originally from Sveinn Björnsson, 'Um afskipti mín af sambandsmálinu við Dani' [About My 'Interventions' in the Union Case with Denmark] Greinargerð, samin í janúar-febrúar 1944, National Archive of Iceland [statement composed in Jan.–Feb. 1944]; BÞ, Annáll [Annals] 14 October 1943.

4 Ibid.

At the beginning of 1944, Sveinn proposed instead that a national convention be appointed to draw up a new constitution for the Republic of Iceland. But this idea did not get off the ground. The Alþing had its way, the nation at large agreed with it, and no national convention was called. Nonetheless, Sveinn Björnsson became the first President when the Republic was established on 17 June 1944. And, as President, he made no attempt to hide his opinions when he spoke about the Constitution of the Republic, insisting that, from the outset, it had been considered a temporary measure that needed revising at the earliest opportunity. In his New Year address in 1949, Sveinn said:

> And now, four-and-a-half years after the foundation of the Republic, there is still no sign of the new constitution which we need to have as soon as possible, and which the people and the political leaders were generally in favour of having enacted at the earliest opportunity. In this regard we are still using a patched garment that was originally designed for another country, with other attitudes, a whole century ago. [. . .] It is to be hoped that the adoption of a new constitution will not be put off for much longer.[5]

Sveinn Björnsson (1944–1952) made his presence very much felt in the political sphere. Nevertheless, he was seen by Icelanders as a 'symbol of unity.' Regarding that role, there was not a single word in the Constitution; in these matters, perception, rather than wording, was the decisive factor.

In many respects, Ásgeir Ásgeirsson, elected after Sveinn Björnsson's death in 1952, followed the same path as his predecessor. Before he became President, Ásgeir had said, regarding the Constitution, that either any changes to it would have to be as small as possible 'or, alternatively, really radical so as to inspire people.'[6] However, all plans for the revision of the Constitution came to nothing during his presidency (1952–1968). The political parties were not wildly keen on making changes, and neither was the general public. Admittedly, an important part of the Constitution was amended when new constituency boundaries were adopted in 1959.[7] This amendment was the subject of bitter confrontation both within the Alþing and outside it.[8]

Apart from that, nothing much happened in the history of the Constitution and the office of President during Ásgeir Ásgeirsson's presidency. The Socialists were

5 Diaries of Sveinn Björnsson, National Archives of Iceland.

6 Jóhannesson, *The First Presidents* (n 1) 89, footnote nr. 292.

7 In 1959, the system of electoral districts was changed drastically. The 28 lower-tier districts under the old system were replaced with eight constituencies with proportional representation in each. As before, 11 members were allocated from the nationwide upper tier.

8 Ólafur Th. Hardarson, 'The Icelandic Electoral System 1844–1999' in Bernard Grofman and Arend Lijphard (eds), *The Evolution of Electoral and Party Systems in the Nordic Countries* (Agathon Press 2002) 101–167.

always antagonistic towards him,[9] but during his final years at Bessastaðir,[10] Ásgeir was an uncontroversial figure, a symbol of unity outside the arena of political conflict.

Revision of the Constitution was still planned during Kristján Eldjárn's presidency (1968–1980). A new constitutional committee was supposed to submit a bill on constitutional reform in 1974. This did not happen, and the committee members complained that the people 'had failed regarding the constitutional issue.'[11] They said they had received little or no response to their approach to organisations and the general public regarding constitutional change. People seemed to be happy with their Constitution.

Kristján Eldjárn himself mentioned the revision of the Constitution in public. His choice of words was cautious, however, as it always was. In his third and final inaugural address, in August 1976, he said:

> Everyone who has read the Constitution knows that at first glance, the President may seem to have considerable power, but it transpires that this is more in theory than in practice, since the President entrusts his authority to ministers and his executive acts are their responsibility. [. . .] A constitutional committee is currently at work in Iceland. I imagine it will examine, amongst other things, how successful the provisions on the role of the President have turned out to be over the years. I do not know whether amendments will be proposed in this area, or whether such proposals would be adopted. I think people will probably be mainly curious to see whether proposals will be made concerning a change in the part that the President plays in forming new governments; this is an area in which he is expected to play an important role.[12]

Early in 1980, after nearly two years of almost constant cabinet crisis and complex attempts to form a government, Kristján Eldjárn asked himself whether the President should not play more of a role in this area. He read the following comments into his tape-recorded diary: 'I'm beginning to find this rather an odd situation, this role of the President as a theatre director where in fact he doesn't make any active proposals, [. . .] I think it could be worth considering just proposing some particular pattern to these people, so giving them some moral support.'[13]

9 The Socialists saw Ásgeir Ásgeirsson as a political promotor for militarisation and for Iceland's membership in NATO in favour of the military American base in Keflavik. Guðni Th. Jóhannesson, *The First Presidents* (n 1) 116, footnotes nr. 366 and 367.

10 Official residence of Icelandic presidents.

11 Jóhannesson, *The First Presidents* (n 1) 147, footnote 456.

12 Guðni Th. Jóhannesson, *Völundarhús valdsins – Kristján Eldjárns presidentsship 1968–1980*, p. 319, footnote 87; see also: *Hjá fólkinu í landinu [With the People of this Country]* – speeches of Kristján Eldjárn (Menningarsjóður 1986).

13 Jóhannesson, *The First Presidents* (n 1) 156, footnote 482; see also: Kristján Eldjárn, cassette nr. 3, 9 February 1980.

However, Kristján Eldjárn stuck to his praiseworthy position of not trying to determine who should and who should not take part in government. To this extent, he was certainly a non-political president. He lived up to the title of a unifying symbol, and that was the sort of Head of State that the people wanted at the time.

Vigdís Finnbogadóttir knew this. As President between 1980 and 1996, she read the Constitution as meaning that 'the President was above politics.' She stated this view formally when she approved the Act on Iceland's membership of the European Economic Area at the beginning of 1993:

> Ever since the establishment of the Republic of Iceland, the office of the President has been in the process of formation. In this, one principal element in the office has been steadily growing stronger: to be independent and above party politics and partisanship, and at the same time to be a common denominator for Iceland's national culture and our educational and cultural policy, a symbol of unity and not disunity.[14]

Constitutional committees were still at work during Vigdís Finnbogadóttir's time as President, and now various amendments found their way into the Constitution: the lowering of the voting age from 20 to 18, the abolition of the bicameral structure of the Alþing,[15] an amended provision on the dissolution of Parliament and a new human rights chapter.[16] However, as before, a comprehensive revision of the Constitution still did not come about.

Ólafur Ragnar Grímsson was the fifth President of the Republic, in office from 1 August 1996 to 31 July 2016. He was the first to exercise the power to refuse to approve legislation on media in accordance with Article 26 of the Constitution; meanwhile, constitutional committees continued their work in the Alþing. Up to the banking collapse in 2008, there was not much to indicate that they would produce any great results, but the economic crisis proved to be a watershed. A Constitutional Commission was appointed in 2010 and asked to organise the National Forum held in November 2010 and to prepare the work of the Constitutional Assembly, which was elected in 2011 (subsequently renamed the Constitutional Council) designed to draft a proposal for revising the 1944 Constitution. In the first days of August 2011, the Constitutional Council submitted its Proposal for a new Constitution to the Alþing, and when parliament was convened that fall, the President expressed his view about the proposals in a way that aroused attention: 'The proposals by the Constitutional Council entail important changes to Iceland's constitutional structure,'[17] said Ólafur Ragnar Grímsson. 'In effect, they would be the basis of a new constitutional structure,

14 Jóhannesson, *The First Presidents* (n 1) 186, footnote 562; see also: the meeting minutes of the Council of the State from 13 January 1993 in the National Archive of Iceland.

15 Act No. 56 of 31 May 1991.

16 Act No. 97 of 28 June 1995.

17 President Ólafur Ragnar Grímsson's New Year's speech, 1 January 2013.

a democratic system different from what the nation is used to, very different from the one we have known for decades.'[18]

More than seven years have passed since the Constitutional Council's Proposal for a New Constitution was unveiled. I cannot predict what will become of them. However, history shows that those who have occupied Bessastaðir have consistently expressed their views on the position of the President in Iceland's constitutional structure. They have gone to varying lengths in doing this and in response to different situations. Each president has shaped the office according to his or her own wishes, the spirit of the times, and the needs of the moment, within the framework set by custom, tradition, and the constitutional structure itself.

In the summer of 2016, another milestone was reached with the election of a new Head of State. In the run-up to the presidential election, I described my position on constitutional change in these words:

> The President should promote consensus regarding the Constitution of Iceland. It needs to include provisions on the right of a specific number of voters to demand a referendum on legislation from the Althing. Also, the powers and responsibilities of the President of Iceland need to be better clarified. On these questions, the President should adopt his own official standpoint, since they have a direct bearing on his position.[19]

In my inaugural speech on 1 August 2016, I drew attention to the responsibility that rests with the Alþing in these words:

> If parliament is incapable of responding to calls from large numbers of voters and the declared will of the political parties for constitutional reform or review, then we are in trouble. In this connection I stress the value of settling for partial victories and making compromises.[20]

I repeat this call now. Politics is the art of the possible.

18 Ibid.
19 National Broadcasting Service RUV X16, information and interviews with candidates to the presidential elections of 2016: www.ruv.is/persona/gudni-th-johannesson
20 www.forseti.is/media/1072/2016_08_01_inauguration_speech_english.pdf

3 The reform of the 1944 Constitution and Icelandic constitutionalism

Ágúst Þór Árnason† *and Catherine Dupré*

Ágúst Þór and I discussed his chapter as part of our general editing work, and we finalised the core issues to be included in it during my last visit to him in April 2019. Ágúst Þór had no time to write it up, so we agreed that I would do this for him. As he left no draft manuscript and no set of notes for me to work with, my role was much more than editing or polishing an unfinished version. I had to write this chapter in its entirety but did so on the basis of ideas and arguments that Ágúst Þór entrusted me to express on his behalf. What I have therefore sought to achieve above all is to let Ágúst Þór's voice and opinions come through as clearly as possible. While he regularly commented on the constitutional reform in Icelandic media until 2018, his last academic publication dates from 2011. Therefore, his overall analysis of the constitutional reform is reconstructed in English for the first time here. His key message was not to reject the 1944 Constitution and the Republic it has established. Rather, he saw the complex reform process between 2009 and 2017 as a unique opportunity to reflect on the path travelled and, in particular, on the significance of two core features of the Constitution, namely the President and the Republic, and their interconnections through the People.

Bearing in mind that the chapter was also designed as an overview of the reform, I decided to provide a broader analytical framework within which Ágúst Þór's arguments could be positioned and take their fuller significance. In terms of style, I have sought to distinguish his voice – by referring to e.g. 'Ágúst Þór's argument' – from mine, which is intended as an editorial voice-over outlining the wider context and issues and seeking to join the dots of some of his unfinished connections. Following the Icelandic custom, I have used his first name. In terms of substance, in addition to our April 2019 work, I have drawn on my own record of our discussions going back to the early months of 2009 and 2010 when Ágúst Þór sat on the Constitutional Commission. In order to supplement this, I have referred to his publications, and, wherever possible, I have quoted his earlier work. In terms of methodology, I have sought to follow Ágúst Þór's approach, which Joakim Nergelius refers to as 'theoretical-historical' [J Nergelius (ed), Constitutionalism: New Challenges *(Martin Nijhoff 2008) xiv], whereby a focus on historical presentation becomes a narrative blending into a theoretical framework, within which the law is understood.*[1] *Ágúst Þór tended to keep his papers short and concise, with an apparent technicality and simplicity that often masked a deeper level of philosophical reflection, though he tended not to refer much to constitutional law theory or political philosophy. I have therefore followed this approach which was also in line with our editorial endeavour not to fit the Icelandic constitutional reform into a pre-existing theoretical box. In addition, I have used my editorial discretion to put together a more substantial footnote apparatus, in order to include as systematically as possible references to his own work, something he rarely did himself, but that was necessary to bring together here his earlier writing with his last thoughts on Icelandic constitutionalism and on the constitutional reform.*

I am immensely grateful to Ágúst Þór's family, his children and his partner: the time he spent discussing his work with me in April 2019 was time they could not spend with him. Special thanks are due to Icelandic colleagues and friends who made it possible for me to complete this chapter: Aðalheiður Ámundadóttir helped me understand the reform's wider context; Skúli Magnússon patiently and thoroughly answered my questions, filling in many gaps in my knowledge of Icelandic constitutionalism, and provided valuable feedback on draft versions of this chapter; and Margrét Elísabet Ólafsdóttir generously let me borrow some key documents from Ágúst Þór's work archive. Thanks are also due to Guðmundur Alfreðsson, Skúli Magnússon, and Sigríður Vilhjálmsdóttir for helping me collate a list of Ágúst Þór's publications in Icelandic, which is presented at the end of this chapter. Outside Iceland, I wish to thank Stephen Skinner, who made helpful suggestions on how best to approach this unusual co-authorship, and Cheryl Saunders who provided insightful and encouraging feedback on a draft version of this chapter. Any errors and misunderstandings are mine.

Introduction

When the question of the constitutional reform reached the political agenda in the early months of 2009, the 1944 Constitution had already been reformed seven times apparently without problems. Indeed, in Iceland, constitutional reform is part of the normal political and law-making discussion, as under Article 79(1) of the Constitution, the procedure for constitutional revision broadly follows the ordinary legislative process, except for the important requirement that a constitutional amendment has to be confirmed by a new parliament after a general election and so involves two parliaments. The reform considered in this collection was unprecedented as it arguably involved an attempt to adopt an entirely new constitution,

1 Typically, see: Ágúst Þór Árnason, 'What Did Icelanders Really Want? The Home Rule Revisited' in Lise Lick (ed), *Socio-Economic Developments in Greenland and Other Small Nordic Jurisdictions* (New Social Science Monographs 1997) 241, and 'The History of the Icelandic Constitution and Some Economic Issues' in Lise Lyck (ed), *Constitutional and Economic Space of the Small Nordic Jurisdictions* (NordREFO 1997) 48.

and to do so by creating, under Act 90/2010 on the Constitutional Assembly, a special body outside Parliament to draft proposals for amendments. In addition, after the 2013 general election, a new – and interim – revision procedure was adopted by Constitutional Act 91/2013 in an endeavour to at least complete some amendments to the Constitution as it had proved impossible to adopt a new constitution under the previous parliament (2009–2013).

This departure from established practice and from Article 79(1), combined with the unprecedently tumultuous financial, social, and political contexts, renders almost impossible any attempt to construct a posteriori an overall narrative that might help make sense of the reform. If anything, the reform process can be seen as characterised by a constantly evolving entanglement of conflicting narratives or underlying logics, with many of them being shaped as spontaneous responses to unpredictable developments. Bearing this in mind and as the historiography of those years is still in flux, this chapter provides a first analytical grid to understand the reform and to assess its significance for Icelandic constitutionalism.

Ágúst Þór did not approach the reform primarily in terms of what it had achieved (or rather did not achieve); nor did he seek to reconstruct a narrative for the reform process itself. Instead, his starting point was to ask *why* the 1944 Constitution should be reformed at all, and if so whether it should be reformed to the extent undertaken by the Constitutional Council (the body especially created by parliament to take over the role of the Constitutional Assembly and to draft a constitutional proposal). Positioning his analysis of the constitutional reform squarely within the framework of the 1944 Constitution and ultimately assessing it by reference to this text, rather than primarily to the context in which it took place, Ágúst Þór had two main arguments. The first was that the financial crisis and its aftermath did not justify replacing the 1944 Constitution by an entirely new text. While he fully acknowledged the seriousness of the situation, he did not think that Iceland in 2008–2009 could, for instance, be compared to Central and Eastern Europe after the collapse of the Soviet bloc or to South Africa at the end of the Apartheid regime. The second argument was that while most, if not all commentators on (and actors in) the reform agreed on the point that the reform process had failed because no change to the text of the 1944 Constitution was ultimately made,[2] a key substantive change tended to be overlooked. That is the veto power of the President vis-à-vis the Parliament demonstrated by the 2010 Icesave referendum held under Article 26 of the Constitution, that was fully implemented for the first time.

In order to understand these two points more fully, the chapter proceeds in three stages. It starts by raising the question *why?* – challenging the construction of a correlation between the 'pots and pans revolution' as a causal link, not only explaining but also justifying a full revision. Secondly, the chapter addresses the question *how?* and discusses the processes of constitutional change and development. The

2 Constitutional Act 91/2013 created a new procedure for amending the 1944 Constitution. However, it ceased to be valid on 30 April 2017 and therefore introduced no lasting change to the Constitution.

chapter argues that the emphasis on formal procedures – there were in total three different frameworks for revising the Constitution – has distracted attention away from the constitutional significance of the first Icesave referendum of 6 March 2010, which was triggered as a result of Article 26 of the 1944 Constitution being fully implemented for the first time. Thirdly, the chapter reflects on *what* was achieved in terms of changes to the Constitution and argues that a core feature of the 1944 Constitution was clarified, namely the powers and status of the President of the Republic.

Ultimately, this chapter contributes to understanding constitutional change both in Iceland and in broader theoretical terms (i.e. drawing on the Icelandic experience to inform theoretical reflection rather than the other way around). In this regard, it highlights the fact that substantial constitutional change can take place outside any formal process of revision of the constitution, when a constitutional power is fully exercised for the first time. Moreover, it emphasises the importance of methodological choices when studying and assessing constitutional reform, a question that calls for greater explication than has been the case for the Icelandic reform both inside and outside Iceland.

Why reform the 1944 Constitution?

The question *why?* was the first question Ágúst Þór raised about the events of 2009–2017. It was one of the first questions he raised with his fellow members of the Constitutional Commission (2010–2011) when they set out to prepare the National Forum and the work of what was at the time called the Constitutional Assembly (subsequently renamed the Constitutional Council).[3] It was also the last question that he raised reflecting upon the entire process nearly a decade after he was first involved in it. It is, of course, the essential question to ask because answering it determines the question *what?* – namely, whether the revision has to be partial or total – and the question *how?* – namely, whether it should occur within the existing constitutional framework or through a specially adopted framework and, if so, how this framework should be designed. Ultimately, addressing this question is necessary for monitoring the reform process and reflecting on whether it is achieving its overall aim(s). The question *why?* is all the more important because in the fast-moving political context of the reform years, it does not seem to have been given much analytical consideration. Ágúst Þór thought that constructing the 'pots and pans revolution' as a call (or even a demand) and as a legitimate reason for the full revision of the 1944 Constitution was at best an oversimplification of the reality, driven by a short-term vision of Icelandic constitutionalism. Such construction of the 'pots and pans revolution' also overlooked the significance of the context in which the 1944 Icelandic Constitution was adopted.

3 This is discussed in this collection by Björg Thorarensen (Chapter 5).

1944 as Iceland's constitutional moment

Calls for an overall reform of the 1944 Constitution stemmed from the fact that it is, in essence, a revised version of the first Icelandic constitution of 1874 (modelled upon the Danish constitutions of 1849 and 1866). Ágúst Þór considered the adoption of the revised constitution in 1944 as Iceland's 'constitutional moment,' a concept that he understood as meaning a unique set of circumstances justifying – and legitimising – the adoption of a new constitution and giving it its distinctive identity,[4] emphasising that 1944 was the culmination of Iceland's long struggle for independence and marked its transformation from a monarchy into a republic. He would also point out that these changes had taken place in a very legalistic manner and would ask rhetorically how many democracies were functioning properly at that point in time.

Icelanders' high level of involvement as one people through a referendum in May 1944 gave the revised Constitution its ultimate democratic seal of approval. In addition, Ágúst Þór would observe that, despite the apparently limited changes to the text of the Constitution, its theoretical significance was clear to its main drafters. These consisted of a committee composed of three Supreme Court judges amongst whom was Einar Arnósson (a key figure in the negotiation of the 1918 Union Treaty with Denmark who became Minister of Education and Justice between 1942 and 1944), and professor of constitutional law, Bjarni Benediktsson (born 1908, mayor of Reykjavik in 1940, and elected to parliament in 1942). This committee was asked by Prime Minister Hermann Jónasson, as early as 1940, to draft a constitution in the event of Iceland being cut off from Denmark because of the war. In particular, Ágúst Þór would point out that Bjarni Benediktsson, who had studied in Berlin in 1932, is understood to have observed Hitler's rise to power and to have been aware of the significance of constitutional law in providing democratic safeguards. The committee's first draft eventually became the basis for the 1944 Constitution, with the major difference (discussed in more detail later in the chapter) being that the President would be directly and universally elected by Icelanders rather than elected by Parliament as originally suggested by Bjarni Benediktsson.[5]

Ágúst Þór described the circumstances of the adoption of the 1944 Constitution in the following way:

> When Iceland became a republic in 1944 the concept of its constitution was still in the making. The Second World War was then in its last phase, and the Icelandic politicians were aware of the possibility that their claim for independence from the Danish Monarchy could be rejected, or even forgotten, in the political turbulences of the times – when the winners of the war would start their wheeling and dealing about the construction of a new world order.

4 Ágúst Þór tended to refer to Bruce Ackerman, *We the People: 1. Foundations* (Belknap Press 1991).

5 With thanks to Skúli Magnússon for these clarifications.

> [. . .] When the German army invaded Denmark on April 9, 1940, Iceland lost contact with its Monarch. The Icelandic parliament declared, the following night, that the Icelandic government would assume the Danish King's duties for the time being and take control over foreign affairs and other matters previously handled by Denmark on behalf of Iceland. The invasion of Denmark had not come as a total surprise to Icelandic parliamentarians, and the political parties seemed to be quite united in their response to those serious happenings in Denmark – but without much debate about where the state of Iceland was heading as a constitutional entity. However, it was made clear that the Union Treaty with Denmark would not be renewed when it expired in 1943.[6]

And:

> The Constitution of Iceland was adopted on June 17, 1944. Two years earlier, the Constitutional Amendment Act (No 97, December 16, 1942) had been enacted to enable the nation to vote on the new constitution. The national referendum was held on May 20–23. The turnout was 98.61 per cent, and 95.04 per cent of the votes cast were in favour of the new constitution. The referendum dealt only with the dissolution of the Danish-Icelandic Union and the establishment of a republic in which Icelanders could assume the highest positions.[7]

As it was mainly intended to sever the remaining ties with the Kingdom of Denmark (rather than being future oriented), the 1944 Constitution was at first considered to be a 'preliminary one'[8] and a 'patched garment,'[9] a critique that was brought back to the fore of the discussion by those requesting the adoption of a new constitution from 2008 onwards. However, subsequent attempts to replace it with a new text consistently failed. Between 1945 and 1972, the Icelandic Parliament (or Alþing) appointed a number of committees with a view to revising the Constitution but with no result.[10] In 1983, a bill on the general revision of the Constitution was proposed by Gunnar Thoroddsen (Independence Party), the then Prime Minister and chairman of the Constitutional Committee, which had been appointed by the Alþing following its 1978 resolution to revise the Constitution.[11] However, the

6 Ágúst Þór Árnason, 'Constitutionalism and the Republic of Iceland and the Role and Status of the President' in Asbjørn Eide, Jakob Th. Möller, and Ineta Ziemele (eds), *Making Peoples Heard: Essays on Human Rights in Honour of Gudmundur Alfredsson* (Martinus Nijhoff 2011) 589.

7 Árnason, 'The History of the Icelandic Constitution' (n 1) 48. This paper discusses the two different visions of Icelandic constitutionalism, respectively put forward by Gylfi Þ Gíslason and Ólafur Jóhannesson, 58.

8 Ibid. 51.

9 Sveinn Björnsson, first President of Icelandic Republic (1944–1952), 1949 New Year's address. See: Guðni Th. Jóhannesson in this collection (Chapter 2).

10 Árnason, 'The History of the Icelandic Constitution' (n 1) 51.

11 Ibid. 51.

Prime Minister's party lost the 1983 parliamentary elections.[12] The 'elaborate bill' for a new constitution was therefore dropped,[13] leaving the 1944 Constitution in place as the Republic's foundational text.

The 'pots and pans revolution': insufficient justification for extensive revision

There is no doubt that the 'pots and pans revolution' (*búsáhaldabyltingin*) was an exceptional moment in Iceland[14] and that it reflected a profound crisis of trust between Icelanders and their politicians which had deeper and more complex roots than its immediate trigger, the collapse of the banking sector. Ágúst Þór would point out that not many Icelanders had read their Constitution at the time and that what most wanted in those months was primarily justice, the bankers' resignation, as well as the resignation of the government and of the Prime Minister, who had led Iceland to this catastrophic situation. Among those calls, the idea that the 1944 Constitution should be revised started being floated in December 2008, when a petition requesting a constitutional reform and early election was circulated.[15] The first idea for full revision has tended to be attributed to Professor Njörður P. Njarðvik who gave a television interview on 11 January 2009, comparing Iceland in 2009 to France in 1789.[16] This period was marked by an effervescence of ideas that was relayed and amplified by the TV, radio, and newspapers, as well as by social media – notably Facebook – which were just beginning to take off at the time. They made it possible for individual people to connect with one another in an unprecedented manner. In this process, social media arguably gave some isolated voices a disproportionate audience and prominence. As Skúli Magnússon notes in his chapter, there were, however, also collective calls for a new constitution:

> In a press-announcement [of 22 January 2009] by Voices of the People ('*Raddir fólksins*'), probably the most influential of various popular movements

12 Baldvin Th Bergsson notes that this was a 'one-man project, which attracted limited interest': 'The Constitution as a Political Tool in Iceland: From the Periphery to the Center of the Political Debate' in Paul Blokker (ed), *Constitutional Acceleration within the European Union and Beyond* (Routledge 2018) 157.

13 For the key changes that this bill would have introduced, see: Árnason, 'The History of the Icelandic Constitution' (n 1) 59–61.

14 Jérôme Skalski, *La révolution des casseroles: Chronique d'une nouvelle constitution pour l'Islande* (La Contre Allée 2012); and Jón Gunnar Bernburg, *Economic Crisis and Mass Protest: The Pots and Pans Revolution in Iceland* (Routledge 2016). This chapter uses the word 'revolution' as it has become the mainstream label for those events, but it does not engage with any consideration of political theory on that concept.

15 Skalski (n 14) 49.

16 See e.g.: One of his articles on the subject 'Nýtt lýðveldi' published on 14 January 2009 on www.visir.is/g/2009133864879 (all webpages accessed 2 June 2020). See also: Bergsson (n 12). Njörður P. Njarðvik subsequently sat on the (2010–2011) Constitutional Commission, but his formal involvement in the constitutional reform seems to have stopped there.

> emerging in autumn 2008, it is stated that the 'will of the Icelandic People is to rebuild the Republic by writing a new Constitution and changing the rules of politics'. It further reads: 'Let us emphasise on building a new Iceland, a new Republic and a new Nation' (www.visir.is on 22.01.2009). Other, albeit less prominent popular movements, carried names referring to a similar ideal, e.g. 'New Times', 'New Iceland' and 'New Republic'. This manifesto was, by and large, taken up by a new political party supported by various popular movements in the beginning of 2009, the 'Citizens' Movement' [*Borgarahreyfingin*], which won four seats in the elections of Spring 2009 and proved to be an ardent supporter of the 2011 Proposal and the 2012 Constitutional Bill submitted to the Alþing.[17]

Ágúst Þór considered these to be insufficiently representative to justify a full or extensive revision of the 1944 Constitution, and he observed that established political parties' engagement with the constitutional reform was rather mixed, and that it dwindled by 2013. The members of the Progressive Party who 'had been looking for a popular idea' were the first to put forward a constitutional bill to amend Article 79(1) of the Constitution on 6 February 2009, which was, however, dropped.[18] Later on and formally, the constitutional revision project came from the interim Prime Minister, Social Democrat Jóhanna Sigurðardóttir, on 4 March 2009 with a constitutional bill providing for a constitutional assembly to be directly elected and a binding referendum to adopt the constitutional proposal that it was intended to elaborate[19]. In short, the power to revise the Constitution would no longer be held by Parliament; instead, it would be jointly exercised by a constituent body and Icelanders with Parliament only playing an advisory role.

While this was, of course, a response to what MPs, and the Prime Minister in particular, perceived as being what Icelanders wanted at that time, Ágúst Þór observed that 'as an MP [she] had for many years fought for the total revision of the constitution by means of a constitutional assembly.'[20] Therefore, Jóhanna Sigurðardóttir's proposal can also be seen as a continuation of her earlier call for constitutional reform in 1994 (when the human rights discussion was taking place),[21] rather than exclusively as her response to Icelanders at this juncture.[22] In this respect, Ágúst Þór noted that the 2009 election manifesto of the Social Democrats

17 Skúli Magnússon's Chapter 8 in this collection, note 9.

18 136. löggjafarþing 2008–2009. Þskj. 512–286. Mál: www.althingi.is/altext/136/s/0512.htm. The February bill provided that a constituent assembly should be established with binding power to adopt a new constitution pending a referendum. This meant that the procedure of Article 79(1) of the Constitution was to be completely overridden, with Parliament not playing any part in the revision procedure.

19 136. löggjafarþing 2008–2009. Þskj. 648—385. Mál, https://www.althingi.is/altext/136/s/0648.html

20 Ágúst Þór Árnason, 'A Review of the Icelandic Constitution: Popular Sovereignty or Political Confusion' (2011) *Bij de Bueren* 342.

21 As discussed later in the chapter.

22 Árnason, 'A Review of the Icelandic Constitution' (n 20) 347.

did not include any reference to reforming the constitution. Having secured a solid parliamentary majority after the election of April 2009, the Prime Minister pursued her project without, however, explicitly focussing on a total revision of the 1944 Constitution, but at the same time the end product, Act 90/2010 on the Constitutional Assembly, did not preclude this option. Ultimately, the 2012 Constitutional Bill, largely drafted on the basis of the 2011 Proposal for a New Constitution, was not even voted on before the term of the parliament expired and the next general election took place in spring 2013.[23]

Apart from the Citizens' Movement, other political parties had mixed views on the constitutional reform.[24] The Independence Party (sometimes referred to in English as the Conservative Party), traditionally very influential in parliament with regard to constitutional issues, was the most consistently reluctant to support, if not opposed to, the constitutional reform over the period. The Progressive Party, which had been the first to table a bill on a constitutional assembly and was initially in favour of this project (perhaps due to its association with the cooperative movement in the early twentieth century and the values of popular or direct democracy inherent to that movement), turned out to be unsupportive of the 2011 Proposal for a New Constitution drafted by the Constitutional Council. The Left-Green party was mostly ambivalent about the reform throughout the revision process, until its new leader Katrín Jakobsdóttir, elected in February 2013, became a member of the 2013–2016 Constitutional Committee.[25] The Pirates Party was consistently in favour of a radical reform; however, having only been founded in 2012, it joined the political and constitutional discussion quite late, when the parliamentary debate of the 2012 Constitutional Bill was grinding to a halt. In addition, there did not seem to have been a consensus amongst its members on how to pursue the reform between 2013–2016, when the Pirates Party had the greatest representation in parliament, and a representative (Aðalheiður Ámundadóttir) on the Constitutional Committee.

Ágúst Þór, writing in 2013 with Skúli Magnússon in their Memorandum to the Venice Commission in response to its Draft Opinion, made it clear that:

> Thus, [. . .] we have maintained that the links between constitutional deficiencies and the financial collapse are, at best [. . .] highly speculative and have been left entirely unexplained by those taking [this] view. [. . .] Although we would concede that certain constitutional issues could be reviewed in light of the financial crisis (e.g. constitutional provisions providing for more transparency with regard to financial interests of MPs), the financial crisis is, as such, insufficient justification for an overturning of the entire Icelandic constitution.[26]

23 This is discussed further in the respective chapters of Skúli Magnússon (Chapter 8), Jón Ólafsson (Chapter 7), and Thorvaldur Gylfason (Chapter 12) in this collection.

24 Bergsson (n 12) 157–158.

25 See: Katrín Jakobsdóttir in this collection (Chapter 13).

26 Ágúst Þór Árnason and Skúli Magnússon, 'Memorandum on the Draft Opinion of the Venice Commission 702/2013 of 11 February 2013', 27 February 2013, para 4 (on file with the author).

Overall, as observed by Baldvin Thor Bergsson, the early calls for a new political system were too fragmented to last. The new political parties (Dawn and Democracy Watch) that emerged in the run-up to the 2013 election to promote the adoption of a new constitution failed to attract enough voters, and the two parties that had led the constitutional reform were defeated.[27]

No technical reason for reforming the constitution extensively

Ágúst Þór argued that, although it was not perfect, the 1944 Constitution functioned effectively and there was no technical need to replace it with a brand-new text. By 2008, the route of partial amendments had been successfully pursued seven times.[28] The first amendment took place in 1959 when the size of constituencies was increased, abolishing those encompassing only one or two representatives.[29] In 1968, the right to vote was brought down to 20 from 21 years of age. The 1984 amendment further dealt with constituencies and political parties and increased the number of MPs from 60 to 63.[30] In 1991, a major institutional reform was introduced when the two chambers of Parliament were merged into one, and its position was strengthened vis-à-vis the cabinet, e.g. with regard to the issuing of interim legislation and dissolution.[31] The next substantial amendment was undertaken in 1995 to mark the 50th anniversary of the Constitution.[32] This was mostly designed to bring the Icelandic Constitution into line with Iceland's international human rights commitments, particularly but not exclusively due to the codification of the European Convention on Human Rights in 1993 (ratified in 1953).[33] The last amendment, on the electoral system, was introduced in 1999, after which yet another constitutional committee was formed by parliament in 2003, 'without yielding any result.'[34]

Consequently, in 2008 at least some of the issues that needed to be addressed through revision had already been dealt with. In addition, the discussion on constitutional revision had continued since 1995, on and off, focussing in particular

27 Bergsson (n 12) 165.

28 L. 51/1959 (tóku gildi 20. ágúst 1959). L. 9/1968 (tóku gildi 24. apríl 1968). L. 65/1984 (tóku gildi 13. júní 1984). L. 56/1991 (tóku gildi 31. maí 1991). L. 97/1995 (tóku gildi 5. júlí 1995). L. 100/1995 (tóku gildi 5. júlí 1995). L. 77/1999 (tóku gildi 1. júlí 1999).

29 Árnason, 'History of the Icelandic Constitution' (n 1) 59.

30 Act 65/1984 of 30 May 1984, discussed by Árnason, 'History of the Icelandic Constitution' (n 1) 61–62.

31 Act 56/1991 of 31 May 1991, discussed by Árnason and Martin Scheinin, 'Republic of Iceland' in Gisbert H Flanz (ed), *Constitutions of the Countries of the World*, Release 99–1 (Oceana Publications 1999) ix; see also: Ágúst Þór Árnason 'Iceland' in Gerhard Robbers (ed), *Encyclopedia of World Constitutions* (Facts on File 2007) volume II 393.

32 Act 97/1995 of 28 June 1995 and Act 100/1995 of 28 June 1995: with a detailed discussion by Árnason and Scheinin (n 31) xi–xvii.

33 Gudrun Gauksdóttir, 'Iceland' in Robert Blackburn and Jörg Polakiewicz (eds), *Fundamental Rights in Europe, The ECHR and Its Member States, 1950–2000* (OUP 2001) 399–422.

34 Árnason, 'A Review of the Icelandic Constitution' (n 20) 346.

on natural resources with the publication of the 2000 Report of the Committee on Natural Resources appointed by parliament.[35] Therefore, when the banking sector collapsed in October 2008, constitutional reform was not particularly on the agenda, nor were there calls to replace the Constitution with a brand-new text. The 1944 Constitution seemed to meet the needs of Iceland to function as a democracy, and it also met international human rights standards. If anything, it can be suggested that the years between 2008 and 2017 proved the remarkable resilience of the 1944 Constitution, which was used successfully to manage a number of serious political crises. As noted by Ágúst Þór and Skúli Magnússon:

> the constitutional order of Iceland provided for sufficient *terra firma* for a democratic 'healing procedure' as well as various difficult decisions in the public domain post 2008.'[36]

For instance, when the government resigned in February 2009 (and in April 2016), an interim prime minister was appointed, and an early election was organised with a minimum of disruption. Similarly, parliament (which was much criticised by those arguing for a total revision based on the 2011 Proposal for a New Constitution) continued to function and to adopt key legislation, notably the so-called Emergency Act of October 2008 to address the financial collapse and an Act setting up an office of a special prosecutor for economic crimes. The combination of the hard framework provided by the 1944 Constitution, with a soft padding arising out of a mix of practices and conventions, as well as MPs' creative minds, made it possible to come up with innovative ways designed to unblock tricky situations, while complying with democratic standards. This included, for instance, the parliamentary resolution 19/139 of 24 March 2011 to appoint the elected members of the Constitutional Assembly to the new Constitutional Council,[37] parliament's resolution of 24 May 2012 to hold an advisory referendum,[38] and the Constitutional Act 91/2013 of 5 July 2013 establishing an interim constitutional reform procedure.[39]

How did constitutional change and development occur? Formal and informal processes

Between 2010 and 2017, constitutional reform was pursued within three distinctive frameworks, namely Article 79(1) of the 1944 Constitution, Act 90/2010 creating the Constitutional Assembly, and Constitutional Act 91/2013 establishing an interim constitutional revision procedure. Given this backdrop, Ágúst Þór would argue that while the 2010 Icesave referendum was mostly considered from financial and

35 See: Chapter 10 in this collection by Ragnheiður Elfa Þorsteinsdóttir.
36 Árnason and Magnússon (n 26) para 5.
37 www.althingi.is/altext/139/s/1120.html
38 www.althingi.is/thingstorf/thingmalalistar-eftir-thingum/ferill/?ltg=140&mnr=636
39 www.althingi.is/altext/142/s/0088.html

political perspectives, its full significance as a key moment of constitutional development has largely been overlooked. Making these points requires distinguishing between formal and informal processes of constitutional change and development.

Formal processes of change

Article 79(1) of the 1944 Constitution

The 1944 Constitution organises the procedure for its own revision under Article 79, which played a key role in the 2008–2017 reform process, and provides the following:

> Proposals to *amend or supplement* [Tillögur, hvort sem eru til breytinga eða viðauka] this Constitution may be introduced at regular as well as extraordinary sessions of Althingi. If the proposal [tillagan] is adopted, Althingi shall immediately be dissolved and a general election held. If Althingi then passes the resolution [Samþykki Alþingi ályktunina] unchanged, it shall be confirmed by the President of the Republic and come into force as constitutional law [stjórnskipunarlög].
>
> If Althingi passes an amendment to the status of the Church under Article 62, it shall be submitted to a vote for approval or rejection by secret ballot of all those eligible to vote.
>
> (emphasis added)

Article 79(1) focusses on what happens *after* a constitutional proposal is adopted by Parliament and is silent on *how* this proposal may be drafted or *what* it may (or may not) involve in terms of substance. Under this framework, the Constitutional revision power is exercised through the interaction of three different entities, none of which holds that power on its own. Parliament is a key actor but has to share the constitutional revision power, which requires two types of confirmation: one indirectly by voters in a general election, the other by the President of the Republic. That is, the constitutional revision process follows the ordinary law-making procedure, with the notable difference that Icelanders are indirectly involved in confirming the constitutional proposal adopted by Parliament, through a general election. As previously mentioned, this process was used successfully seven times in the past. However, if voters do not elect a parliament supporting the constitutional proposal, this puts an end to the reform process and the proposal is deemed not to have existed. Finally, it can be noted that Article 79(1) does not provide for any independent referendum to be part of this process, nor does it provide for any special quorum in Parliament to adopt the constitutional proposals before or after the general election.

Act 90/2010 on the Constitutional Assembly

The Act 90/2010 on a Constitutional Assembly was adopted to open up the normal revision procedure to Icelanders in an explicit attempt to rebuild their trust in public institutions. As it is discussed at length in this volume,[40] it is only briefly set out here. Act 90/2010 focussed on the drafting process, taking it outside Parliament and entrusting it to an ad hoc body, the Constitutional Assembly,[41] to be elected directly and through a voting system that had never been used in Iceland before (single transferrable vote).[42] Article 6 of the Act explicitly stated that 'the President of the Republic of Iceland, members of Parliament, their alternates, cabinet ministers and members of the Constitutional Commission and the organising Committee are not eligible to stand for the election.' The novelty of the voting system, perhaps as well as its complexity, may have contributed to the defects which led the Supreme Court to invalidate the elections in January 2011. Parliament continued the reform project regardless of that ruling by appointing through a resolution the originally elected members (except one) to a Constitutional *Council*, created to replace the Constitutional Assembly.[43]

Under Act 90/2010, the substance of the constitutional proposal to be drafted by the Constitutional Assembly was framed in three different ways. Firstly, Article 3 of the Act listed eight groups of issues that the Assembly was to 'specifically address' and further provided that it 'may decide to address additional matters to those referred to in the first paragraph.' Secondly, the substance of these changes was to be shaped on the basis of the views of a random sample of 'approximately one thousand people' to come together in what was called a National Forum. Thirdly, the Act created a seven-member Constitutional Commission to organise that Forum and to 'process the information collected at the National Forum and deliver it to the Constitutional Assembly when it convenes.' These last two features of the revision procedure were tacked on at the end of the Act under a section entitled 'interim provision' (*Ákvæði til bráðabirgða*). Ágúst Þór was one of the seven members of that Commission and contributed to preparing the 2011 two-volume Report ultimately delivered to the Constitutional Council on 6 April 2011.[44]

40 The Act is available at www.thjodfundur2010.is/other_files/2010/doc/Act-on-a-Constitutional-Assembly.pdf, and it is further discussed by Björg Thorarensen (Chapter 5) and of Salvör Nordal (Chapter 6).

41 'The idea of [. . .] establishing a Constitutional Assembly was proposed for the first time in the time of the Republic by a member of the Parliament in 1948. This idea seems to have been inspired by the Constitutional Assembly (Thjóðfundurinn) that had been held at the beginning of the struggle for national freedom in 1851. It does not seem as if the idea was widely discussed at that time, and there are only few traces of similar ideas [until 2009]': Árnason, 'A Review of the Icelandic Constitution' (n 20) 346–7.

42 Most of Act 90/2010 is taken up by the detailed organisation of the election of the Constitutional Assembly.

43 Resolution 19/139 of 24 March 2011: www.althingi.is/altext/139/s/1120.html. Act 90/2010 was repealed with immediate effect by Act 31/2011 of 12 April 2011: www.althingi.is/altext/139/s/1280.html

44 The text of the Report is available online: Volume I: www.stjornlagarad.is/other_files/stjornlagarad/skyrsla-stjornlaganefndar/skyrsla_stjornlaganefndar_fyrra_bindi.pdf-; and Volume II: www.stjornlagarad.is/other_files/stjornlagarad/skyrsla-stjornlaganefndar/skyrsla_stjornlaganefndar_seinna_bindi.pdf

While this Act was quite detailed about the Constitutional Assembly's election process, and about what should constitute the basis of the Constitutional Assembly's work, it was silent as to the exact constitutional status of the proposal to be drafted by the Assembly. Article 27 simply provided, 'When the Constitutional Assembly has passed the constitutional bill [frumvarp til stjórnarskipunarlaga], it shall be sent to the Alþing to be processed.' This omission created much uncertainty and political controversy.[45] Finally, it has to be noted that the Act 90/2010 and the Act's Explanatory Notes were also silent in relation to the normal constitutional revision procedure and made no reference to Article 79(1) of the Constitution. This can arguably be understood as meaning that there were two procedures existing in parallel, with Act 90/2010 organising the first stage of the revision process (namely *how* the constitutional proposal was to be drafted and *what* issues it should address) and Article 79(1) providing for its adoption. However, that view was far from being generally accepted, with the Prime Minister Jóhanna Sigurðardóttir being one of those who advocated a limited role for Parliament in this respect.

Constitutional Act 91/2013 Amending the Constitution of the Republic

This Act, which amends the Constitution for a temporary period, was adopted in compliance with Article 79(1), in two stages: it was initially passed shortly before the dissolution of parliament in April 2013, and after its election, the new parliament confirmed it on 5 July 2013. The first stage of adoption (before the 2013 election) was marked by a general sense of underachievement, as parliament had not been able (or willing) to progress the 2011 Proposal for a New Constitution beyond the 2012 Constitutional Bill that was not voted on before the 2013 election, making it impossible to turn it into a new constitution. Constitutional Act 91/2013 Amending the Constitution of the Republic has two articles and is summarised in the following terms by Páll Þórhallsson:

> If Parliament approves a constitutional bill with at last 2/3 of votes cast it shall be submitted to a *binding referendum*. The referendum shall take place no sooner than 6 months after the parliamentary approval and no later than 9 months. In order to pass, the bill needs to be approved by the majority of valid votes which is not less than 40% of all registered voters. Subsequently it shall be confirmed by the President of the Republic and become a valid constitutional law.[46]
>
> (emphasis added)

This special constitutional revision procedure envisaged a referendum as a response to the controversy arising out of the 2012 advisory referendum. This Act was followed by the appointment of a Constitutional Committee with cross-party

45 See: Jón Ólafsson (Chapter 7) and Thorvaldur Gylfason (Chapter 12) in this collection.
46 www.althingi.is/altext/142/s/0088.html. See: Chapter 9 by Páll Þórhallsson in this collection, note 6.

representation expected to take the constitutional reform forward in the new 2013–2017 parliament. Establishing an exceptional procedure for revising the 1944 Constitution, Constitutional Act 91/2013 was explicitly declared to be valid only until 30 April 2017, the expected normal end of that parliament's term. As discussed elsewhere in this volume, the political crisis of the Panama Papers led to an early election on 29 October 2016, and another crisis triggered the collapse of the coalition government, resulting in another early election on 28 October 2017. In the meantime, the validity of Constitutional Act 91/2013 expired with no formal change to the text of the Constitution being made at all.

While Act 90/2010 and Constitutional Act 91/2013 were adopted in an attempt to respond to a set of specific circumstances and issues, it has to be noted that the overarching revision framework, at least from a formal legal point of view, remained Article 79(1) of the 1944 Constitution. However, there were a number of political arguments according to which the 'pots and pans revolution' amounted to a constitutional moment for Iceland and justified the adoption of a new constitution, regardless of the procedures specified by Article 79(1). The advisory nature of the 2012 referendum is emblematic of this tension. Despite the political turbulences and technical challenges that characterised the reform period, it seems clear that parliament sought to remain within the boundaries of the formal constitutional revision framework. This focus on formal revision processes may have distracted attention away from the constitutional significance of the 2010 Icesave referendum under Article 26 of the Constitution. While not a formal process for revising the Constitution, the full exercise of this provision for the first time arguably signified a crucial development with regard to the substance of the Constitution.

The 2010 Icesave referendum: an informal process of constitutional development

The 2010 Icesave referendum was essential in Iceland's effort to recover from the collapse of its financial sector and to regain political control over its financial affairs.[47] In terms of the wider chronology of events, it took place between the adoption of the so-called Emergency Act coming into force on 6 October 2008 and the EFTA Court ruling of 28 January 2013, which cleared Iceland of all claims in the Icesave dispute, holding that the Icelandic state (i.e. the taxpayers) was not liable for payment of the minimum guarantees to British and Dutch depositors.[48] It was followed by a second Icesave referendum on 9 April 2011.[49] The financial significance of these referenda has been well studied and discussed

47 See: Kristrún Heimisdóttir in this collection (Chapter 4).

48 *EFTA Surveillance Authority v Iceland*, 28 January 2013, Case E-16/11.

49 Helga Kristín Hallgrímsdóttir and Emmanuel Brunet-Jailly, 'Contentious Politics, Political Expediency, and the Real Cost of the Icesave Debt' in Valur Ingimundarson, Philippe Urfalino, and Irma Erlingsdóttir (eds), *Iceland's Financial Crisis: The Politics of Blame, Protest and Recognition* (Routledge 2016) 103.

elsewhere.[50] What interested Ágúst Þór was that the 2010 Icesave referendum was held under Article 26 of the Constitution, which was exercised fully for the first time and provides the following:

> If Althingi has passed a law, it shall be submitted to the President of the Republic for confirmation no later than two weeks after it has been passed. Such confirmation gives it force of law. If the President rejects a law, it shall nevertheless become valid but shall, as soon as circumstances permit, be submitted to a vote by secret ballot of all those eligible to vote, for approval or rejection. The law shall become void if rejected, but otherwise retains its force.

There had been two previous occasions when Article 26 came close to being fully implemented. The first was when Iceland joined the European Economic Area,[51] a decision ultimately taken by Parliament alone, adopting the 'EEA-Act' 2/1993, with a majority of 33 out of 63 MPs. Ágúst Þór described that development in the following terms:

> Another occasion when the president sought to act independently was on 13th January 1993. [President] Finnbogadóttir signed the law on the Agreement on the European Economic Area despite a petition from over 34 thousand Icelanders asking her not to do so. In a declaration which she published when signing the law, Finnbogadóttir gave the explanation that it was not the role of the president to question Parliament by not signing, and that it would also be in contradiction with the tradition of how to manage the unifying role of the presidency. Thus, she did not give the nation the possibility of having the last word in a referendum, in accordance with Article 26 of the Constitution.[52]

The second occasion when Article 26 came close to being fully implemented was in 2004. Then President Ólafur Ragnar Grímsson refused to sign the law on the media, but no referendum was held as parliament withdrew the controversial law. Ágúst Þór noted:

> Almost 32 thousand had signed a petition to the president not to sign the [media] law. After some debate about how to run a referendum, the government decided to withdraw the bill on July 4th 2004.[53]

50 Ibid. 105–106. See also: P Ørebrech, 'The Icesave Bank of Iceland: From Rock Solid to Volcano Hot: Is the EU Deposit Guarantee Scheme Resisting Financial Meltdown?' (2010) 6 *Croatian Yearbook of European Law and Policy* 127–152.

51 Ágúst Thór Árnason, 'The European Union Seen from the Top: The View of an Inside-Outsider' in Joachim Nergelius (ed), *Nordic and Other European Constitutional Traditions* (Martin Nijhoff 2006) 27, 32–34.

52 Árnason, 'Constitutionalism and the Republic of Iceland and the Role and Status of the President' (n 6) 595.

53 Ibid. 595–596.

In 2010 at the height of the financial dispute with the UK and the Netherlands, this episode was still fresh in the memory of Icelanders. It is also significant to note that the same president was in office in 2004 and 2010.[54] Ágúst Þór described the first Icesave referendum in the following terms:

> On January 5th 2010 president Ólafur Ragnar Grímsson refused to sign the law allowing the government to fulfil an agreement which it had made with the governments of the United Kingdom and the Netherlands about the Icesave accounts which the Icelandic bank Landsbankinn had established in those two countries before the bank was taken over by the Icelandic Financial Supervisory Authority. Around 60 thousand Icelanders had signed a petition to the president not to sign the law.[55]

The petition was not required under Article 26, but it arose as a spontaneous and informal development and arguably reflected Icelanders' appetite for justice and for political change.[56] The figure of 60,000 signatures takes its full significance when compared to the overall Icelandic population (c. 300,000) and to the total number of voters (c. 200,000). It also represents about twice the number of Icelanders who had petitioned the president about the media law in 2004. As a result of the president's refusal to sign the contested Act, parliament adopted Act 4/2010 on the technical basis of which the referendum was held. Article 3 of the Act raised two questions, one about the disputed Icesave law and the other about the president's power vis-à-vis the Alþing:

> Act No 1/2010 amends Act No 96/2009, regarding the authorisation for the Minister of Finance, on behalf of the State Treasury, to issue a state guarantee of the loans granted by the governments of the UK and the Netherlands to the Depositors' and Investors' Guarantee Fund to cover payments to the depositors of Landsbanki Íslands plc. Althingi adopted Act 1/2010, but the president refused to sign it. Should Act 1/2010 remain in force?[57]

The result of the 2010 Icesave vote – 98% rejected the Icesave law – demonstrates the highest level of consensus among Icelanders ever, being higher even than the 1944 referendum (95.04%) confirming the 1944 Constitution. In addition, the voters' turnout was high (63%) and higher than the 2012 advisory referendum on the 2011 Proposal for a New Constitution (49%).[58] Beyond the substance of the

54 President of the Republic between 1996 and 2016, re-elected in 2012.

55 Árnason, 'Constitutionalism and the Republic of Iceland and the Role and Status of the President' (n 6) 596.

56 Hallgrímsdóttir and Brunet-Jailly (n 48) 112–113; Bernburg (n 14) 88–115.

57 Finnur Magnússon, 'Opening Pandora's Box: The Refusal of a President to Sign a Bill from Parliament' (2010) *Zeitschrift für öffentliches Recht* 203–224, 213.

58 Figures from Valur Ingimundarson, Philippe Urfalino, and Irma Erlingsdóttir (eds), *Iceland's Financial Crisis: The Politics of Blame, Protest and Recognition* (Routledge 2016) 14.

question and financial issues at stake in the referendum, Ágúst Þór saw it as a significant development of the 1944 Constitution that took place outside any formal constitutional revision framework. In the timeline of the constitutional reform, the first Icesave referendum took place at the very start of the process, even before the adoption of Act 90/2010 on the Constitutional Assembly on 16 June.

Considering the full exercise of Article 26 as what could be called a key moment of constitutional development or change, I suggest, might be a useful way of capturing what Ágúst Þór had in mind.[59] While discussing this in theoretical terms falls outside the scope of this chapter, some of the defining characteristics of this key moment may be noted here. Firstly, the rare use of a referendum in Icelandic constitutionalism makes the 2010 Icesave vote stand out. Indeed, a referendum or 'vote by secret ballot of all those eligible to vote, for approval or rejection'[60] had seldom featured in Icelandic constitutional history.[61] Moreover, while the 1944 Constitution provides for a referendum in two additional situations, under Article 11(3)[62] and Article 79(2),[63] no referendum had taken place since 1944. Therefore, being the only one held since then, the 2010 referendum may arguably be seen as a parallel to the constitutional moment of the 1944 referendum, which established the Icelandic Republic and confirmed the adoption of the Constitution. In both instances, voters' turnout was high, and the issues at stake were of unprecedented political significance for Icelanders.

In addition, to continue the metaphor, the 2010 Icesave referendum gave the key for fully understanding the 1944 Constitution, and Ágúst Þór saw its significance as clarifying the constitutional status of the President by confirming that not only can the President refuse to sign a contested law (which was known since the 2004 media law), but that when he (or she) refuses to sign it, Parliament has to hold a referendum (which had not happened in 2004 as the parliament withdrew the contested media law). While both the Constitutional Commission (2010–2011) and the Constitutional Assembly/Council were explicitly asked to address the

59 Ágúst Þór did not use this phrase, nor did he elaborate on the theoretical distinctions between 1944 and 2010 'moments.' I chose to label the 2010 Icesave referendum as a 'key constitutional moment' both by reference to and in distinction with neighbouring concepts such as 'constitutional moment' (B. Ackerman, n 4) and 'founding moments' (Richard Albert, Menaka Guruswamy, and Nishchal Basnyat (eds), *Founding Moments in Constitutionalism* (Hart 2019)).

60 The Icelandic original does not use the word 'referendum.'

61 'The referendums were held in 1908 (whether to impose a ban on the importation of alcohol; approved), 1916 (whether to implement work duty for men 17–25 years of age; not approved), 1918 (whether to adopt the Union Act with Denmark; approved), and 1933 (whether to repeal the ban on the importation of alcohol; approved).' F. Magnússon (n 57) 213.

62 Article 11(3): 'The President may be removed from office before his term expires if approved by a majority vote in a plebiscite ['þjóðaratkvæðagreiðsla': litt. a vote by the people] called pursuant to a resolution adopted by three-fourths of the Members of Althingi. This plebiscite shall be held within two months from the date of adoption by Althingi of the resolution. The President shall not perform his duties from the time the resolution is adopted by Althingi until the results of the plebiscite are known.'

63 Article 79(2): 'If Althingi passes an amendment to the status of the Church under Article 62, it shall be submitted to a vote for approval or rejection by secret ballot of all those eligible to vote.'

constitutional power of the President according to Article 3 of Act 90/2010 and both actively engaged with this, no change was ultimately made as the formal revision process was not completed.[64] As Ágúst Þór observed in 2013, the 2011 Proposal for a New Constitution 'offers no clear vision' for the institution of the President of the Icelandic Republic.[65] By contrast, the Icesave referendum contributed to completing the construction of the 1944 Constitution by revealing the extent of the President's power and clarifying the concept of Icelandic Republic.

What changed: the President's power, the People, and the Republic

As one of Ágúst Þór's analytical intentions was to emphasise the significance of the Icesave referendum in clarifying the role and power of the President of the Republic, in this section I have drawn on his chapter, 'The Constitutionalism of the Republic of Iceland and the Role and Status of the President,' which was published in 2011.[66] Although that chapter was most likely written in the immediate aftermath of the 2010 Icesave referendum, Ágúst Þór did not directly discuss that referendum in it. Nevertheless, that chapter provides a useful analytical framework that sheds light on the significance of the 2010 Icesave referendum for understanding the President's constitutional identity and role in their connections to both the Parliament and the People. While in relation to the former I was able to follow Ágúst Þór's thinking quite closely as it is well documented, discussing the latter has required a little more reconstruction on my part and joining the dots between his reflections.

The President's uncertain constitutional status since 1944

Although the creation of the President was key to Iceland's transformation into a republic,[67] his or her exact role and status were not fully clarified when the Constitution was adopted in 1944. In terms of drafting, it seems that the institution of the President was mostly designed by replacing the word 'King' with the word 'president.' In addition, Article 3 of the Constitution states that 'the president of Iceland shall be elected by the people.' In terms of powers, it was decided to give the newly created President somewhat comparable powers to the King, including the power to veto legislation under Article 26, which was substantially revised for that purpose.[68] As the King had not used his veto power since 1914, that power was generally considered to be only formal,[69]

64 This is further discussed by Björg Thorarensen (Chapter 5) and Skúli Magnússon (Chapter 8).

65 Árnason and Magnússon (n 26), para 23. See also: Skúli Magnússon (Chapter 8) in this collection.

66 Árnason, 'Constitutionalism and the Republic of Iceland and the Role and Status of the President' (n 6) 589–597.

67 Article 1: 'Iceland is a republic with a parliamentary government.'

68 F Magnússon (n 57) 214.

69 Ibid. 206.

and since the President replaced the King, one view was that the President's power under the revised Article 26 of the Constitution was also only formal. As a result, the institution of the President was criticised by some for being weak and old-fashioned, while Parliament was seen as the real holder of the power under the new constitutional arrangement.

Ágúst Þór did not subscribe to this view and argued that with the changes to Article 3 and Article 26, the President 'was completely reinvented' and placed in a radically different position from the King.[70] However, he continued, this 'reinvention' was not fully realised until the President exercised his power under Article 26 for the first time with the Icesave referendum. Until then, the academic and political discussion was structured in two broad camps:

> [I]t is fair to say that the powers of the President and, in particular her or his constitutional role have been debated ever since the foundation of the Republic in 1944. Under one view [. . .] the President's role is first and foremost a unifying symbolic role in the line of Scandinavian Monarchy. Under this view, it has been argued, mainly by politicians but also a few legal scholars, that the President's power of veto has become *desuetudo* and that the President's real powers are limited to certain minor functions with regard to the forming of Government.
>
> Under the opposite view, the President of the Republic constitutes a key element in the institutional balance of the Icelandic Constitution. Being directly elected, he/she acts as a check on parliamentary legislation and also ministerial powers. This latter view is supported both by the preparatory materials of the 1944 Constitution, the text of the Constitution as well as the actual role of those who have served as presidents, in particular the first one, Sveinn Björnsson, and [the present one in 2013] Ólafur Ragnar Grímsson.'[71]

The 2010 Icesave referendum put an end to these discussions, by bringing to life crucial features of the President's power that, until then, some had thought no longer existed.

The republican president

The 2010 Icesave referendum clarified essential features of presidential power and status, both vis-à-vis Parliament and vis-à-vis the People, and in so doing it arguably completed the constitutional construction of the emblematic institution of the 1944 Constitution and of the Icelandic Republic.

70 Ágúst Þór also referred to the seminal paper of Sigurður Líndal, 'Stjórnskipuleg staða forseta Íslands' [The President of the Republic in Constitutional Law] (1992) 166 *Skírnir* 425–439.

71 Árnason and Magnússon (n 26), paras 24 and 25. See also: F. Magnússon (n 57) 214–216.

The President and Parliament

The confirmation of the President's power in relation to Parliament is perhaps the most visible contribution of the 2010 Icesave referendum to changing constitutional practice. This is largely due to the configuration of Article 26, which is designed to settle a disagreement between Parliament and the President about a specific law. This is also due to the fact that Article 26 was the locus of the political and academic controversy about the exact scope of the presidential power in relation to Parliament. The 2010 referendum clarified three core features of these powers. Firstly, it confirmed that the President had the power to veto an Act of Parliament and the repeated exercise of the presidential veto on three separate occasions (2004 with the media law, 2010 the first Icesave law, and 2011 with the second Icesave law)[72] has now unquestionably embedded this practice in Icelandic constitutionalism. Secondly, the Icesave veto confirmed that in taking his or her decision to refuse to sign a law, the President does not have to consult Parliament or the government.[73] Thirdly, the 2010 Icesave referendum demonstrated that Parliament has no discretion with regard to implementing Article 26 and that it must take the practical steps necessary for a referendum to be held, as it did with Act 4/2010. This follows the letter of Article 26 and appears to confirm that withdrawing the contested law (as parliament did in 2004 with the media law) is no longer an option. Consequently, the President is confirmed as a distinct and autonomous actor in the law-making process; his or her power to go against the will of Parliament is also asserted beyond doubt. Ágúst Þór therefore considered that these developments clarified the constitutional status of the President sufficiently so as to put to rest the ongoing discussion about his or her powers and to render further reform of presidential powers unnecessary:[74]

> [As discussed previously], academics have disagreed about the constitutional position of the President, in particular whether he/she can refuse to confirm legislation under Article 26 of the Constitution and refer it to a national referendum. *After the referendum of 6 March 2010 on the so-called Icesave Act, this dispute, as well as most of the other related issues discussed by these academics, must be considered as resolved.* [. . .] All in all, the only provisions of the Constitution that can be considered the Icelanders' own input in the making of the Republic [in 1944], i.e. Article 3 (the election of the President

72 The second Icesave referendum was held on 9 April 2011: the turnout was 75%, and 58.9% voted against the contested law.

73 Hallgrímsdóttir and Brunet-Jailly (n 49) 110–112. For a critical analysis, see: Svanur Kristjánsson, 'Hið nýja Ísland eftir hrunið eða geðþóttavald forseta Íslands?: Forsetatíð Ólafs Ragnars Grímssonar 2008–2012' [New Iceland Post Financial Melt-Down or Arbitrary Powers of the President: The Time of Ólafur Ragnar Grímsson as President from 2008–2012] (2015) 189 *Skírnir* 307–359.

74 The 2011 Proposal of a New Constitution drafted by the Constitutional Council introduced many changes to the powers of president of the Republic and to the overall institutional balance. These are discussed by Skúli Magnússon in his Chapter 8 in this collection.

> by universal suffrage) and Article 26 (the President's right to refer legislation to a national referendum), have withstood the test of time and the pressure of turmoil resulting from legislation that seemingly divided the nation. Against this backdrop, any ideas to significantly change the current constitutional position of the President should be approached with suspicion.[75]
>
> (emphasis added)

In this instance, the processes of constitutional change and of development are therefore very close. While no change was made to the text of the 1944 Constitution, the presidential power to veto legislation was brought to life. Taken out of the sort of constitutional limbo in which it had been confined since 1944, that first exercise may be seen as transforming both the role of the President and the academic and political understanding of it. Assessing the scope of the constitutional change introduced in this instance depends on the prior view adopted on what the President's power was or should be. For those who thought, as Ágúst Þór did, that the President was 'completely reinvented' on paper in 1944, the Icesave referendum can be seen as completing this institution. For those with the opposite view (the President as a formal figure with limited law-making power), the 2010 referendum can be seen as changing the substance and practice of the Constitution. In addition, the Icesave referendum further clarified the constitutional identity of the President in relation to the Icelandic People.

The President and the People

It is argued that the coming together of the President and Icelanders through the 2010 Icesave referendum introduced a major change to the 1944 Constitution, which affects the constitutional identity of Icelanders and also clarifies the Republican identity of the President.

Ágúst Þór was very clear that the President ought not to be construed as a sort of non-monarchical King because his or her constitutional identity and role are embedded in and shaped by the Republic, a concept that Ágúst Þór observed was not fully grasped.[76] Understanding the concept of republic in general political and constitutional terms is challenging enough.[77] Discussing it in relation to Icelandic

75 Ágúst Þór Árnason 'Lýðveldið, stjórnskipun og staða forseta' [The Republic, the Constitution and the position of the President] (2010) 4 *Lögfræðingur* 20–30 (24, 28). Translated by Skúli Magnússon.

76 Árnason, 'Constitutionalism and the Republic of Iceland and the Role and Status of the President' (n 6) 590–591, 593–594.

77 At a constitutional theory level, Ágúst Þór found the work of Günter Frankenberg particularly compelling and *Die Verfassung der Republik* in the 1997 Suhrkamp edition was one his favourite go-to books in the early years of the revision process. In his 2011 chapter (n 6), he also referred to the work of Quentin Skinner, *The Foundations of Modern Political Thought* (Cambridge University Press 1978) and *Liberty before Liberalism* (Cambridge University Press 1997), as well as Philip Pettit, *Republicanism: A Theory of Freedom and Government* (Clarendon 1997).

constitutionalism is particularly difficult as the Icelandic language has no specific word for 'republic.' The 1944 Constitution uses the word '*lýðveldið*' (literally 'the rule of the people'), a word that is very similar to the Icelandic word for 'democracy' (*lýðræði*). Ágúst Þór believed that understanding the concept of 'republic' required understanding better who 'the People' were in terms of constitutional law and theory.

Building on Ágúst Þór's unfinished reflection, I suggest that the 2010 Icesave referendum created an opportunity to see both of those concepts in action for the first time and that it brought to light the role of the President in connecting the two with each other. In other words, the 2010 referendum triggered as a result of the presidential veto of the first Icesave law arguably brought Icelanders into existence as a constitutional People for the first time. In so doing, it gave them a distinct constitutional identity from that of the mathematical sum of their parts and from that of voters in a general election divided according to political parties' preferences. With this distinct identity comes a special power to be involved in the law-making process, including, and significantly so, the power to override Parliament. Following the logic of Article 26, the People, as appealed to by the President, are the ultimate collective sovereign, with the President operating only as a catalyst, namely as the institution making this process possible.

The specific republican identity of the President (and arguably his or her ontological distinction from the King) therefore lies in his or her constitutional power to convene Icelanders as a sovereign People. Unlike that of the Monarch, the discretion of the President under Article 26 is arguably not absolute, as his or her decision to veto a law is bounded in two complementary ways: the presidential veto will necessarily bring the Icelanders as a constitutional People into existence, and the President (as well as Parliament) is bound by the People's expression of sovereignty as reflected in the referendum results. Seen in this light, the President and the People are mutually constitutive (i.e. they give each other their respective constitutional identities and powers). As may be recalled, the promotion of Icelanders as key actors in constitutional reform were issues at the core of that process between 2009 and 2017, with several attempts to formalise their involvement in reforming the Constitution. The significance of the 2010 Icesave referendum in triggering constitutional change outside a formal revision framework is further highlighted as, paradoxically perhaps, it arguably generated a greater and deeper degree of constitutional change than the formal processes managed to achieve.

Some questions remain open about the exact scope of the President's power under Article 26 as well as that of the People. Ágúst Þór was certainly well aware of the risk of presidential powers being misconstrued and abused by their holder and that, even in a Republic, the will of the People might need some careful framing.[78] In addition, he resisted any simplistic equation between, on the one

78 'The only thing which is perfectly clear is that in a republic, the head of state cannot be a king, a military general or a self-appointed dictator. Yet some of the *worst tyrannies and dictatorships in the world have decorated themselves with this name, seemingly without any moral concerns*' (emphasis added): Árnason, 'The History of the Icelandic Constitution' (n 1) 53.

hand, allowing 'the People' some constitutional mechanism through which they might exercise their sovereignty against the will of a parliament elected by the same people, albeit through a different (i.e. mediated) process and, on the other hand, the argument (or belief) that 'the people' are always right in their direct democracy configuration or necessarily better than their indirect democratic configuration through Parliament. The 1944 Constitution is silent about the degree of presidential discretion in triggering Article 26, and this might be read as granting the President total discretion. This would be in line perhaps with the monarch's power. However, Ágúst Þór distinguished clearly between the monarch and the republican president. In this regard, his alternative and complementary approach to the concept of a republic by reference to its Latin origin as *res publica*, the 'public thing' or public good (contrasting with family matters to be dealt with inside the family circle)[79] might be informative here. Considering the concept of a republic in that sense might provide a useful starting point to reflect on whether and, if so to what extent, the subject matter of a referendum under Article 26 (or indeed perhaps under other frameworks elsewhere) might be bounded so that the People may not exercise their sovereign power in a way detrimental to the Republic. In seeking to define these boundaries, Ágúst Þór was thinking about the relevance and possible usefulness of the concept of human dignity.[80] While he raised this issue with fellow members of the Constitutional Commission, his reflection was a work in progress and remained unfinished.

Conclusion: the wider theoretical significance of Ágúst Þór's analysis of the constitutional reform

This chapter has reflected on a fundamental dimension of constitutional law and theory, namely how constitutions change and, more precisely, how major constitutional change happens outside the formal revision framework. Constitutional (as well as political) theory is still profoundly influenced by the French and American revolutions, which led to the adoption of what are considered to be the first two modern constitutions establishing democracy after (absolute) monarchy. Flowing from those unique historical developments and their contemporary analyses, two broad theoretical categories still permeate the current analytical imaginary: one is the distinction between *pouvoir constituant* and *pouvoir constitué*,[81] and the other is the idea that radical constitutional change takes place in a unique set of radical circumstances, broadly understood as the constitutional moment.[82] Icelandic

79 Árnason, 'Constitutionalism and the Republic of Iceland and the Role and Status of the President' (n 6) 593.

80 Ágúst Þór Árnason, *'Fundur um mannréttindi og stjórnaskrá 1. desember 1994 í Súlnasal Hótel Sögu'* in Ágúst Þór Árnason (ed), *Mannréttindi í stjórnarskrá* [Human Rights in the Constitution] (Mannréttindaskrifstofa Íslands 1994) 3–4. His philosophical thinking on this was mostly inspired by the work of Ernst Tugendhat and Ingeborg Maus.

81 Claude Klein, *Théorie et pratique du pouvoir constituant* (PUF 1996).

82 Ackerman (n 4).

constitutional developments, however, have followed a very different route from the U.S. and French experiences. Iceland became a republic and a democracy through a sort of constitutional glissando from one constitutional status to another, with 1944 as the moment (for want of a better word) that both crowned decades (or centuries) of pursuit of sovereignty and independence, and marked the beginning of the Icelandic Republic.

From a more abstract point of view, this chapter has addressed two distinct questions. One question is whether a set of exceptional circumstances should trigger radical constitutional change (e.g. the adoption of a new constitution) and to what extent they can legitimise bypassing the constitution in force for doing so. The other question is whether changes to core constitutional features, albeit of a lesser scope, can take place outside the formal revision framework, and, if so, what sort of circumstances are necessary to trigger and to justify these changes. Both of these questions have given rise to a third question, namely how different degrees of constitutional change can be identified and assessed. As the chapter has shown, the unique experience of the Icelandic constitutional reform process of 2009–2017 brought to light new ways of understanding and answering those questions.

In relation to Iceland, Ágúst Þór thought that there had been only one constitutional moment, the one leading to the Republic's foundation. He did not exclude, however, that other sets of circumstances might subsequently trigger change to core constitutional features outside the formal amendment procedure, and his analysis of the 2010 Icesave referendum broadly fits with more recent theoretical reflections characterising these as 'founding moments'[83] or 'founding acts.'[84] I have used the phrase 'key moment' when referring to the 2010 referendum in this chapter to avoid any hasty association with either approach, while seeking to convey its special significance for the Icelandic constitution. From a theoretical perspective, the idea of a 'key moment' echoes that of the original constitutional moment, albeit to a lesser extent, in terms of the substantive change at stake. Reflecting on the Icelandic process of constitutional change suggests that such a 'key moment' can be said to have three sorts of features: firstly, it has to be about a first, unprecedented exercise of constitutional power; secondly, it has to complete or clarify a core feature of the constitution; and thirdly, it has to involve the People to an extent similar (but not necessarily identical) to that of the foundational constitutional moment. This outline analysis of a concept of 'key moment' in constitutional terms arguably has two sorts of applications. One is, as indicated here, a descriptive or classificatory application to past events, which can provide a tool of analysis when reflecting on major constitutional change processes that do not necessarily fit the existing theoretical models. The other is more prescriptive and

83 Richard Albert, Menaka Guruswamy, and Nishchal Basnyat (eds), *Founding Moments in Constitutionalism* (Hart 2019).

84 Serdar Tekin, *Founding Acts: Constitutional Origins in a Democratic Age* (University of Pennsylvania Press 2016).

prospective, in that this set of features could be used to frame a discussion of the necessity and, crucially, the political legitimacy, of major constitutional change when it takes place outside the revision framework set out in a constitution. In that regard, this analysis of Icelandic constitutional reform is not only a sui generis discussion, but also a way of developing broader reflection on key matters of constitutionalism with potential relevance to other contexts.

On Icelandic constitutionalism and constitutional reform: List of publications by Ágúst Þór Árnason

Chronological order

Edited work

Mannréttindi [Human Rights] (Icelandic Red Cross, 1994)
Mannréttindi í stjórnarskrá [Human Rights in the Constitution] (Mannréttindaskrifstofa Íslands 1994)
Member of the original Editorial Board of the *Yearbook of Polar Law* (Brill/Nijhoff, from 2009)

Authored and co-authored book chapters, academic and journalistic articles

'Lýðræði og sjáflstæði Svisslendinga' [Democracy and Independence in Switzerland] (1992) 10 *Vísbending* 2
'Mannréttindi í sögu og vítund Íslendinga' [Human Rights in the History and Conscience of Icelanders] (1994) 168 *Skírnir* 472–478
'Fundur um mannréttindi og stjórnaskrá 1. desember 1994 í Súlnasal Hótel Sögu' in Ágúst Þór Árnason (ed) *Mannréttindi í stjórnarskrá [Human Rights in the Constitution]* (Mannréttindaskrifstofa Íslands 1994) 3–4
'Mannréttindi og lýðræði í skólastarfi' [Human Rights and Democracy in Schools] *Mannréttindi Barna* [The Rights of the Child] (1995) 63–83
'Frjáls félagasamtök hafa mikilvægu hlutverki að gegna' [Civil Society Plays an Important Role] (1995) 44 *Vinnan* 12–15
'What Did the Icelanders Really Want? The Home Rule Revisited', in Lise Lyck (ed), *Socio-Economic Developments in Greenland and other Small Nordic Jurisdictions* (New Social Science Monographs 1997) 241–271
'The History of the Icelandic Constitution and Some Economic Issues' in Lise Lyck (ed), *Constitutional and Economic Space of Small Nordic Jurisdictions: The Aaland Islands, the Faroe Islands, Greenland, Iceland* (NordREFO 1997) 48–73
'Stjórnarskrárfesta: grundvöllur lýðræðisins' [Constitutionalism: The Basis of Democracy] (1999) 173 *Skírnir* 467–480
With Stéphanie Lagoutte, 'Article 16' in Guðmundur Alfreðsson and Asbjørn Eide (eds), *The Universal Declaration of Human Rights. A Common Standard of Achievement* (Martinus Nijhoff Publishers 1999) 325–357
With Martin Scheinin, 'Constitution of Iceland (English translation)', in Gisbert H Flanz (ed), *Constitutions of the Countries of the World* (Oceana Publications 1999)

'Constitutionalism: Popular Legitimacy of the State?' in Martin Scheinin (ed), *The Welfare State and Constitutionalism in the Nordic Countries* (Phønix-Trykkeriet A/S 2001) 29–79
'Lögvísindi norðan heiða' [Legal Science in North Iceland] (2004) 1 *Lagakrókar* 12
'Den Gode Staten: Menneskerettigheter i Norden' [The Good State: Human Rights in the Nordic Countries] (2004) 22 *Nordisk Tidsskrift for Menneskerettigheter* 129
'Háskólinn á Akureyri' [The University of Akureyri] (2006) 1 *Lagakrókar* 18–19
'The EU Seen from the Top: The View of an Inside-Outsider', in Joakim Nergelius (ed), *Nordic and Other Constitutional Traditions* (Brill 2006) 27–45
'Iceland' in Gerhard Robbers (ed), *Encyclopedia of World Constitutions*, Volume II (Facts on File, 2007) 393–396
'The Good State or Constitutional Innocents of the Nordic Societies' in Joakim Nergelius (ed), *Constitutionalism – New Challenges: European Law from a Nordic Perspective* (Martin Nijhoff 2008) 155–160
'Lýðveldið, stjórnskipun og staða forseta' [The Republic, the Constitutional Order and the Position of the President] (2010) 4 *Lögfræðingur* 20–30
'Samband ríkis og kirkju' in Guðrún Pétursdóttir (ed), *Skýrsla Stjórnlaganefndar*, Vol I (Alþingi 2011) 258–267
'Upphaf stjórnarskrárfestunnar og áhrif hennar á stjórnskipun einstakra ríkja' [The Origins of Constitutionalism and Its Influence on National Constitutions] in Guðrún Pétursdóttir (ed), *Skýrsla Stjórnlaganefndar*, Vol II (Alþingi 2011) 305–316
'Jón Sigurðsson og stjórnskipun Íslands' [Jón Sigurðsson and Iceland's Constitutional Order] (2011) 1 *Andvari* 109–123
'Lýðveldi, stjórnarskrá og þjóðaratkvæði' [The Republic, the Constitution and Referenda] (2011) 1 *Lögfræðingur* 8–26
'A Review of the Icelandic Constitution: Popular Sovereignty or Political Confusion' (2011) 3 *Tijdschrift voor Constitutioneel Recht* 342–351
'The Constitutionalism of the Republic of Iceland and the Role and Status of the President' in Asbjørn Eide, Jakob Th. Möller and Ineta Ziemele (eds), *Making People Heard: Essays on Human Rights in Honour of Gudmundur Alfredsson* (Martin Nijhoff 2011) 589–597
'Stjórnskipun lýðveldisins, lýðræði og þingræði' [The Constitution of the Republic, Democracy and Parliamentarianism] *Morgunblaðið* 28 February 2011, p 17
'Ábyrgðarleysiskenning úr lausu lofti' [Theory of Non-Responsibility from Thin Air] *Fréttablaðið* 19 April 2011, p 17
'Jón Sigurðsson og stjórnarskráin' [Jón Sigurðsson and the Constitution] *Morgunblaðið* 17 June 2011, p 28
'Tillögur Stjórnlagaráðs – Spor í rétta átt?' [The Proposal of the Constitutional Council – A Step in the Right Direction?] *Fréttablaðið* 28 July 2011, p 20
'Hvaðan koma mannréttindi?' [From what Do Human Rights Emanate?] *Morgunblaðið* 7 September 2011, p 19
'Hvers konar lýðræði?' [What Kind of Democracy?] *Morgunblaðið* 17 December 2011, p 39
'Hvers er að vænta af Feneyjanefndinni?' [What to Expect of the Venice Commission?] (2012) 8 *Þjóðmál* 42–48
'Endurskoðun eða uppstokkun?' [Revision or Revolution?] *Fréttablaðið* 7 February 2012, p 14
With Skúli Magnússon, 'Pólitísk hlutverk forsetans' [The Political Role of the President] *Fréttablaðið* 23 May 2012, p 16

'Lýðveldi kvatt?' [Goodbye to a Republic?] *Morgunblaðið* 30 August 2012, p 21

With Skúli Magnússon, 'Ný eða endurskoðuð stjórnarskrá?' [New or Revised Constitution] *Fréttablaðið* 17 October 2012, p 14

'Hvað sagði þjóðfundur 2010?' [What Did the National Forum of 2010 Say?] *Morgunblaðið* 19 October 2012, p 25

'Feneyjarnefnd og sjálfsvirðing' [The Venice Commission and Self-Respect] *Fréttablaðið* 28 November 2012, p 12

'Hvers er að vænta af Feneyjarnefndinni?' [What Is to Be Expected of the Venice Commission?] (2012) 8 *Þjóðmál* Vol 4 pp 42–49

With Skúli Magnússon, 'Sátt um stjórnarskrárbreytingu?' [Consensus on a Constitutional Amendment] *Fréttablaðið* 17 December 2012, p 16

With Skúli Magnússon, 'Á að breyta breytingarákvæði?' [Should the Amendment Procedure Provision Be Amended?] *Fréttablaðið* 18 February 2013, p 14

With Skúli Magnússon, 'Endurskoðun stjórnarskrár' [The Revision of the Constitution] *Fréttablaðið* 3 May 2013, p 18

With Skúli Magnússon, 'Er þörf á endurskoðun kosninga- og kjördæmaskipunar?' [On the Need for a Revision of the Electoral System] *Morgunblaðið* 13 May 2014, p 21

With Guðmundur Alfreðsson, Rachael Lorna Johnstone, Timo Koivurova and Natalia Loukacheva, 'Memoriam: In Memory of Kari A Rogvi' (2015) 7 *Yearbook of Polar Law* xii

'Þjóðaratkvæðagreiðsla um rýniskýrslu?' [A Referenda on Screening Report?] *Fréttablaðið* 1 May 2015, p 22

Ágúst Þór Árnason and Giorgio Baruchello, 'Europe's Constitutional Law in Times of Crisis: A Human Rights Perspective' (2016) 10 *Nordicum-Mediterraneum*. https://nome.unak.is/wordpress/volume-10-no-3-2016/conference-paper-10-3/europe-s-constitutional-law-in-times-of-crisis-a-human-rights-perspective/

With Skúli Magnússon, 'Vegvísir að heildarendurskoðun stjórnarskrárinnar' [A Roadmap for a Concise Constitutional Revision] *Morgunblaðið* 10 November 2016, p 26

With Guðmundur Alfreðsson, 'Fullveldið og heimskautarétturinn' (Sovereignty and Polar Law), in Svala Ísfeld Ólafsdóttir (ed), *Fullveldi í 99 ár. Safn ritgerða til heiðurs dr. Davíð Þór Björgvinssyni sextugum [99 Years of Icelandic Sovereignty. Essays in Honour of Dr David Thor Björgvinsson at Sixty]* (Hið íslenska bókmenntafélag 2017) 267–282

With Skúli Magnússon, 'Endurskoðun stjórnarskrárinnar – Eftir hverju er beðið?' [The Revision of the Constitution – What Are We Waiting for?] *Fréttablaðið* 7 September 2017, p 20

With Ragnheiður Elfa Þorsteinsdóttir, 'Fullveldi og auðlindir' [Sovereignty and Natural Resources] *Morgunblaðið* 2 August 2018

4 Iceland's near-death experience

Kristrún Heimisdóttir

Introduction: a national constitution challenged by financial crisis

For this collection dedicated to the Icelandic constitutional reform, I was asked to contribute a chapter about the constitutional reform's financial crisis context. My analytical framework is marked by the enormity of the financial crisis that hit Iceland with full force in the late summer of 2008 and triggered, among so many other things, an experiment in constitutional reform. In style and essence, this is a report of certain political actions executed to respond to the crisis, and the methodology used is to seek to transpose and verify which goals were reached and which were not.

Crisis – the word belongs in our time to countless languages. It has at least two different meanings: either it means imminent danger caused by a particular dangerous event or, as in ancient Greek Hippocratic medicine, *krisis*, the turning point in the progress of a disease, when either the patient dies or is fully cured. In order to understand why the Icelandic constitutional reform stalled, researchers must take note both of its paralyzing design failure throughout its four-year leap and of the broader context of Iceland's crisis decade 2008–2018 when financial crisis led to political crisis.

Iceland had a near-death experience in 2008, and its *krisis* cure was not constitutional reform but rather the Icelandic state's application of state prerogatives in accordance with the 1944 Constitution as a means of resistance.

Near-death experience as a constitutional event

The Icelandic financial crisis was in 2008 seen by the rest of the world as the worst in any of the countries hit by the Great Financial Crisis (GFC), which was a global phenomenon. Various self-induced weaknesses contributed to this unfortunate situation and made it a crisis *extraordinaire* in Iceland's history.[1]

1 On 12 April 2010, a report was issued by the Special Investigation Commission established by Act 142/2008 by Althingi, the Icelandic Parliament. The commission's mandate was to investigate and analyse the processes leading to the collapse of the three main banks in Iceland.

The financial crisis constituted a threat to Iceland's statehood, as will be further explained. The circumstances revealed how state prerogatives, as defined by a national constitution, became a last defence of seminal importance. The three legal institutions of statehood, sovereignty, and constitution are all intertwined and reliant upon one another. For Iceland in 2008–2011, two important and unprecedented actions, both nationally and internationally, were the 2008 Emergency Act[2] and the 2010 and 2011 referendums on Icesave.[3] Iceland managed with these measures to come to its own rescue. All branches of government had a role in this and acted at some point: Parliament, Government, the Supreme Court, as well as the President of Iceland, who enabled the demos to act decisively twice by calling two referendums on a law granting the government permission to pay the UK and the Netherlands the cost of a deposit guarantee due to the collapse of Landsbanki and its Internet bank accounts, Icesave. These referendums took place in 2010 and 2011, and that law was rejected both times. President Ólafur Ragnar Grímsson had applied his powers according to Article 26 of the 1944 Constitution once before in 2004, but the government retracted the contested media law, and no referendum was held at that time.

According to Article 26 of the Constitution of Iceland, the President can submit to a national referendum a law, passed by the Althingi, by refusing to sign such a law. The outcome of the national referendum decides whether the approved law is upheld or ceases to have effect as law. In 2010 and 2011, the public vote was decisive, and the laws passed by the Althingi ceased to have effect. The referendums were decisive not only within Iceland but also internationally, as their result was generally respected. It meant that a state guarantee was ruled out. The Emergency Act had, by giving deposits priority status in the bankruptcy procedure of the Icelandic banks, ensured that in due course the claims concerning the deposit guarantees would be paid out from the estate of the fallen Landsbanki. The governments of the UK and the Netherlands had decided immediately in October 2008 to pay out deposit guarantees to their citizens. In 2015, they were paid in full by the estate of Landsbanki and Icelandic Deposit Guarantee Fund from funds held by Landsbanki before its collapse.

The challenge to Iceland's Constitution by the financial crisis was, as it happened, marked by three distinguishable and different processes, all of constitutional significance going on simultaneously, two of them throughout nearly a decade. It is a story of a national constitution challenged by financial crisis, foreign creditors, and political distrust and upheaval. The three processes are (1) resurrecting the domestic financial system which collapsed in its entirety; (2) the serious international dispute concerning the cross-border banking crisis particularly between

2 Act 125/2008.

3 Icesave was the name of Internet deposit banking accounts run by the Icelandic bank Landsbanki in two countries, the UK and the Netherlands. When Landsbanki collapsed in October 2008, these cross-border accounts closed, and an international dispute ensued concerning deposit insurance and European law. In Iceland, an all-encompassing and rigourous public debate lasted for at least five years, on whether or not a state guarantee should be accepted by Iceland.

Iceland and the UK and the Netherlands; and (3) the constitutional reform process to adopt a new constitution via the Constitutional Assembly changed into Constitutional Council, which only had powers delegated from Parliament. This chapter deals with these three processes and the issues of constitutionalism, democracy, and the crisis of finance and money, which they brought forward. The aspects of finance and of constitutional affairs interacted consistently and are in this chapter dealt with in correlation, which is common neither in research nor theory – and therefore probably novel for many readers.

The financial crisis was the trigger that started the constitutional reform process. In November 2008, a movement calling for a French-style 'new republic' began to gather political momentum demanding a constitutional assembly to be directly elected eventually to replace the 'ruins' that was the crisis-ridden, shamed, and catastrophically indebted Icelandic Republic. The 1944 Constitution was in effect blamed for the financial crisis, and a new constitution was presented both as a solution to the problems that had caused the crisis in the first place and as the right way to resolve the vast currency, banking, and debt crisis that Iceland was faced with. As it turned out, the constitutional reform process achieved neither. It did not produce any substantial ideas of change to the economic aspects of the Constitution, nor did the process have any influence on the crisis resolution. While this was truly an exceptionally important period in Icelandic constitutional history, it unfolded in a way that differed greatly from the vision of the instigators.

Indeed, the financial crisis proved to be a much more complicated constitutional event than the architects of a 'new republic' constitutional reform ever fathomed. The Althingi had a decade-long stretch ahead dealing with the consequences of the financial crisis and its ramifications. By contrast, the popularly elected Constitutional Assembly (which then became the Constitutional Council) sat for only little less than four months in the summer of 2011.

While internationally famed as an interesting democratic experiment in constitution-making, a significant novelty as regards constitutional assemblies, and an example of positive empowerment through social media, in particular Facebook, these accolades are a very much romanticised version of the reality of the constitutional reform process. The Constitutional Council, which drafted a new text for a constitution (the 2011 Proposal for a New Constitution), was never granted a mandate to effect constitutional change. That power remained with the Althing, in accordance with the existing Constitution's Article 79. The Constitutional Council's text was not a proper parliamentary bill either in form or substance. Handed over to the Icelandic Parliament on 27 July 2011 it was not a fully worked-through constitutional bill with explanations of legal concepts, effects of rulings with regards to institutions, legal rules, precedents, traditions, etc. The advisory referendum in 2012 did not resolve these problems since at the time of voting there was still no proper bill to vote on and no clarity as to the verified final text of the "draft" that voters were meant to refuse or accept. The mandate remained with the parliament which had made various sweeping changes and was to continue to add a considerable amount of changes after the referendum. A blend of the Constitutional Council's text and numerous changes by the Althingi was harshly criticised by the

Council of Europe Venice Commission.[4] Ultimately both time and parliamentary support ran out.

The constitutional significance of the reconstruction of financial sovereignty, of a national financial system, of financial assets within the Icelandic economy, of the currency itself, and of state access to global markets was a process eventually carried through by five governments in the ten-year period of 2008–2018. The Icelandic Constitution of 1944 proved essential in this greatest challenge ever to Iceland's statehood. Iceland became a sovereign state in 1918 after a period of at least 70 years of active demands for independence from Denmark in which a constitution was a key element. The Icelandic Constitution of 1944 is rooted in the European liberal tradition of the revolutionary nineteenth century. It has been amended regularly, and the Icelandic constitutional inheritance encompasses steps taken through law to strengthen the state-building process – law being the only tool and defence that such a small country can ever master in international arenas of statecraft.[5]

The Icesave dispute should be understood as another separate constitutional event also, of course, triggered by the financial crisis. It was in essence a cross-border banking crisis that struck three countries: Iceland, Holland, and the United Kingdom, but it turned into the most difficult and severe international feud in Icelandic history and provoked a public initiative first via a national collection of signatures, and eventually instigating two national referendums called by the President of Iceland, applying his powers according to Article 26 of the 1944 Constitution. The turnout in these referendums was much higher than in either the elections for a Constitutional Assembly in October 2010 or the 2012 referendum on the draft proposal for a new constitution and five topical questions. The Icesave dispute also created more debate by far and generated broad civil society interest, with civil society groups submitting detailed and comprehensive reports to the Althing concerning various aspects of the dispute. Without the context of these three processes, observers can be easily misled to see only a part of the picture that is Iceland's political arena in the time of the Icelandic constitution reform process.

4 Opinion on the Draft New Constitution of Iceland Adopted by the Venice Commission at its 94th Plenary Session (Venice, 8–9 March 2013). The Venice Commission uses unusually strong wording warning against a serious and general lack of clarity in the human rights chapter of the draft. The Commission finds the proposed electoral system very complicated (para 78) and stresses that a careful impact assessment is an essential requirement prior to its adoption. It expresses similarly grave concerns about the chapter on courts and judges. The strongest wording is, however, used to warn against the sweeping changes of the Icelandic institutional system that the draft entails. It states that 'the Commission believes that the government organization should be carefully reconsidered with a view to achieving a more unified and coherent system' (para 105). Furthermore, it warns about the design giving rise to 'problems in the administration of the country and the design of coherent policy' and that a system such as the draft proposes carries an obvious risk of political instability (para 112).

5 Ágúst Þór Árnason and I agreed on Iceland making respect for the rule of law the guiding principle of all its international relations.

Iceland's failed statehood[6]

The Republic of Iceland was in a state of powerlessness by October 2008. It had neither resources to save its banks, nor had it had much assistance to do so from other nations ex ante before the crisis. Acquiring assistance ex post turned out to be a great struggle. Where they operated or had ownership across borders, the Icelandic banks were all overtaken by authorities in the respective countries without collaboration or cooperation with the Icelandic Central Bank or other Icelandic government institutions. Iceland was considered to be to blame for being the weakest link in integrated financial systems and as such constituting a threat that had to be eliminated. It was an extraordinary situation for a highly developed wealthy nation to be in.

Devastation due to financial crisis comes to nation states in many guises: social turmoil, lawlessness, unemployment and recession, bankruptcies, and national trauma are common elements. A study made in 2015, which covered all financial crises in the Western world since the late 1900s, found that all democracies shift to extremism in elections after a financial crisis in a way that is not shown to happen when an ordinary recession (not caused by financial crisis) occurs.[7] Indeed, the aftermath of the Great Financial Crisis has brought on a seismic shift of the political landscape in the Western world towards authoritarian style of governance as trust towards political parties and democratic institutions evaporated. International relations and foreign policy have changed in ways that nobody expected before 2008, with changed alliances, trade wars, and severe challenges to the system of international organisations, be it NATO, the EU, or supranational collaboration to stall climate change.

6 I refer to loss of statehood here as absolute loss of sovereignty, e.g. that a national bankruptcy under harsh duress from foreign creditors can result in a loss of independent statehood, i.e. that a country loses its position in the international community that sovereign statehood brings. I also refer further on to state prerogatives – an element of sovereignty, which Iceland exercised when issuing the Emergency Act and following through on the results of the two Icesave referendums. Then there is the particular aspect that is financial sovereignty and economic sovereignty. Those refer to privileges, freedoms and capabilities of developed countries to issue a currency, run a Central Bank and a national financial system. Such privileges, enough resources and national wealth, tend to ensure that a state is economically on solid ground. This entails being solvent. Iceland risked all this in the run up to the crisis.

7 Manuel Funke, Moritz Schularik, and Christoph Trebesch, 'Going to Extremes: Politics after Financial Crises, 1870–2014' (2016) *European Economic Review* 227–270. 'We will present three main stylized facts from 140 years of modern political economy. First, politics takes a 'hard right turn' after financial crises. Both before *and* after World War II, we observe a significant increase of votes for far-right parties. In contrast, parties on the far left of the political spectrum did not have comparable electoral successes after crises. Second, we also find that political polarisation increases substantially after financial crises as measured by weaker government majorities, a stronger opposition, and a greater fractionalisation of parliaments. These effects are considerably more pronounced after World War II than before. Finally, we show that street protests typically increase after financial crises, then and now.'

Furthermore, a financial crisis of a state can prove devastating to the point of annihilation. Newfoundland, which was an independent dominion within the British Empire from 1907 to 1949, is an example of how a sequence of events led to loss of self-rule. The country's default was a key event, creating a vulnerability that in effect usurped the authority of a constitutional assembly that had been elected to decide the future of the country and to put two suggestions to the electorate in a national referendum in 1948. Neither of the two options put to the people suggested that Newfoundland should become a part of the sovereign state of Canada as a province, but nevertheless that is what happened due to the influence of the creditor country, the United Kingdom.

A sovereign default in certain circumstances usurps a country's sovereignty even though the theory of international law of nations does not recognise this as a function of sovereignty. The reality of economic power, as opposed to legitimate authority, serves to enable an outside actor to usurp authorship and write their own altogether alternative text concerning the sovereignty of individual countries. It should be pointed out that we are here not discussing circumstances of war or secession or any other example from the general typology of diplomacy; our topic is money interests and economic power in the interactions of nations, which is in essence ruled more by private law and limits of jurisdictions than by public law, be it either national or international.

Did the 2008 Icelandic financial crisis constitute a sovereign debt default for Iceland? The question was existential. In the autumn of 2008, news headlines around the world overstated as much, and the perception of governments, central banks, and international organisations was unequivocal. They viewed Iceland as bankrupt, a failed state and near death. The outrage was that Iceland had no capability to back up all its banking system, the size of which was believed to be, at the point of time when the crisis hit, nine times the gross national product of the country.[8] The bankruptcies of the three main banks, Glitnir, Landsbanki, and Kaupthing, all occurred in three days from 6 to 8 October 2008 and rate as among the largest corporate bankruptcies in recorded history. Iceland was broken in the eyes of the world. Time would tell that the Republic of Iceland avoided sovereign default by ring-fencing domestic banking and financial assets and by providing them with state backup, while allowing foreign assets to go into arrears and orderly bankruptcy procedures.[9] This is what the Emergency Act 125/2008 succeeded in doing.

A run on the banks in Reykjavik began for real on Monday 29 September and was increasing throughout the next two weeks but ceased completely on Monday 13 October. The Prime Minister issued a statement on 6 October that all deposits

8 Richard Z Aliber and Gylfi Zoega (eds), *Preludes to the Icelandic Financial Crisis* (Palgrave Macmillan 2011).

9 The Bank of Canada published a list based on thorough analysis of sovereign defaults and debt crisis, with particular emphasis on the great financial crisis period, but Iceland does not get a mention. See: David Beers and Jamshid Mavalwalla, 'Database of Sovereign Defaults, 2017' Technical Report No. 101 (Bank of Canada, n.d.).

in banks in Iceland were guaranteed. This was a so-called blanket guarantee, the only method known to halt a bank run. This was to become a matter of debate in the Icesave dispute. Iceland's key emergency measure was the Act that came into force on the evening of 6 October 2008. Part of the legislation had been prepared as early as in 2006. However, the final decisions were only taken during the preceding weekend, and some of them and not until the last minute on Monday 6 October. The legislation entailed the following:

1 Deposit holders were given priority to the bondholders of the three fallen banks. In 2016, because of this changed priority through the Emergency Act, the UK and the Netherlands received 100% full payments from the estate of the fallen banks.
2 All domestic assets were transferred along with deposits to new banks at a 'fair' value.
3 The new banks capitalised by the state then assumed the role of the old banks in the payment system.
4 International operations of the old banks were put into liquidation in an orderly bankruptcy procedure.
5 The banking system shrunk from being ten times GDP to being two times GDP.

After the Emergency Act came into force, both Landsbanki on Tuesday 7 October and Kaupthing on Wednesday 8 October handed in their banking licence to the Icelandic Financial Services Authority. Thus all the three banks involved were subjects to the processes of ring-fencing, default, and orderly bankruptcy procedure that the Emergency Act entailed; this amounted to 85% of the Icelandic banking sector. Others were to follow two to three years later. The Financial Authority divided each bank into one 'new' and one 'old,' and the Ministry of Finance formally created three new banks that all opened up the next morning without any hiccup. The Icelandic banks had operations in Norway, Sweden, Finland, Austria, Germany, the UK, Netherlands, Denmark, Luxembourg, Belgium, and Guernsey. By far the most serious issues of the cross-border banking crisis concerned the Internet accounts run by Kauphting, i.e. Kaupthing Edge and by Landsbanki, i.e. Icesave.[10] The British government was particularly fierce as they launched a public relations war on Iceland on 7 October 2008 and applied terrorist legislation to freeze all Icelandic assets in the UK. This was the start of a five-year international dispute and arguably probably the most serious conflict with other nations in Iceland's history. The stakes were existential for Iceland as the initial debt burden was crippling, and Britain and the Netherlands used harsh methods to enforce a state

10 For a detailed description in Icelandic of the international dispute and how it proceeded from 2008 to 2017, see: Skýrsla starfshóps um EES-samstarfið, September 2019, útgefandi Utanríkisráðuneytið, pp. 189–196. A working Group Report on the European Economic Area Collaboration issued by the Foreign Ministry of Iceland.

obligation on Iceland to pay, denying it access to court for years. Iceland's escape route was a constitutional clause unique to the Icelandic Constitution, namely Article 26 giving the President of the Republic power to bring formally enacted law to the vote of the electorate and suspending his signature until a referendum has been held in which the law has either been accepted or refused by the said referendum. It was through two such referendums that Iceland got its day in court and won in the EFTA Court in Luxembourg on 28 January 2013.[11] When the International Monetary Fund (IMF) seemed closed to Iceland, a decision was made to send a negotiating committee to Moscow, as government officials there were understood to be interested in offering a loan. In the end, nothing came of it.

As explained later in the chapter, I borrow the 'near-death' epithet from an IMF official to underline the fact that a danger of such magnitude is conceivable and real to sovereign states under the circumstances of a severe financial crisis. Although sovereign state bankruptcy is not a procedure clearly defined in law and is therefore never actualised as such. As sovereign states are not programmed by capitalism to die and rise again, unlike firms and corporations, there is no limited liability to ensure that sovereign states are never hit too hard socially, financially, and politically by crises, as is possible for corporations. There are, history shows, serious consequences inflicted on sovereign states when finance is hit by crisis. Such crises are capable of leaving sovereign states overwhelmed and devastated.

Still, the notion that a banking crisis or a currency crisis is, by its very nature, a crisis of statehood and political legitimacy had not enjoyed recognition in Western economic thought in the last few decades before the Global Financial Crisis. The lessons of the 1920s and 1930s of deep financial crisis, causing the functioning of both the political and the financial systems to collapse, were forgotten – financial crises were not supposed to happen anymore except in developing countries.

A book published in 2009, *This Time Is Different*,[12] brought home how out of touch with facts of history such complacency was. When Queen Elizabeth II visited the London School of Economics (LSE) after the crisis had struck in 2008, she asked why nobody had foreseen it. The LSE economists had only unclear answers to offer. A special meeting was called at the British Academy, after which this explanation was given in a special letter:

> So in summary, Your Majesty, the failure to foresee the timing, extent and severity of the crisis and to head it off, while it had many causes, was principally a failure of the collective imagination of many bright people, both in this country and internationally, to understand the risks to the system as a whole.[13]

11 *EFTA Surveillance Authority v Iceland*, 28 January 2013, Case E-16/11.

12 Carmen M. Reinhart and Kenneth S. Rogoff, *This Time Is Different Eight Centuries of Financial Folly* (Princeton University Press 2009).

13 British Academy, 'Letter to Her Majesty Queen Elizabeth,' 20 July 2009.

The use of the wording 'near-death experience' to describe the status of a sovereign state, namely the Republic of Iceland at the height of its twin financial crisis in the autumn of 2008, was made by the International Monetary Fund's top-crisis interlocutor when he looked back three years later on his first arrival in Iceland, in a blog post published by the IMF on its website in 2011.[14] By that time, his prime locus operandi had been moved to Athens via various other capitals in Europe, and the financial crisis was getting a new name: Great Financial Crisis (GFC for short). His name is Poul Thomsen, and he wrote in his blog post:

> When I travelled to Reykjavik in October 2008 to offer the IMF's assistance, the situation there was critical. The country's three main banks – which made up almost the entire financial system – had just collapsed within a week of each other. The sense of fear and shock were [sic] palpable – few, if any countries had ever experienced such a catastrophic economic crash.

As one among those who received Thomsen in the Ministry of Foreign Affairs, which was then the Crisis Coordination Centre of the Republic of Iceland, the author of this chapter can attest that we felt that Iceland might not survive as a sovereign country. All ministries, the Financial Surveillance Authority, the Central Bank, and all other organisations or institutions, when and if relevant, were called upon to step up and contribute. Each day and night seemed to bring new horrors, and everybody willingly worked around the clock to take on whichever project they were asked because everyone felt what Thomsen put into words three years later: Iceland was near death. There were loyalty and willingness to embrace responsibility and to do whatever had to be done.

For the general public, the shock, anxiety, and uncertainty were tremendous. In the time span of three days, the banking system collapsed, and in the next weeks and months the economy came to a standstill. Unemployment rose dramatically, and arrears seemed to loom all over society; both household debt and corporate debt were extraordinarily high, one reason being the foreign-denominated loans that mushroomed with the collapse of the currency the ISK (*króna*). Students abroad were unable to pay their fees, and their credit cards did not work. Icelandic companies lost contracts and most if not all access to lending. Everybody was fearful of a horrible depression or of something even worse to come. The situation also released a wave of public initiatives all around the country. The near-death epithet may now seem to the reader a mere dramatising metaphor since Iceland remains a rich and prosperous country having quickly recovered economically. However, nobody predicted that when Iceland hit rock bottom. In Icelandic, that event has its own name – *Hrunið*, which means 'The Collapse' – a reference to something much more than a regular economic recession.

14 Poul M. Thomsen, 'How Iceland Recovered from Its Near-Death Experience' *IMFdirect* (blog), 26 October 2011. https://blog-imfdirect.imf.org/2011/10/26/how-iceland-recovered-from-its-near-death-experience/

The Icelandic state proved its capability to resurrect

Systemic financial crises are not resolvable without capabilities that only sovereign states have, yet economic theories that view the state only and simply as a weakest link and as merely a source of corruption still dominate economic thinking. The discourse evolves around the idea of a moral hazard in financial and monetary markets due to the assumed backup of the state. Rethinking is therefore much needed since state backup of finance has been immense in the Great Financial Crisis. Across continents, a socialisation of losses took place, and only a few countries escaped the crisis altogether. The crisis has destabilised political systems everywhere as states were burdened with the necessity of applying power and consuming legitimacy in order to stabilise exchanges throughout all parts of society. The ways and means of state backup also developed radically throughout the crisis, which started as a banking crisis but turned into a sovereign debt crisis in some European countries and into a crisis of the Euro within the European Union. Central bank collaboration, by means of e.g. currency swap lines and the invention of quantitative easing (QE) with interest rates lowered in the United States and the Euro Area of the EU in an unprecedented way, will be among the legacies of the GFC.

In the Great Financial Crisis, the Republic of Iceland became for some a symbol of a people's revolt against global finance. When the crisis spread to southern Europe, in Spain and in Greece people marched in demonstrations carrying flags and signs with reference to Iceland. Primarily, this mythical status stemmed from news of economic recovery, criminal prosecutions against bankers, and in particular the two national referendums in Iceland where the payment of deposit guarantee costs to two other countries was rejected by a big majority of the popular vote. This turn of events and its resolution through direct democracy were not usual in this crisis, and similar historical precedents are difficult to find.

The real events are more complicated than the myth implies. Those hoping for or even expecting a clear-cut example to follow were not to find what they were looking for. Legal precedents created by referendums through direct democracy are not the same thing as judicial precedents since the applicable reasoning can never be as exacting as within a rigourous tradition of adjudication in a particular legal system and jurisdiction. Elements of adjudication, either formal or substantive, may translate into international systems of law if those systems entail institutions possessing power of adjudication.

However, the example of referendum results being accepted and adhered to by other nations and by international organisations does become a recorded precedent in international law and in this case a precedent which forms a part of EU/EEA and IMF history. As such this is not a legal rule of any kind but forms part of the living law and is a political milestone in how the division of power between a member country and the organisation is to be understood. Moreover, in the case that we are discussing, the added element is that direct democracy has seemingly enforced legitimacy beyond what the government or Parliament could achieve within the supranational European system. This is of substance when evaluating, after these events occurred, the theory of implied and attributed powers in the EU and the EEA, and deciding which institution has the final word in any dispute or matter at hand. Anyhow, the Icelandic precedent is not a clear or easy act to follow since the opportunity to apply democracy in such a way is far from being always or easily available. There has to be a legal authority within a country's system of government, in Iceland's case the unusual authority given to the President of Iceland through Article 26 of the Constitution.[15] Moreover, in Iceland's case, this meant that the President was able to turn to the public through a referendum on an issue that the government had negotiated with two other nations by virtue of its constitutional power to represent Iceland and that the parliament had turned into law. It was the free and personal decision of the President of Iceland to send the Icesave law passed by parliament to a referendum twice, in 2010 and in 2011. In spite of what has already been explained above about the near impossibility of applying this as a precedent, there is no doubt that the Icelandic example influenced the idea of the proposed Greek economy referendum of 2011, which the Greek government called but later suspended under pressure, and eventually four years later the bailout referendum which took place in Greece on 5 July 2015.

For Iceland, the results of the two referendums concluded the matter at hand. More often than not, however, such referendums are constrained by the way in which the hierarchy of law is constructed within a particular constitution or legal system. I know of no other constitution where the different institutions of state power could stage a similar interplay between their actions as happened in Iceland with the Icesave dispute. In general, questions put to a referendum do not involve issues of this kind, i.e. economic issues including everything that has to do with state loans, payments of financial obligations, and, importantly, all dealings on behalf of member states of the International Monetary Fund or similar EU programmes, organised ad hoc in a time of crisis as a temporary measure. All this creates a hierarchy of law that constrains not only the issue and question put to a referendum but also the effect that such a decision may have. Thus it is likely to be capable only of demonstrating a democratic majority opinion rather than a decisive final say and is therefore more political than legal in its effect. That depends on the constitutional norms in each case.

The Emergency Act and the Icesave referendums are examples of a country exercising its state prerogative. In both cases, it was severely tested within the international system, both legally and geopolitically, and it withstood the pressure. The change of priority in case of bankruptcy became valid viewpoints in EU law, and so did changes concerning the deposit guarantee system. In that way, the actions of Iceland were vindicated by the evolution of international financial regulation.

To sum up, Iceland's use of state prerogative on these issues succeeded on all fronts. The international community tolerated it and had in the end no choice but

15 See: Chapter 3 by Ágúst Thór Árnason and Catherine Dupré in this collection.

to adhere to it. However, international recognition was by no means to be taken for granted. Both the Netherlands and the United Kingdom, as well as a vast number of creditors, attempted to strike down the Emergency Act, but the only courts where they could have its legality challenged were Icelandic. Thus, it became a legal question for the Supreme Court of Iceland, which ruled that it was not only a right of the Icelandic Parliament to legislate in this manner but positively a duty under the Constitution.[16] The referendums were not testable in courts anywhere. They were a democratic act of referral, with one clear question on the ballot requiring an absolute majority of either yes or no, which decided the issue at stake.

There were great fears of the consequences that this would have on the country's position in the global financial system and money markets. It was predicted that Iceland would have to endure its position as a pariah state for a long time, unable to finance itself on international markets, with a detrimental effect on its economy. But it turned out differently. Somehow, the punitive power of global finance did not materialise or strike back. The small country on the periphery was in effect powerless but able to make use of the law in its defence; and because of the drastic measures of ring-fencing the national banking system and economy, the ground was laid for more comprehensive 'haircuts' and debt restructuring for both households and corporations than in most other countries during the crisis. Thus Iceland fairly soon got rid of the fallen assets and cleaned up the balance sheet accounts throughout its economy. There were huge losses, but the economy was able to revitalise and invest again gradually. This was one reason of many for the relatively quick economic recovery.

The financial crisis triggered the construction of the experimental special process of constitutional reform in Iceland which, as it turned out, was flawed in that its specially made processes were fundamentally inconclusive. Government actions were announced and publicised with considerable public participation but were never fully executed accordingly because of ex ante failure in procedural design. Since no one owned the process, the question of who was to blame took prominence, with claims of political corruption and vested interests pushing out constructive bona fide constitutional debate.[17] The democratic discourse on constitutional reform was thus transformed into a maze of half-truths. This was obviously also a direct result of the general crisis atmosphere in the country. A financial crisis cannot be resolved without the state taking measures to provide a backstop to the financial system in a process that lacks rules, transparency, constitutional legitimacy and legal foundation and inevitably, as both recent experience and history show, the result is often a damaged democracy.

In Iceland's case of financial crisis, the circumstances were so dire that it took extreme measures to save what could be saved. And the key to these measures

16 Supreme Court Ruling, known as 'the Emergency Act judgment' (Neyðarlagadómar) of 11 October 2011 (H 340/2011). See: Eyvindur G. Gunnarsson, 'The Icelandic Regulatory Response to the Financial Crisis' (2011) 12 *European Business Organization Law Review* 1–39.

17 Valur Ingimundarson, Philippe Urfalino, and Irma Erlingsdóttir (eds), *Iceland's Financial Crisis: The Politics of Blame, Protest and Recognition* (Routledge 2016).

turned out to be the application of the Constitution in force, referendums, and various other legal acts. The existing 'normal' procedures and processes were stepped up, so to say, and in the case of the international Icesave dispute, Icelanders exercised sovereignty to regain power over their destiny. In 2015, a spokesperson for the IMF summed up Iceland's economic recovery in this way:

> This year, Iceland will become the first 2008–10 crisis country in Europe to surpass its pre-crisis peak of economic output. The key differentiating factors supporting Iceland's relatively strong recovery are worthy of further study, but rapid external adjustment through depreciation and limited government absorption of private financial sector debt were likely important factors. Iceland also had a low debt ratio going into the crisis. Relative to past financial crises in Nordic countries, Iceland's experience has been rather similar.[18]

The following timeline situates the Icesave dispute in its wider context from 2008 to 2015 and summarises the key steps towards its resolution:

6 October: Act 125/2008 (Emergency Act) passed by parliament.
6–10 October: The British government demands state guarantee and lashes out at Iceland.
8 October: The Landsbanki freezing order and the freezing of all Icelandic assets. Gordon Brown: 'We have frozen all Icelandic assets in the UK.'
11 October: Memo agreed at the annual meeting of the IMF in Washington by Finance Ministers Wouter Boos of the Netherlands and Árni Mathiesen of Iceland. Geir H. Haarde informs the Dutch Prime Minister that Iceland will withdraw from that agreement.
4 November: ECOFIN meeting of EU's Finance Ministers in Brussels: Demands for arbitration and involvement of the IMF. Geir H. Haarde announces Iceland's refusal.
5–12 November: Agreed guidelines. The IMF released Letter of Intent.
25 November–5 December: Parliamentary resolution.
5 June 2009: The signing of an agreement.
28 August 2009: First law passed by parliament permitting state payments to the UK and the Netherlands according to the agreement signed on 5 June but with new conditions.
30 December 2009: Second law passed by parliament permitting state payments to the UK and the Netherlands according to the 5 June agreement with certain alterations
6 March 2010: The law is defeated by a referendum. Turnout is 62.7%, with Yes 1.8% and No 93.2%.

18 Karin Hammar, 'IMF Survey: Iceland Makes Strong Recovery from the 2008 Financial Crisis', 13 March 2015. The cited spokesperson is Peter Dohlman, then IMF Mission Chief to Iceland.

16 February 2011: Third law passed by parliament permitting state payments according to a new agreement considerably different from the previous ones.

9 April 2011: Law defeated in a referendum. Turnout is 75%, Yes 39.7% and No 58.9 %.

European Economic Area Surveillance Authority (ESA) decides to bring Iceland to the EFTA court. Until then, Iceland had been denied its day in court.

28 January 2013: ESA, the UK, and the Netherlands lose their case in the EFTA court. There was no state guarantee.

17 September 2015: Payments that began in 2011 from the estate of Landsbanki in accordance with the Emergency Act of 2008 are finalised along with an agreement between the the Icelandic Deposit Guarantee Fund and the UK and the Netherlands, which adds the amount that the fund had gathered from the Icelandic banks before the collapse in 2008. The UK gets 2.403 million pounds. The Netherlands gets 1.479 million Euros. For both countries, the amount is considerably higher than their cost of providing around 300.000 depositors with a guarantee in October 2008.

The aborted revolution

By the end of 2008, calls for a new republic to be established by enacting a new constitution had begun to be heard. In February 2009, when the government resigned, the perception of a revolution and the use of that concept as in 'the pots and pans revolution' (*Búsáhaldabyltingin*) became widespread. I apply a legal analysis of revolution to the ensuing sequence of events.[19]

A new government came to power immediately in the traditionally orderly manner as before, within the mandate of the parliament elected in May 2007 and through negotiations among three parties in parliament that together constituted a majority. Thus, it fulfilled all the requisites of a parliamentary government. This new government, in particular the new Prime Minister Jóhanna Sigurðardóttir, made the election of a Constitutional Assembly its priority and thus assumed at that time political ownership of the project of establishing a new republic by enacting a new constitution. In the coalition agreement, the Social Democratic Alliance and the Left-Greens declared that they would amend Article 79 of the Constitution and set up a Constitutional Assembly. A parliamentary bill for a constitutional law was put forward jointly by four parties in parliament. The reasoning for the parliamentary bill made references to Iceland as a failed state and broken beyond

19 There is, of course, a vast literature on the revolutions of their tasks and methods, but I stress that my analysis is strictly of the legal aspect and in the context of legal theory and constitutionalism. Suri Ratnapala puts these questions of law into a modern global perspective analysing different historic events and comparing the transition methods and their effect on legitimacy. Suri Ratnapala, *Jurisprudence* (Cambridge University Press 2009).

repair; the legitimacy of the Republic of Iceland was being called into question. Had Iceland's legitimacy been de facto usurped by the financial crisis? The substance of such a declamation constituted a new existential paradox of extraordinary proportions. Legitimacy was the salient point of weakness of Iceland's position in the world, of its policies and actions – inasmuch as a powerless backup state with a collapsed currency and national financial system had only the law to build on. In effect the outside world's harsh evaluation of creditors had entered the text of the Althing itself. Was Iceland in the same predicament as Newfoundland had been 60 years earlier?

The parliamentary proposal drew comparisons from revolutions and wars:

> Such constitutional assemblies have been held around the world at various times in history and are preferably a new beginning of the foundation of a new state or new regime of government in the aftermath of war, revolution or a collapse of the social order and a resulting constitutional crisis.[20]

The bill defined the project as an act of direct democracy and cited the recent events as its motivation:

> Widespread discussion on the necessity to re-evaluate the foundations of the system of government in Iceland because of the banking crisis last autumn and the ensuing harm to the economy.

As a result, the financial crisis was used as a justification for sidestepping the Althing as the instigator of constitutional amendments and taking action to hold a national election of a constitutional assembly in spite of the legally valid Constitution. A legal classification of revolution depends on whether the legal order continues or is disrupted, whether the norm is changed without adhering to the basic norm, whether the rule of recognition is upheld or not – in sum, whether the constitution in force is respected. Under its Article 79(1), the 1944 Constitution prescribes how constitutional changes are made, which in a very clear manner leaves no doubt that the power to bring forward and enact, in law, any changes to the Constitution rests exclusively with the Althing:

> Proposals to amend or supplement this Constitution may be introduced at regular as well as extraordinary sessions of Althingi. If the proposal is adopted, Althingi shall immediately be dissolved and a general election held. If Althingi then passes the resolution unchanged, it shall be confirmed by the President of the Republic and come into force as constitutional law.

20 Parliamentary proposal document no. 648, year 2008–2009. Frumvarp til stjórnarskipunarlaga þskj. 648, 136. Löggjafarþing 2008–2009, bls. 23. Jóhanna Sigurðardóttir, Steingrímur J. Sigfússon, Birkir Jón Jónssson, and Guðjón A. Kristjánsson: https://www.althingi.is/altext/136/s/0648.html

Contrary to the rationale of the 2009 parliamentary bill, it is in accordance with Article 79 that referendums, except those based on the authority of the President of Iceland under Article 26, can only be advisory to the Althing. The sequence of legal acts required to amend, change, or replace the Constitution is thoroughly spelled out in Article 79.

The parliamentary bill's process entailed having two elected national assemblies at work at the same time, with the Constitutional Assembly being only temporary, and a unique ad hoc process of consultation between the two, as well as a referendum. The idea was, by deliberate design, that democratic support in the envisaged national referendum would somehow trump or usurp the lawful process of constitutional change according to the 1944 Constitution. The exact legal basis for doing so was never clarified, and no constitutional moment ever came to the rescue by revealing itself. According to the Constitution, the (proposed) referendum could only be consultative. Eventually, the government and the Prime Minister accepted that fact but only in deeds not in words. This resulted in public duplicity that marred the process from that moment on. The pretence that Article 79 could be sidestepped was upheld in fierce rhetoric, but a lawful shortcut has yet to be designed. The attempt to get this bill through parliament before the general election, which was set for 25 April 2009, failed as minority parties applied filibuster tactics to prevent it. Such tactics were and still are frequent, well-known, and foreseeable and within the frame of procedure in the Althing.

At that point in time in March 2009, five months had passed since the crisis had struck with full force. Before that crisis point, no one had voiced or probably even contemplated the idea of the Republic of Iceland as a broken legal order or as a democracy without legitimacy. This was therefore not a movement with a deep-rooted political programme of constitutional reform, nor were there comprehensive ideas of change of e.g. the human rights chapter or of the system of government that had been advocated by any organised group or political party. At best, there were in the public sphere fragmented views entailing suggestions of changes to individual articles of the Constitution. The need for a comprehensive rethinking of the system of government had from time to time been acknowledged but always by lone voices. This was sometimes done with reference to the 1940s discussions according to which Iceland should eventually write its own constitution from scratch instead of retaining the basic structure provided by the King of Denmark and Iceland in 1878 as was done in 1944, with the main difference between the two being the establishment of a President of the Republic of Iceland and the creation of that same Republic. Moreover, the project to replace the 1944 Constitution was not supported by research or analysis. Rather, the tasks were defined by applying methods of pooling public opinion through social media and a national meeting or 'crowdsourcing.'

The revolutionary reasoning for directly electing a Constitutional Assembly never materialised in the drafting of the statute eventually passed by the parliament (Act 90/2010). In the end, the pushback was too strong for the parliament's political majority to withstand it. When a bill on the Constitutional Assembly was introduced in July 2009, there was no mention of a binding referendum anymore.

Althing's adherence to the existing Constitution as the valid norm was apparent in the fact that the Constitutional Assembly was to be only advisory. Thus, the lawful authority of Parliament was recognised, as was the present Constitution's rule of recognition and method of change.

The Supreme Court ruling that annulled the election of the Constitutional Assembly in January 2011 refuted any claim to special legitimacy, not to mention creating a supra-legal constitutional structure. The government and parliament complied with the Supreme Court ruling. Once the Constitutional Council (formally replacing the Constitutional Assembly) handed its finished Proposal for a New Constitution over to the Speaker of Althing in the summer of 2011, it also stated that its Proposal should be put to a public vote that is to be understood as advisory, thus accepting that a binding referendum was not in accordance with present constitutional norms, as in the Act 90/2010 on the Constitutional Assembly. The revolutionary rationale, however, lives on as rhetoric, creating a divide between legal reality and political fiction. The process was not based on precedent, and time has revealed the inability to design a viable process for writing a new constitution involving a directly elected constitutional assembly.

When the Proposal of the Constitutional Council is analysed, one thing is striking, namely that it contains no direct reference to the lessons Iceland learned from the experience of the financial crisis, a particularly stark contradiction to the declared reason for the endeavour.[21] There was no time to do so since the crisis resolution was still in its early stages when the work on the new constitution was to be ready. Whatever the intentions of the elected members may have been, this is an understandable and foreseeable result. An added factor is the absence of research in conjunction with the project. Icelandic society was overwhelmed with questions of constitutional law that were being fought, tried, and tested in every state institution. These are issues that were not comprehensively addressed by the Constitutional Council. With time, however, it becomes much easier to analyse these in a constitutional context.

The following timeline brings together the key steps in the constitutional reform process and situates the work of the Constitutional Council in its wider context:

January–March 2009: Mass protests, a new government, and election of a new parliament.

16 June: Adoption of Act 90/2010 establishing an advisory Constitutional Assembly, agreed in the Committee of Judicial Affairs on 14 June 2010.

Appointment of the Constitutional Commission of seven members to prepare an analysis of the strengths and weaknesses of the 1944 Constitution and to organise a National Forum.

6 November 2010: National Forum.

27 November 2010: Constitutional Assembly election. Turnout is 37%.

21 For further discussion of the 2011 Proposal, see: Chapter 8 by Skúli Magnússon in this collection.

25 January 2011: Ruling of the Supreme Court annulling the elections as unlawful in breach of the election law.

24 March 2011: Parliamentary resolution to appoint a Constitutional Council to replace the Constitutional Assembly. Parliamentary document 930. Memorandum 2 March 2011.

29 July 2011: The Proposal for a New Constitution handed over to parliament by the Constitutional Council after four months of work.

4 October 2011: Report from the Parliamentary Presidium. Dispatched to the Supervisory and Constitutional Committee on 11 October 2011. Closed on 20 February 2012.

5 December 2011: Individual members of the Constitutional Council meet with the Supervisory and Constitutional Committee. Attempt to hold a referendum alongside presidential elections (due in summer 2012) fails.

8–11 March 2012: Meeting between members of the Constitutional Council and members of parliament.

20 March 2012: Parliamentary resolution on an advisory referendum put forward, adopted on 24 May 2012.

20 October 2012: Advisory Referendum. Turnout is 48.4%.

16 November 2012: A bill on the proposal for a new constitution drafted by legal scholars presented in parliament.

26 January 2013: Proposed amendment by the majority of the Supervisory and Constitutional Committee left stranded in parliament.

March 2013: An extraordinary Constitutional Act of Parliament wins the vote in parliament making it possible the revise the Constitution in line with its Article 79. It will be confirmed by parliament after the April general election on 5 July 2013 as Constitutional Act 91/2013.

Example of financial crisis constitutionalism

The 1944 Constitution's legitimacy survived the national turmoil. Furthermore, it was the 1944 Constitution and its powers that ultimately sustained Iceland's statehood. Constitutions develop and change by events, precedents, and evolving custom. This is particularly evident for Iceland in the decade between 2008 and 2018 with the success of the Emergency Act of 6 October 2008 and the two referendums made possible by Article 26. This idiosyncratic Article made a significant difference, and the 1944 Constitution as a whole, with its institutions adhering to it, managed to withhold the immense pressure of one of the worst financial crisis situations on historic record and all the turmoil that followed.

Iceland is never referred to as a failed state in international forums anymore; instead it is most often now hailed as a success story by those same actors who before blamed Iceland as a failed state. As has been previously mapped out, has the 1944 Constitution was adhered to at all times, and the Icelandic constitutional reform process has had to comply with it. Still, Prime Minister Jóhanna Sigurðardóttir (2009–2013) never stopped hinting at the original legal revolution argument of circumventing the 1944 Constitution and Parliament. This duplicity remains present in public debate, upheld in particular by a vocal group of former Constitutional Council members and their ongoing campaign for their 2011 Proposal to be adopted by parliament without complying with Article 79 of the 1944 Constitution. As Thorvaldur Gylfason puts it: 'The game is not up. If Parliament wants to retain Iceland's place among democratic European nations, it must relent. It must respect the will of the people. This must happen.'[22] The Constitutional Council's Proposal for a New Constitution does exist but only as a fallen victim of a broken procedure that could not be rectified in the referendum of 20 October 2012, since it was by law advisory, and more importantly by design, inconclusive with no finished bill to vote on.

The 2012 referendum is the only one in Iceland's history that was not designed in a way that ensured a decisive political outcome. The public was not informed about the complicated bargaining that had to take place in parliament on the text itself and the comprehensive changes that were made to it; nor was the public informed of the work that legal experts had done on the Proposal for a New Constitution. Public debate on the substance of the 'new constitution' was therefore very limited. In its Opinion on the Icelandic constitutional reform, the Venice Commission chose to underline its concern about this, while stating that it was not its role to intervene in political controversy or to intervene in or take positions on political choices:

> [T]he adoption of a new good Constitution should be based on the widest consensus possible within society and [. . .] a wide and substantive debate involving the various political forces, non-government organisations and citizens associations, the academia and the media is an important pre-requisite for adopting a sustainable text, acceptable for the whole of the society and in line with democratic standards. Too rigid time constraints should be avoided and the calendar of the adoption of the new Constitution should follow the progress made in its debate.[23]

Article 79 of the Constitution gives the Althing the power to amend the Constitution; that is, once a constitutional bill has been accepted, elections must be called immediately, and, in order to take effect, the bill has to be accepted unchanged by the newly elected parliament. This rule is designed to protect the minority and to ensure that constitutional amendments enjoy broad political support. It is a lawful hurdle, a measure to ensure a stable democratic constitution of a parliamentary government. Compare the Icelandic case to that of Hungary and its 2010–2011 constitutional

22 See: Thorvaldur Gylfason, 'Iceland's Ongoing Constitutional Fight:' 'Is there a lesson for other countries to be learned from Iceland's now six-year-long constitutional impasse? I think so. When political parties act like interest organizations of politicians and as obedient servants of their paymasters, and when (as in Iceland) *two-thirds* of Gallup respondents view government corruption as pervasive, such misbehavior by politicians can have serious consequences to the point of undermining democracy. If this could happen in Iceland, it *can happen* elsewhere as well. Stay on guard.' *Verfassungsblog.de*, 29 November 2018. https://verfassungsblog.de/?s=gylfason

23 Venice Commission, Opinion 702/2013 of 11 March 2013, Paragraph 17.

turnaround, which was also triggered by the Great Financial Crisis.[24] Iceland and Hungary were both among the very first countries to enter into a programme with the IMF. The two countries had a lot in common with, in particular, the problem of currency-denominated loans to households, which exploded into a major crisis resolution challenge once the national currency had lost value. Both Iceland and Hungary were given junk status by ratings companies at some point during the crisis. In Hungary, the whole constitution was rewritten and a new constitution enacted in 2011. Such sweeping change was enabled by one landslide election victory and an ensuing two-thirds parliamentary majority, and the constitution became a tool of the political camp ruling the country. This may have been attempted in Iceland but did not happen. Instead, constitutional democracy held up – tried and tested by the severe financial crisis.

Recent history shows that devastation due to financial crisis is generally a destructive rather than a constructive circumstance to trigger the writing of a new constitution. The Backstop-State[25] inevitably faces such turmoil, difficulty, and public distrust that it may crumble. History tells us that peace, justice, tempered power, human rights – constitutional democracy as such – may suffer immense backlash along with it. The Icelandic Constitution should be understood as a framework for state building. The quest for statehood – i.e. being a nation among nations – is the alpha and omega of the legal reasoning that was the battle for independence in the nineteenth century and the state-building of the twentieth century. A black letter law view on the Constitution as text only is way too narrow, and, if we do not consider the Icelandic State as a three-dimensional organ of all the modern functions of states, we miss the real lessons of the Icelandic financial crisis.

Conclusion

The Icelandic financial crisis was total in the sense that the whole financial system collapsed. It meant that the state had the final say on all contracts, the value of which depended on how the state-owned banks or the courts would treat them. In such times of crisis, the currency has no value, and everyone capable rushes to buy gold. Democratic institutions are never prepared for this. No constitution has rules to apply in case of financial emergency. History tells us that authoritarianism often replaces democracy in such circumstances. The story of Iceland's three processes of constitutional reassessment and application in the Great Financial Crisis and of the country's crisis decade provides interesting examples and is, as a whole, a positive illustration of institutions surviving the odds and proving their effectiveness and benefit to human society.

24 See: Zoltán Szente, 'Breaking and Making Constitutional Rules: The Constitutional Effects of the Financial Crisis in Hungary' in Xenophon Contiades (ed), *Constitutions in the Global Financial Crisis: A Comparative Analysis* (Ashgate 2013) 245–262.

25 'Backstop State' refers to the mode which a sovereign state takes on in times of financial crisis where its function as a backstop to money and finance, i.e. its currency, its banks, households, and corporations, becomes an absolute and all-encompassing priority, law's elasticity increases, and constitutional principles are tested.

Part II

Drafters and drafting processes

5 The role and impact of the Constitutional Commission in preparing the constitutional revision

Björg Thorarensen

Introduction

One of the main actors contributing to the preparation phase of revising the Icelandic Constitution was the Constitutional Commission, an independent body of seven individuals appointed by the Althing. The Commission was given a threefold task. Firstly, it was to prepare and organise a National Forum on constitutional matters. Secondly, it was expected to process the results of the National Forum and undertake the collection and preparation of available materials and information relating to constitutional matters which could be useful to the Constitutional Assembly (subsequently renamed the Constitutional Council). Thirdly, the Commission was to submit ideas to the Constitutional Assembly on amendments to the Constitution. The Constitutional Commission operated for eight months and delivered an extensive report on 24 February 2011. Amongst other things, it contained an analysis and summary of the conclusions of the National Forum and two sets of comprehensive proposals for a new constitution.

This chapter will explore the objective of the establishment of the Constitutional Commission, why it came about, and how it performed its tasks. Then an assessment will be made of how this objective was achieved and of the impact it had on the final Proposal for a New Constitution adopted by the Constitutional Council in July 2011.[1]

Establishment of the Constitutional Commission under the 90/2010 Act on the Constitutional Assembly: context and last-minute amendment

Wider tasks and the narrower time frame for the Constitutional Assembly

The proposal to establish the Constitutional Commission and to convene a National Forum came up very late in the discussion of the bill on the Constitutional

1 This is further discussed in Chapter 6 by Salvör Nordal and Chapter 8 by Skúli Magnússon in this collection.

Assembly in the summer of 2010. In fact, the entire structure of the Assembly as eventually adopted in Act 90 of 16 June 2010 was completely different from that initially proposed by the new coalition government, the first cabinet of Ms. Jóhanna Sigurðardóttir, which took office on 1 February 2009 and the bill which Ms. Sigurdardóttir introduced a month later on a Constitutional Assembly and on the amendment of the 1944 Constitution.[2]

When the second bill on the Constitutional Assembly was introduced in November 2009, extensive discussions took place in the Althing concerning the Assembly's structure, procedures, the scope, and time frame of its operation. As a result, the bill underwent various amendments by the Judicial Affairs Committee in charge of it.[3] It discussed the six points which should be examined specifically by the Assembly according to Article 3, paragraph 1 of the bill, namely: (1) the foundations of the Icelandic constitution and its fundamental concepts, (2) the structure of the legislative and executive branches and the limits of their powers, (3) the role and position of the President of the Republic, (4) the independence of the judiciary and its supervision of the other branches of state power, (5) provisions on elections and electoral districts, and (6) public participation in the democratic process. It was also stated in paragraph 2 that the Assembly could 'decide to address matters other than those listed in paragraph 1.' The Judicial Affairs Committee considered that these tasks were too limited, and two more were added: (7) the transfer of sovereign powers to international organisations and the conduct of foreign affairs, and (8) environmental matters, including the ownership and utilisation of natural resources.[4]

A desire to limit the cost entailed by the work of the Constitutional Assembly became clear in the Althing's debates on the bill. Mainly for this purpose, it was decided to shorten its working time drastically. The result was that the Assembly was given only two months to carry out its work, though the Althing was ultimately permitted, under Article 2 of the 90/2010 Act, to extend this to as much as four months. This abridgement of the Assembly's maximum possible working

2 Bill amending the Constitution of the Republic of Iceland No. 33/1944 with later amendments introduced in the Althing on 4 March 2009. See: Althing 2008–2009, No. 385, doc. 648, www.althingi.is/altext/pdf/136/s/0648.pdf. This bill contained a special provision, Article 4, on the establishment of a Constitutional Assembly, and draft proposals on its structure. All webpages last accessed 1 June 2020.

3 The Judicial Affairs Committee is one of the standing committees of the Althing, according to Article 13 of the Standing Orders of Althing. No. 55/1991. Like other standing committees, it is composed of nine members of parliament and is elected by the Parliament for the whole parliamentary term after the general elections. The majority of the members of standing committees in the Althing represents the majority parties in the Parliament supporting the government. See: Björg Thorarensen, 'Mechanisms for Parliamentary Control of the Executive' in Helle Krunke and Björg Thorarensen (eds), *The Nordic Constitutions: A Comparative and Contextual Study* (Hart Publishing 2018) 84.

4 See: Breytingartillaga allsherjarnefndar [Amendment Proposed by the Judicial Affairs Committee]. Althing 2009–2010, No. 152, doc. 1296, 11 June 2010, 1: www.althingi.is/altext/pdf/138/s/1296.pdf

time from the initially envisaged 11 months to four meant a fundamental change regarding the time it would have to make a revision of the current constitution.

Objectives of the establishment of the Constitutional Commission and the National Forum

In the last stages of the Althing's examination of the bill on the Constitutional Assembly, directly connected with the amendment of the time frame allowed for the Assembly to do its work, was its decision to add new players into the process, arranging for the National Forum and establishing the Constitutional Commission. This was suggested by the Judicial Affairs Committee following the second reading of its proposal adopted on 11 June 2010.[5] Accordingly, a new final provision was added to the bill:

> On the passing of this Act, the Althing shall appoint a Constitutional Commission of seven members; the Commission shall work independently. The Commission will have the role of preparing and organising a National Forum on constitutional matters. The National Forum shall be held in good time before elections to the Constitutional Assembly pursuant to the Act. Participation of approximately one thousand people should be assumed for the National Forum, selected by means of random sampling from the National Population Register, with due regard to a reasonable distribution of participants across the country and an equal division between genders, to the extent possible. The sample shall be restricted to persons who have the right to vote in the election to the Constitutional Assembly and who are domiciled in Iceland. The National Forum shall endeavour to call for the principal viewpoints and points of emphasis of the public concerning the organisation of the country's government and its constitution; the Constitutional Commission shall process the information collected at the National Forum and deliver it to the Constitutional Assembly when it convenes.
>
> The Commission shall also undertake the collection and processing of available material and information relating to constitutional matters which could be useful to the Constitutional Assembly and furthermore present ideas on amendments to the constitution when the Assembly convenes.

This introduced a fundamental change in the constitutional revision process. Rather little was stated in the way of reasoning for these innovations, and it is clear that there was insufficient time to elaborate them in further detail. Nevertheless, the Judicial Affairs Committee stated the following regarding the National Forum

5 Breytingartillaga meirihluta allsherjarnefndar [Amendment Proposed by the Majority of the Judicial Affairs Committee]. Althing 2009–2010, No. 152, doc. 1301, 1: www.althingi.is/altext/pdf/138/s/1301.pdf

in its argumentation for this amendment in its supplementary opinion adopted on 14 June 2010:

> The [Judicial Affairs] Committee considers it important to hold a National Forum prior to convening the Constitutional Assembly to call for the public's main perspectives and emphases regarding the constitutional structure of the state, the constitution and amendments thereto. The National Forum should be held in good time before the election of the Constitutional Assembly as provided for under the Act. Participation of approximately one thousand people should be assumed for the National Forum, selected by means of random sampling from the National Population Register, with due regard to a reasonable distribution of participants across the country and an equal division between genders, to the extent possible. [. . .] Regarding other aspects of preparing and publicising the National Forum, the committee is of the opinion that consideration should be given to the experience gained from the 'National Gathering' [*Þjóðfundur*] held in 2009 by 'The Anthill.'
>
> The [Judicial Affairs] Committee considers it important that the National Forum should last for some consecutive days, e.g. three days, so as to promote efficiency in its work and elicit proposals that can be used as a basis for the work of the Constitutional Assembly.[6]

As can be seen from this, the National Forum was modelled to a certain extent on the 2009 'gathering' organised by 'an informal group of individuals sharing similar interests' calling themselves the Anthill (*Maurapúfan*) that had gained great attention in the public debate in Iceland.[7] No further explanation was provided in the Judicial Affairs Committee's opinion about the reasons why that 'gathering' could serve a model for the 2010 National Forum. Held in autumn 2009, it lasted for one day and was attended by about 1,500 people largely selected at random from the National Population Register. Its aim had not been specifically to discuss the constitution; rather, it was to discuss what values should be adopted as guidelines in the rebuilding of society after the economic crisis and to stimulate discussion of principal social institutions. Thus, it was intended to make the government aware of what the Icelandic people regarded as the most important fundamental values and the main issues to be tackled.[8] The 2009 National Gathering was generally considered to be a success and its conclusions were widely publicised. It was apparently in the light of this that the Althing's Judicial Affairs Committee thought another gathering of this type should be involved in

6 Framhaldsnefndarálit allsherjarnefndar [Supplementary Opinion of the Judicial Affairs Committee]. Althing 2009–2010, No. 152, doc. 1354, 1: www.althingi.is/altext/pdf/138/s/1354.pdf

7 This will be referred to as National Gathering, to distinguish it from the 2010 National Forum.

8 The Anthill's homepage: www.thjodfundur2009.is/thjodfundur/maurathufan/

the constitutional revision process; however, no further guidance was provided as to how this could be useful.[9]

Rather more of a surprise, without any direct model, was the other body provided for in the final provision, namely the Constitutional Commission. On this point, the Judicial Affairs Committee said in its previously mentioned opinion of 14 June 2010:

> The committee proposes that Althing elects, when the [90/2010] Act comes into force, seven members of good reputation in a commission which shall work independently. The role of the Constitutional Commission shall be to prepare the actual work of the National Forum and of the Constitutional Assembly, to collect preparatory materials, such as academic articles and writings on these matters, both Icelandic and foreign, and to collect materials on earlier work done on the revision of the constitution, foreign models, etc. Furthermore, it shall organise the work of the National Forum so as to make it efficient and produce conclusions and proposals. Finally, the Constitutional Commission shall prepare concrete proposals from the conclusions reached by the National Forum which shall be submitted to the Constitutional Assembly. The committee underlines that the Constitutional Commission may advise the Constitutional Assembly if the Assembly so requests. The committee considers that, by these means, the work of the National Forum, and also that of the Constitutional Assembly, will be made more efficient and there will be a greater likelihood that the Constitutional Assembly will produce results in the form of a proposal [*frumvarp*] which will have been approved, at least by a majority of the Constitutional Assembly, and which will be submitted to the Althing.[10]

The Act on the Constitutional Assembly was adopted by the Althing only two days later, on 16 June 2010, including the aforementioned amendments proposed by the Judicial Affairs Committee, listed under an additional provision entitled 'interim provision' inserted after the last article of the 90/2010 Act.

From this it can be seen that the Constitutional Commission was expected to assist the Assembly by carrying out various preparatory tasks and seeing to the collection of documents and academic materials to be used in connection with the proposals made by the Assembly; it was also to distil proposals from the National Forum's conclusions. This was designed to make the Constitutional Assembly's work more focussed and effective as it could be expected that the four months

9 James S Fishkin, 'Rökræðulýðræðið og 'lýðvistaða stjórnarskráin.' Tilaunastarfsemin verður að halda áfram' [Deliberative Democracy and the 'Crowdsourced Constitution.' The Experiment Must be Continued] in Jón Ólafsson (ed), *Lýðræðistilraunir. Ísland í hruni og endurreisn [Experiments in Democracy. Iceland in Collapse and Restoration]* (Háskólaútgáfan 2014) 23.

10 Framhaldsnefndarálit allsherjarnefndar [Supplementary Opinion of the Judicial Affairs Committee]. Althingi 2009–2010, No. 152, doc. 1354, 1–2: www.althingi.is/altext/pdf/138/s/1354.pdf; www.althingi.is/altext/138/s/1354.html

allowed for this would be nowhere near enough for the Assembly to start from scratch and end up producing coherent proposals. Moreover, the 90/2010 Act left open the possibility that the Constitutional Commission could advise the Constitutional Assembly in its work, but only if the Assembly so requested.

Composition and qualification of the members of the Constitutional Commission

As stated in the 'interim provision' of Act 90/2010, the Althing was to appoint the Constitutional Commission. No mention was made of professional qualifications that the members of the Constitutional Commission could be expected to hold. Thus, for example, it was not clear whether it was supposed to be composed of experts or of political representatives. It is only in the supplementary opinion of the Judicial Affairs Committee of 14 June 2010 that a reference was made to seven members of 'good reputation.' This wording in Icelandic usually refers to certain individual merits, such as being known for being sensible and reliable, but it does not refer to formal requirements, such as education or official position.

Four women and three men were chosen to serve on the Constitutional Commission. Most of them were connected with the country's universities, though not all had connections with the disciplines of law or political science, which would have been the most relevant qualifications for working on revising the Constitution. Four were connected with the University of Iceland: Ms. Björg Thorarensen (the author of this chapter) a professor of constitutional law;[11] Mr. Skúli Magnússon, the Registrar of the EFTA Court and an associate professor; Ms. Guðrún Pétursdóttir, an associate professor of cell biology and director of the Institute for Sustainability Studies; and Mr. Njörður P. Njarðvík, an emeritus professor of literature.[12] Two members of the Commission were from the University of Akureyri: Mr. Ágúst Þór Árnason (co-editor of this collection), who was an employee of the faculty of law, and Ms. Aðalheiður Ámundadóttir, who was studying for a master's degree in law. The seventh member of the commission, Ellý Katrín Guðmundsdóttir, was a lawyer and manager of environmental issues with the City of Reykjavík. None of the Constitutional Commission's members were members of the Althing; neither had they direct connections with political parties.

There was no official appointment procedure or documentation regarding the selection of these individuals, but apparently this was discussed informally among the political parties in the Althing. The composition of the Constitutional

11 Ms. Thorarensen had been involved in previous committees appointed by the government to revise certain parts of the 1944 constitution, one operating between 2005 and 2007 and another advisory working group appointed by Prime Minister Johanna Sigurðardóttir in February 2009, which submitted the bill for amendment on the Constitution in March 2009.

12 Njörður P. Njarðvik had actively participated in the public debate about his ideas to establish a new republic in the wake of the pots and pans revolution in January 2009. See e.g.: One of his articles on the subject 'Nýtt lýdveldi' was published on 14 January 2009 (www.visir.is/g/2009133864879).

Commission was eventually discussed and decided within the Judicial Affairs Committee of the Althing. In the minutes of the meetings on 14 and 15 June 2010, it is simply noted, without any further explanation, that the Committee discussed the composition of the Constitutional Commission.[13] At a meeting of Althing on 16 June, the Speaker of the Althing, Ms. Ásta Ragnheiður Jóhannesdóttir, announced the list of members of the Constitutional Commission, which was adopted by the Althing without discussion and without voting. No further documentation regarding proposals or the selection of these individuals can be found in the Althing's archives. Eventually, the members of the Constitutional Commission received a letter dated 21 June 2010 signed by the Speaker of the Althing, informing them of their appointments at the Commission.

The Constitutional Commission met for the first time on 8 July 2010 and elected Ms. Guðrún Pétursdóttir as its chairperson from among its own members. The chairperson's role was not defined; however, it was decided by the Commission that she would be responsible for organising and conducting the discussions on the Commission's meetings. The chair was also the Commission's spokesperson. In the first weeks of its work, the Constitutional Commission hired a secretary, Ms. Guðbjörg Eva Baldursdóttir, a lawyer who worked closely with the chairperson throughout.

In the following months and until it submitted its final report on 6 April 2011, the Constitutional Commission held a total of 40 meetings. Thereof 19 meetings were held before the National Forum on 6 November 2010. In addition, in the first phase of its work (i.e. before the National Forum), the Commission organised seven open meetings between 4 and 20 October 2010 in all parts of the country to encourage public debate and to distribute information about the Constitution and the reform process. At these meetings, the members of the Commissions introduced and discussed its task with the public.[14]

The appointment of a Preparatory Committee and its role

The interim provision of Act 90/2010 also provided for the appointment of a special Preparatory Committee (*Undirbúningsnefnd stjórnlagaþings*) as part of the Constitutional Commission, staffed with three members. The sole task of the Committee was to assist the Constitutional Commission with practical and organisational matters; this included presenting the work of the Assembly and setting up its website, securing premises, and preparing the appointment of its staff. It was not intended to have any input in the substantive proposals regarding the revision process of the Constitution.

13 Minutes of the 61st, 62nd, and the 63rd meetings of the Judicial Affairs Committee, 14 and 15 June 2010.

14 These meetings were held in Akureyri, Borgarfjordur, Egilsstadir, Hvolsvöllur, Ísafjordur, Saudarkrokur and Reykjavik. See in *Skýrsla Stjórnlaganefndar*, 1. bindi [Report of the Constitutional Commission, Vol. 1], 16.

The Preparatory Committee was appointed by the Speaker's Committee of the Althing following the adoption of Act 90/2010[15] and included Þorsteinn Magnússon, Assistant Secretary General of the Althing; Páll Þórhallsson, Director of Legislative Affairs, Department at the Prime Minister's Office;[16] and Sigrún Benediktsdóttir, attorney. The Preparatory Committee played an important role in various practical aspects of the preparation and execution of the National Forum and the Constitutional Assembly, but no further account will be given of its work here.

Organising the National Forum and processing its results

Preparation and process of the National Forum

The Constitutional Commission faced a huge challenge at its first meeting. Its immediate task was to decide a date for the National Forum, organise the meeting in cooperation with the Preparatory Committee mentioned above, and ensure that it would produce the desired results. In the first three months of the Constitutional Commission's work, its time was to a large extent devoted to the preparation of the National Forum. One of the main issues discussed in the Commission was how to gather the opinion of the participants on constitutional matters and whether or to what extent participants should be prepared.

In light of the fact that the Althing had in its discussion of Act 90/2010 referred specifically to the 'Anthill' project as a model for the National Forum, the Commission looked first into how the Anthill had prepared and run the National Gathering convened on 14 November 2009. The Anthill project had been a grassroots initiative, organised by a non-partisan group of people from all areas of the society. All preparations for the Gathering were done by volunteers. As stated on the Anthill's home page, the National Gathering of 2009, the idea was to bring people together for a whole day of discussions and to seek their opinion generally on the values Icelandic society should be based upon, as well as on their vision for Iceland's future and possible actions to rebuild the country's economy and society.[17] Some 1,500 individuals over 18 years of age had been invited to participate in the Anthill Gathering, including 1,200 chosen at random from the national registry and 300 who were representatives from companies, institutions, and other groups. The project was mostly financed through multiple donations. The event's total cost of 27 million ISK was covered by approximately 70 bodies, including individuals, companies, Reykjavik municipality, and other institutions, with the Icelandic government contributing 7 million ISK.[18]

15 The Speakers' Committee is a parliamentary committee responsible for organising the conduct of work in the Althing and for preparing a schedule for each session of Parliament according to Article 10 of the Standing Orders of Althing. No. 55/1991.

16 Páll Þórhallsson subsequently became the chairman of the parliamentary Constitutional Committee (2013–2016). See: Chapter 9 in this collection.

17 www.thjodfundur2009.is/fraedsluefni/lesa/item1877/index.html

18 www.thjodfundur2009.is/frettir/lesa/item1645/index.html

The Constitutional Commission decided early on to seek the advice of the organisers of the Anthill project regarding the organisation of the National Forum and the methodology and structure of the discussion. As a result, it was decided that the participants should not be requested to prepare for the National Forum and that they would not be sent the 1944 Constitution beforehand to formulate their opinion on their issue. It was also decided early on during the Commission's work that the National Forum should be held over one day only. The date and place chosen for the National Forum was 6 November 2010 in the largest sports hall of Reykjavik. The 1,000 participants were to be chosen at random from the National Population Register. For this, one 1,000-person sample was chosen, and then four others were added, meaning that behind each principal participant in the original sample, there would be four alternatives, who could be summoned in turn only if the need arose; if none of these was able to step in, then that seat at the Forum would remain vacant. As a result, the number of participants did not exceed one thousand. Invitations were sent out in September. Eventually, 950 people aged 18–91 attended the National Forum, with an almost equal gender balance and representation of all parts of the country. Every participant was paid a low fee for his or her role, and full travel cost was paid for those who travelled to Reykjavik.[19]

The Constitutional Commission strove to ensure that everyone would play an active part in the discussions and formulation of views. In this respect, advice was largely sought from the organisers of the 2009 Gathering, and an agreement was made with two individuals who had been in charge of that meeting to make necessary preparation for discussion techniques in the Forum. On the basis of their proposals, participants were seated in groups of eight, and each of the 128 tables had a so-called guide (*lóðs*), whose role was to explain the three main topics and to help the discussion along, though without directing it or actually taking part in it. The guides were prepared and trained by the organisers of the Anthill, many of them were selected from a group of guides from the 2009 Anthill Gathering.

The discussion agenda was decided by the Constitutional Commission following consultation with the Preparatory Committee and the organisers of the 2009 Gathering. The agenda was divided into a number of topics (or rounds), with each being allocated a certain amount of time: *ideals and values* (45 minutes), *contents of the new constitution* (70 minutes), and *recommendations from the National Forum* (most part of the afternoon). With the first topic, the aim was to create a positive atmosphere and break the ice among the participants. Each of them wrote one ideal or value on a small card and could ask for as many cards as they wanted. Then they put them forward at their respective table, one at a time, giving a brief account of each ideal or value. The guide then selected the ten qualities or concepts that had been most often mentioned around that table and summarised these on a result sheet for that topic.

While participants were making their suggestions on the contents of the new/revised constitution (second topic or round), the members of the Constitutional

19 Webpage of National Forum: www.thjodfundur2010.is/english/

Commission and of the Preparatory Committee were busy grouping the values that had received the most support into eight main categories. These categories were relatively wide and could cover the points suggested. The participants then grouped their ideas on the contents of the new constitution under these main categories, with the aim being to stimulate discussion on how the values and ideals that emerged from the first round were to be given expression when it came to amending the Constitution. Discussion on the values in each of these eight categories continued according to rules which made the debate more focussed. Then these were ranked and put to a vote at each table so as to produce some concrete conclusions for the second round. At the third round, 'recommendations,' i.e. advice or instructions designed for those who were to discuss proposals for a new/revised constitution were distilled from the material that had been gathered.[20] At the end of the day, the Constitutional Commission and the preparatory committee summarised the main conclusions of the National Forum. These reflected what participants wished to see form the basis of Iceland's new/revised constitution. They were listed under eight separate themes: (1) country and nation, (2) morality, (3) human rights, (4) justice, well-being, and equality, (5) Iceland's natural resources, their conservation, and utilisation, (6) democracy, (7) division of power, responsibility, and transparency, and (8) peace and international cooperation.[21]

As was further explained in the summary conclusions in the Constitutional Commission's Report on the outcome of the National Forum, the participants laid great emphasis on honesty and integrity, particularly in the public sector and among public officials. Overall, there was a desire to see ethics and morality become more integral concerns in Icelandic society and for this to be promoted via various channels such as introducing morality and ethics into education at an early age.[22] Participants also expressed the wish to see a separation between church and state. Human rights featured prominently among their concerns, as did equal access to health care and education. Participants wished to see Iceland play a role in international cooperation and to take a stance on the side of peace, as being a military- and nuclear-free zone. There was a strong call for protection of the country's natural resources and environment and for clear laws and regulations to ensure that the resources remained under Icelandic control. Finally, there was a call for democracy to be a strong force in Icelandic society, based on principles such as a clear separation of powers and transparency.[23]

The National Forum's website had been opened on 7 September 2010. Its preliminary conclusions were published there the day after the meeting, on 7 November.[24] In the following days, all the documents and materials produced at

20 A detailed description of the procedure can be found in Icelandic in *Skýrsla Stjórnlaganefndar,* 1. bindi [Report of the Constitutional Commission, Vol. 1], 23–31.

21 An English version of these themes and main conclusions was published on the website of the National Forum on 7 November 2010. http://thjodfundur2010.is/english/

22 *Skýrsla Stjórnlaganefndar,* 1. bindi [Report of the Constitutional Commission, Vol. 1], 28.

23 Ibid. 27.

24 www.thjodfundur2010.is/other_files/2010/gogn/Samantekt-Thjodfundur-2010.pdf

the National Forum were made available online.[25] This included a list of 2,759 personal recommendations that each participant was invited to submit relating to different institutions, including the Althing and the Constitutional Assembly. Finally, it has to be noted that the total cost of the National Forum was 63.5 million ISK, about 70% of the estimated cost, which was paid out of the State Treasury.

Significance of the National Forum

In the organisation of the National Forum, priority was attached to finding ways of allowing people with no experience in politics and no chance of ever obtaining such experience in the normal way to contribute towards shaping a major political document.[26] Much has been written and said about the National Forum, including the question of whether or not the participants reflected the general public's opinions adequately.[27] Admittedly, no study has been made to compare the demographic composition of the participants with that of the rest of the population who did not attend the Forum or to determine the reasons why some people declined to take part in it. It has been questioned whether those who participated were more dissatisfied or felt they were more marginalised than those who declined to take part or than the public as a whole, and doubt has been raised about whether the sample can be regarded as microcosm of society in terms of the strength of the opinions expressed.[28]

The methodology used at the Forum has also been criticised. Although discussion went ahead in small groups under the direction of guides, their role was confined to ensuring that everyone had a chance to her or his ideas. This worked well as far as the discussions themselves were concerned, yet participants expressed their opinions largely in the form of brief declarations which the leader recorded and collected. This arrangement was therefore focussed on identifying opinions and values together with their ranking by the participants rather than finding out why they held these opinions or whether they might be prepared to modify them after testing them against others. It was pointed out that it would have been preferable for the participants to have been given more opportunity to discuss the topics, to come into contact with viewpoints other than their own, and to make independent assessments of the methods and measures that were to be taken in the process as planned.[29]

In addition, it would obviously have been desirable to have had more thorough preparation for the National Forum during which these points could have been dealt with in greater detail. As with the entire constitutional reform process,

25 www.thjodfundur2010.is/heim/

26 Hélène Landemore, 'Inclusive Constitution-Making: The Icelandic Experiment' (2005) 23 *The Journal of Political Philosophy* 173.

27 Fishkin (n 9) 26–28.

28 Ibid. 25.

29 Landemore (n 26) 184.

the time frame allowed to the Constitutional Commission and the Preparatory Committee for setting up the National Forum was extremely narrow, namely less than four months, during which the Commission had started working fully on its other main task involving the collection of materials and preparation of ideas for amending the Constitution. Moreover, even though the plan had been to copy the Anthill's Gathering of 2009, it was ultimately not possible to do so. In other words, while the Anthill's Gathering was intended to reflect, in general terms, some basic values about society and to identify some direction for the future, the outcome of the National Forum had to be more focussed and to reflect the participants' principal viewpoints concerning the organisation of the country's government and the contents of its constitution. More space should perhaps have been made for more structured discussion, focussing directly on the 1944 Constitution's contents and for opinions on possible amendments. Instead, quicker methods were used in order to arrive at a picture of the common values and perspectives of the group and to establish their priorities. With this in mind, together with other methodological weaknesses in how the Forum was held, it may be considered as overstating the case to say that the general views and suggestions arising out of the Forum can be understood as 'the will of the people' and expected to have a decisive influence on the writing of a new/revised constitution.

The preparatory work by the Constitutional Commission in 'presenting ideas on amendments to the constitution'

The Constitutional Commission's ideas on amendments

By mid-November 2010, when the National Forum was over, the full energy of the Constitutional Commission went into preparing the Constitutional Assembly which was to debate the substantive aspects of the constitutional revision. As can be recalled, under the 'interim provision' of Act 90/2010, the Commission's mandate was 'to submit ideas to the Constitutional Assembly on the revision of the constitution.' A similar statement in the Explanatory Notes was the only further indication of the Commission's role in this connection. What this involved was therefore not particularly clear. Was the Commission to prepare comprehensive proposals on amendments, perhaps some sort of draft for a constitutional text which the Assembly would then examine and elaborate? Or was it only to submit ideas of a general nature, perhaps together with materials in which the Assembly could find further information? There was considerable difference of opinion among the members of the Commission regarding this. It was decided to tackle the task in the light of circumstances and the fact that the Commission had been established to offset the short time that the Assembly had been granted to revise the Constitution: a maximum of four months.

The way the Constitutional Commission saw itself as being of greatest assistance to the Assembly was that its members should discuss and submit reasoned alternatives which could serve as a basis for the Assembly. As the discussion on the National Forum and the public debate related to the Constitutional Assembly had focussed largely on 'a new constitution' which also could fall under the Assembly's open mandate in this respect under Act 90/2010, the Commission decided to draft examples of how a new constitution could be structured and its contents might be. In this, it attempted to reflect the main points of view expressed at the National Forum, while also making a priority of the tasks of the Constitutional Assembly enumerated in Article 3 of Act 90/2010. These were:

1 The foundations of the Icelandic constitution and its fundamental concepts;
2 The structure of the legislative and executive branches and the limits of their powers;
3 The role and position of the President of the Republic;
4 The independence of the judiciary and its supervision of branches of state power;
5 Provisions on elections and electoral districts;
6 Public participation in the democratic process, inter alia the timing and organisation of a referendum, including a referendum on a legislative bill for a constitutional act;
7 The transfer of sovereign powers to international organisations and the conduct of foreign affairs;
8 Environmental matters, including the ownership and utilisation of natural resources.

As the Commission regarded each of these points as deserving extensive discussion, it was decided to divide them into 13 subsections.[30] Various alternatives were considered in relation to amendments, e.g. whether there was any need for amendment at all and, if so, what courses of action were open, the pros and cons of each, etc. Following discussions on each of the 13 subsections, a text was drafted by individual members between meetings and considered and approved in the following session.

The Commission laid out the choices and discussed their strong and weak points, stating the reasons for its views. On certain issues, it sought opinions from experts outside its own ranks; these were published in 12 detailed analyses and discussions in Section V of the Commission's report.[31]

To make it easier for the representatives in the Constitutional Assembly to obtain an overview of various combinations of these alternatives, the Commission decided to submit two alternative versions (*dæmi*), A and B, of possible

30 *Skýrsla Stjórnlaganefndar,* 1. bindi [Report of the Constitutional Commission, Vol. 1], 59.

31 Ibid. 215–366. These experts were Birgir Gudmundsson and Gretar Thor Eythorsson (University of Akureyri); Eirikur Tomasson, Gunnar Helgi Kristinsson, and Dora Gudmundsdottir (University of Iceland); Bryndis Hlödversdottir (University of Bifrost); and Ragnhildur Helgadottir (University of Reykjavik).

constitutions, which were published in their entirety as appendices to the Report. In addition, references were made to individual articles in these versions in the discussions in each of the sections. Each of the alternatives, A and B, embodied ideas for a comprehensive revision of the Constitution. The Commission itself adopted no position; no majority or minority opinion accompanied the alternatives, either as a whole or in their individual articles.

Although the Constitutional Commission did not express any position or preference for either alternative, e.g. by indicating majority or minority support for them, the move of presenting two comprehensive versions instead of one obviously meant that unanimity had not prevailed regarding a single draft of the new constitution. The Commission pointed out in its report that it was completely up to the Constitutional Assembly whether and, if so, how it intended to use these proposals or whether it ended up combining parts of each in the draft it would finally approve. It also needs to be noted that this solution, i.e. setting forth alternative comprehensive versions, A and B, did not command the Commission's full support, and some members cautioned against encroaching on the role of the Constitutional Assembly regarding the preparation of proposals on a new constitution. For this reason, Njörður P. Njarðvik recorded a special reservation, which was published in the introduction to the Commission's Report, regarding the submission of the two comprehensive versions A and B, arguing that the Commission's mandate had not been to compile a comprehensive text of the constitution.[32]

For each of the 13 subsections of its proposals, the Commission strove to give an account of the main considerations and reasons, and the same structure was followed throughout. It started with a short introduction describing the provisions on the point in question in the current Constitution. Then came an account of the National Forum's main priorities and views on the matter, followed by the principal options available for revising the existing constitutional provisions and a brief mention of the exchanges of opinions that had taken place within the Commission. At the end of each section, the Commission summed up its proposals and described how they were embodied in versions A and B.

Substantive emphases in the Commission's proposals and materials employed

In its work and its proposals, the Commission aimed at certain goals about which there seemed to be a general consensus on a need for change or revision; the conclusions of the National Forum were one indication of this.[33] They include:

> To enshrine in the constitution certain basic values and concepts that underpin the structure of the Icelandic state, these also expressing the main features of the country and the nation.

32 *Skýrsla Stjórnlaganefndar,* 1. bindi [Report of the Constitutional Commission, Vol. 1], 3.

33 Ibid. 59–61. See also: Press release issued by the Constitutional Commission on 6 April 2011: www.stjornlagarad.is/frettir/lesa/item33141 (author's translation).

To ensure that the constitution is clear, easy to read, and approachable for the ordinary public, that it gives an accurate picture of state power and how it is administered and the role of the representatives of state power.
To enshrine in the constitution provisions on the nation's ownership of natural resources and the right of all citizens to a healthy environment.
To emphasise the government's obligation to implement international human rights agreements through legislation and other measures to ensure their effect.
To set out a clearer framework for the organs of government and define the role of each of the main branches of government.
To enhance the standing, role and independence of the Althing as the supreme institution in the democratic structure, particularly by giving it a broader supervisory role over the executive and setting clearer provisions on its powers of financial control.
To promote the sophisticated processing of legislative bills and to entrust a new body, the Advisory Council of Constitutional Issues (*Stjórnlagaráð*), with a special role if there is a question of whether provisions in draft legislation are compatible with the constitution.
To promote the separation of the legislature and the executive by means including the possibility of having government ministers who are not MPs.
To enshrine the principle of parliamentary primacy clearly in the constitution.
To clarify the position of the president of Iceland and his or her personal powers, e.g. as regards the formation of governments and the right to decide not to approve legislation passed by the Althing.
To set clearer rules for the top levels of government and clearer provisions on the appointment and release of governments from office, the role of the Prime Minister and the position of the ministers.
To reinforce the independence of the judiciary by means of rules on the appointment of judges and to set clearer provisions on the supervision by the courts of legislation and executive decisions.
To define Iceland's standing as a participant in international collaboration, ensure that the Althing will exert an influence on the conduct of foreign affairs and attend to the status of international agreements in domestic law.
To ensure the right of the citizens to decide directly, through a referendum, changes in the structure of the National Church of Iceland.
To increase public participation in the democratic process through broader authorisation for the holding of referendums and ensure that amendments to the constitution will at all times be decided in referendums.
To strengthen the standing of the local authorities in the Constitution and promote citizen democracy.

Both versions A and B, included these main themes, and the disposition of material in their sections and articles was comparable. There were nevertheless certain differences, such as regarding the powers accorded to the president, electoral system, public finances, the position of international treaties and various details of implementation. In the following table the main differences are summarised:

Ideas for a new constitution/ constitutional revision	*Example (Dæmi) A*	*Example (Dæmi) B*
Foundations and values	No preamble. Main foundations and values set forth in Article 1	Main foundations and values in a preamble
Order of chapters	Chapter on general elections and rights and duties of MPs in Chapter III following the Human Rights chapter	Chapter on the President of the Republic and the executive power in Chapter III following the Human Rights chapter
Provision concerning freedom of the media	No such provision	A paragraph on the subject in the provision on freedom of expression (Article15)
Provision a new electoral system	Revision of the electoral system shall be completed within a certain period (final provision)	A provision providing for a fundamental reorganisation of the electoral system (Article 50)
Decisions in dispute regarding validity of elections	Remains with the Althing (Article 26)	Decisions of the Althing can be appealed to the Supreme Court (Article 54)
Competencies of the Althing	Definition of the main tasks of Althing (Article 32)	No such provision + Article 2: legislative power jointly between Althing and President
Separation of legislative and executive powers	Ministers may not be members of Parliament (Article 43)	Participation of ministers in parliamentary work shall be decided in statutory law (Article 70)
Role of the President of the Republic	Remains largely unchanged (Article 2) Appointment of new Advisory Council of Constitutional Issues (Article 80) Stipulated that the President shall act in accordance with the government's foreign policy (Article 84)	New personal powers granted, e.g. concerning appointment of judges (Article 91), appointment of and referring bills to a new Advisory Council of Constitutional Issues (Article 47) and power to decide certain issues related to the state budget (Article 75)
Court of Impeachment (Landsdómur)	Continues to exist but rules concerning investigation of charges shall be stipulated in law (Article 73)	Abolished but the Supreme Court shall adjudicate all cases of criminal conduct of ministers in office (Article34)
Status of international treaties	The dualist approach towards international treaties remains unchanged	Immediate legal effect in domestic law following ratification and priority over domestic law (Article 86)

In the Commission's view, all the main points of its proposals listed in the table came under Article 3 of Act 90/2010. Revision of the human rights provisions, however, was not listed there as a specific task. As mentioned above, the Explanatory Notes of Act 90/2010 identified the constitutional provisions that had changed least since 1874 as those most urgently in need of attention. The Commission took account of the fact that the relevant section of the Constitution had been completely revised in 1995, bringing it into line with international human rights conventions. New provisions had been added, the scope of some provisions had been expanded, and the wording and presentation of the section had been harmonised with international obligations deriving from human rights treaties.[34] These changes mostly reflected the provisions of the European Convention on Human Rights and the main UN human rights agreements. The Constitutional Commission also cited the fact that since 1995, the human rights provisions of the Constitution had worked well and had achieved the intended results.[35] During the same period, the influence of international human rights agreements on Icelandic law had increased greatly, with the judiciary interpreting domestic legislation in the light of international provisions in this field.[36]

Accordingly, the Commission's proposals on substantive amendments to the human rights provisions were very minor. They involved an expansion of the principle of equality as expressed in the 1944 Constitution and the introduction of more detailed provisions on children's rights, as well as a new provision on the right of access to information (version B also suggested in this context a special provision on the freedom of the media). The Commission proposed moving the human rights section to the beginning of the constitution, arguing that these provisions belonged with those on the fundamental structure of the state, as all power derives from the people. It also proposed adding a provision on the right to a healthy environment, protection of the natural environment and the right of the public to participate in decisions which impact the environment; all of this was listed as part of the Commission's special tasks under Article 3 of the Act 90/2010. Finally, under the first section on fundamental matters and fundamental rights in both A and B versions, the Commission included a new provision about the national ownership of natural resources and their utilisation.

Material gathered by the Commission to prepare the work of the Constitutional Assembly

The Constitutional Commission gathered an extensive body of material on constitutional matters as a basis for discussion and proposals in its own work. Furthermore, one of its special tasks under Act 90/2010 was to gather and process

34 Tuomas Ojanen, 'Human Rights in the Nordic Constitutions' in Helle Krunke and Björg Thorarensen (eds), *The Nordic Constitutions: A Comparative and Contextual Study* (Hart Publishing 2018) 141.

35 *Skýrsla Stjórnlaganefndar,* 1. bindi [Report of the Constitutional Commission, Vol. 1] 82.

36 Ibid. 83.

available materials relating to constitutional design that might be of use to the Constitutional Assembly. To this end, the Commission prepared an electronic database which was used to collect these materials and make them available. These included academic articles, book chapters, reports, mostly in the fields of constitutional law and political science, with a bearing on constitutional theory and practice. These materials were grouped by topic, and efforts were made to ensure that it would be easy to find relevant literature and information that had a bearing on the principal tasks of the Constitutional Assembly. This database included copies of most of the articles written on constitutional matters in the last decades published in Icelandic law journals and journals of social science, chapters from textbooks, reports, and the legislative bills and constitutions of other states.[37]

As previously stated, the Commission additionally sought opinions on selected issues and constitutional questions from experts outside its own ranks, and four members of the Commission (Ágúst Þór Árnason, Björg Thorarensen, Ellý Katrín Guðmundsdóttir, and Skúli Magnússon) also prepared written opinions on some points; these opinions were published in 12 studies in Section V of the Commission's report, in the first volume, which is 367 pages long.[38] The opinions where meant to be concise and to address arguments and options regarding concrete issues. The authors who were not members of the Commission attended the Commission's meetings to discuss their opinions. These opinions were between seven and 30 pages long each and dealt with the following topics:

1 Constitutional provision regarding the Icelandic language (Björg Thorarensen)
2 Constitutional provision regarding natural resources and some legal aspects (Skúli Magnússon)
3 The environment and the constitution (Ellý Katrín Guðmundsdóttir)
4 The connection between state and the church (Ágúst Þór Árnason)
5 The impact of making voting rights equal (Birgir Guðmundsson and Grétar Þór Eyþórsson)
6 Proposals that ministers shall not be members of Parliament (Gunnar Helgi Kristinsson)
7 Althing's control over the executive (Bryndís Hlöðversdóttir)
8 Rules regarding legal responsibility of ministers (Ragnhildur Helgadóttir)
9 Constitutional provisions regarding the judiciary (Eiríkur Tómasson)
10 Treaty powers and foreign affairs in the constitution (Björg Thorarensen)
11 Referendum; comparison between states (Dóra Guðmundsdóttir)
12 The local self-government of municipalities and the constitution (Ellý Katrín Guðmundsdóttir)

37 These files and documents are still accessible on the home page of the Constitutional Council: www.stjornlagarad.is/gagnasafn/

38 *Skýrsla Stjórnlaganefndar,* 1. bindi [Report of the Constitutional Commission, Vol. 1] 82.

Additional material and surveys issued by the Commission were to be found in the second volume of the Commission's Report which is 345 pages long.[39] The second volume is divided into three parts. The first part is a summary of all the proposals for amendments that had been put forward since the 1944 Constitution was adopted, written by Aðalheiður Ámundadóttir, one of the members of the Commission.[40] This was a special survey of all the proposed amendments to the Constitution since 1944. It reflects the work of several parliamentary committees and committees of experts appointed by the Althing or the government to complete a comprehensive revision of the Constitution, and many MPs' bills on the amendment of individual provisions which were presented without ever being adopted. The second part included a report by Páll Þórhallsson on European trends in constitutional matters, amendments during recent decades in the most important European states and the dominant emphases in the design of the most recent constitutions.[41] The third part was a comprehensive commentary on all the current constitutional provisions with notes on their origin, substance and implementation compiled with the assistance of a group of experts in law and political science engaged by the Commission.[42] This was the largest part of volume 2 of the Report. Two members of this group of experts and editors of the commentary sat in the Commission (Björg Thorarensen and Skúli Magnússon). Other experts were selected by the Commission and came from the University of Iceland and University of Bifröst, the administration and the parliamentary ombudsman.[43]

Finally, it should be noted that all the experts who cooperated with the Commission and contributed to its work were paid from the Commission's budget.

The Constitutional Commission's Report and its impact on the Constitutional Council's work

The Constitutional Commission completed its work by issuing a Report, in two volumes running to a total of 700 pages, on 24 February 2011. The aim had been to submit the Report to the Constitutional Assembly, as provided for in

39 *Skýrsla Stjórnlaganefndar,* 2. bindi [Report of the Constitutional Commission, Vol. 2]: www.stjornlagarad.is/other_files/stjornlagarad/skyrsla-stjornlaganefndar/skyrsla_stjornlaganefndar_seinna_bindi.pdf

40 A. Ámundadóttir, 'Samantekt tillagna um breytingar á stjórnarskrá frá lýðveldisstofnun til 2010' [Summary of Proposals on Amendments of the Constitution from the Foundation of the Republic until 2010] in *Skýrsla Stjórnlaganefndar*, 2. bindi [Report of the Constitutional Commission, Vol. 2] 227–300.

41 Páll Þórhallsson, 'Stjórnskipunarþróun í Evrópu' [Constitutional Developments in Europe] in *Skýrsla Stjórnlaganefndar*, 2. bindi [Report of the Constitutional Commission, Vol. 2] 316–345.

42 Skúli Magnússon, Björg Thorarensen, and Páll Þórhallsson, 'Skýringar við stjórnarskrá lýðveldisins Íslands' [A Commentary on the Constitution of the Republic of Iceland] in *Skýrsla Stjórnlaganefndar*, 2. bindi [Report of the Constitutional Commission, Vol. 2] 7–225.

43 The additional experts in this work were Eiríkur Tómasson, Elín Ósk Helgadóttir, Gunnar Páll Baldvinsson, Hafsteinn Dan Kristjánsson, Hafsteinn Þór Hauksson, Kristján Andri Stefánsson, Sigurður Líndal, and Sigrún Jana Finnbogadóttir.

Act 90/2010. However, when the Commission finished its Report, there was uncertainty about the next move in the process and where it should submit its proposals. On 27 November 2010, the Supreme Court of Iceland had invalidated the election of the Constitutional Assembly, in which 25 individuals had been elected out of 523 candidates as Icelanders' representatives to the Assembly.[44] The election to the Constitutional Assembly was annulled on the ground of various electoral defects in its execution, including violation of the right to vote by secret ballot.

The Althing responded to the Supreme Court's decision on 24 March 2011 by appointing the 25 candidates who had been elected to take their seats in a new body, the Constitutional Council, which was given the same consultative role as the Assembly had been intended to perform. At the same time, the Althing reiterated that the Council's task was specifically to examine the same eight points as enumerated in Article 3 of Act 90/2010 on the Constitutional Assembly, but that it was also free to 'decide to address additional matters' under paragraph 2 of Article 3. It was also stated that the Council was to submit its report to the Althing in the form of a proposal for a constitutional act.[45]

Eventually, the Constitutional Commission submitted its Report to the newly created Constitutional Council on 6 April 2011. The Constitutional Commission also held a press conference at which it stressed that it was submitting neither a fully processed proposal nor a commentary of the type that usually accompanies draft legislation but rather a foundation which the Constitutional Council could build on if it chose to or use in other ways.[46]

With the submission of its Report, the Constitutional Commission's work came to an end. As a whole institution, it had no further involvement in the work of the Constitutional Council. However, two members of the Commission, Ágúst Þór Árnason and Björg Thorarensen, later submitted expert opinions to the Constitutional Council and attended its meetings in an individual advisory capacity. Björg Thorarensen attended one meeting with each of the three working groups of the Council (A, B, and C) and submitted opinions to working groups B and C. Ágúst Þór Árnason attended one meeting of working group C and submitted one opinion.[47] The Council did not request any advice or cooperation from the

44 Decision of the Supreme Court of Iceland of 25 January 2011. www.haestirettur.is/akvardanir/2011/

45 Resolution on the appointment of a Constitutional Council. Althing 2010–2011, No. 549, docs. 930 and 1120. www.althingi.is/altext/pdf/139/s/1120.pdf. This decision was criticised and considered by many to undermine the legitimacy of the Council in the revision process. This is further discussed by Salvör Nordal (Chapter 6) and Jón Ólafsson (Chapter 7) in this collection. See also: Thorarensen (n 3) 108.

46 Constitutional Commission, press release issued on 6 April 2011: www.stjornlagarad.is/frettir/lesa/item33141/

47 Stjórnlagaráð, *Frumvarp til stjórnarskipunarlaga ásamt skýringum* [Constitutional Council. A Proposal for a Constitutional Act, with Commentary] 28 and 29: www.stjornlagarad.is/other_files/stjornlagarad/Frumvarp_med_skyringum.pdf

Constitutional Commission as such, even though such advisory role had initially been suggested in the preparation work of Althing in relation to the establishment of the Commission by Act 90/2010.[48]

When assessing the impact of the Constitutional Commission's work on the Constitutional Council, it is important to consider the main emphasis of the Council. Its approach towards the Commission's Report was formulated early on, as its first step in April 2011 was to set out a policy on how it was to work and what its priorities were to be. Based on the Commentary[49] accompanying the Council's Proposal for a New Constitution, it is clear that its work on substantive amendments to the Constitution soon took a direction that was different from that of the Constitutional Commission's preparatory work. As stated in the Commentary's introduction:

> In particular, the Constitutional Council's members expressed, from the outset, a firm desire to revise the human rights section of the constitution, as well as to address several matters that were not mentioned in the 2011 parliamentary resolution appointing its members, but which had been discussed in the Constitutional Commission's Report, e.g. the status of the National Church and that of the local authorities. Furthermore, the Council stressed that its Proposal was a good basis for further work and not a set of binding instructions or options.[50]

Regarding the inclusion of a new human rights section, the Commentary on the Proposal regarding that section went on to state:

> The Constitutional Council decided at one of its first meetings that a revision of the human rights section of the constitution was one of the tasks on which it wanted to concentrate. This decision was based, amongst other things, on the powerful undertow of opinion at the National Forum, where various human rights were very much in the participants' minds, and many of the emphases on which the revision of the human rights section was based may be traced back to the National Forum.[51]

The Council also stated that various lawyers had long urged that the human rights section of the Constitution needed revision. It was not sufficient, said the Council, for the Constitution to ensure only the protection of civil and political rights:

48 Supplementary opinion of the Judicial Affairs Committee of 14 June 2010. Althingi 2009–2010, No. 152, doc. 1354: www.althingi.is/altext/pdf/138/s/1354.pdf; www.althingi.is/altext/138/s/1354.html

49 'Skýringum' is also sometimes translated as 'Explanatory Notes'.

50 Stjórnlagaráð, *Frumvarp til stjórnarskipunarlaga ásamt skýringum* [Constitutional Council. A Proposal for a Constitutional Act, with Commentary] 28.

51 Ibid 39.

its provisions on economic, social and cultural rights were, taken as a whole, inadequate.[52]

The structure of the 2011 Proposal for a New Constitution largely followed the disposition of material proposed in the Constitutional Commission's Report. As previously discussed, examples A and B presented by the Commission were very similar in structure. The commentary on each separate provision of the Council's 2011 Proposal generally referred to the corresponding provision in the Commission's proposals, and some sections were also largely based on those in the Commission's 2011 Report. This is well illustrated by Section V, on government ministers and the government, even though some crucial innovations were proposed by the Council that went further than those originally suggested by the Commission. An instance of this is Article 90 of Council's Proposal for a New Constitution, on the formation of governments, under which, following the arrangements in Finland and Sweden as models, the Althing would elect the Prime Minister, acting on a proposal of the President. By contrast, the Constitutional Commission had proposed that the principle of parliamentarism (*Þingræði*) should be enshrined in the revised constitution (as it is not stated expressly in the 1944 Constitution) in the form in which it has appeared in practice since the beginning of the twentieth century. The existing tradition in the Icelandic constitutional system was based on negative parliamentarism; namely, the President appoints the government after it has been established that the majority in Parliament is not opposed to the choice; in this detail, Iceland's application of parliamentary primacy is the same as has been customary in Denmark.[53]

It is clear from the Commentary on the Constitutional Council's Proposal that the materials prepared by the Commission were of assistance to the Council, as had been the intention of Act 90/2010. The most significant factor in assessing the value of the Commission's preparatory work to the Council, however, was the great weight which the Council gave to the outcome of the National Forum. The change in emphasis adopted by the Council in its decision to make a revision of the human rights section of the Constitution into one of its priorities, with reference to the undertow of opinion expressed at the National Forum, meant that the Council took on a far more extensive task than had been envisaged. In this, the Council made a fundamental change to its own brief as compared with the tasks entrusted to it. Contrary to Article 3 of the Act 90/2010, the main focus ended up being on the human rights provisions, with the work of one of the Council's three working committees being mainly devoted to this task.

As a result of this emphasis in the work of the Council, by far the longest section of its Proposal for a New Constitution, amounting to nearly a third of all the text, was Section II, entitled *Human Rights and the Natural Environment*, spanning 31 articles (Nos. 6–36). This section included a proposal for a detailed new provision

52 Ibid.

53 Thomas Bull, 'Institutions and Divisions of Powers' in Helle Krunke and Björg Thorarensen (eds), *The Nordic Constitutions: A Comparative and Contextual Study* (Hart Publishing 2018) 58.

on natural resources, which included little that had been proposed by the Constitutional Commission but laid out a new approach to the way the state would collect fees for the utilisation of the nation's natural resources.[54] The Council's reference to the National Forum's conclusions regarding human rights as a justification for adopting this course of action may be questioned. The conclusions of the Forum contained a whole section devoted to human rights.[55] The list of rights referred to by the National Forum were, however, already guaranteed in the existing human rights provisions and through general provisions on equality among individuals, the prohibition against discrimination, the principle of respect for the individual, etc.[56] Thus, it is not possible to see a real causative connection between the general attitudes expressed and directional pointers given by the National Forum and many of the new human rights provisions put forward in the Constitutional Council's Proposal.

The Constitutional Council's adoption of a change in policy regarding its brief under Act 90/2010 may be said to have had two consequences. Firstly, as no preparatory materials relating to human rights provisions and no proposals on them had come from the Constitutional Commission, which had based its work on the tasks entrusted to it by law, the Constitutional Council essentially had to begin this work from scratch. In particular, no substantive examination had been made of the need for changes in human rights provisions, the advantages they might bring, or the possible disadvantages they might entail. What is more, the Council's proposals on new human rights provisions had the appearance of random changes rather than of a cohesive revision. Little or no account was taken of the extensive body of case law developed in Iceland over the previous 10–15 years involving the interpretation of the constitutional provisions on human rights or of the case law of the European Court of Human Rights. Many of the proposed amendments generated uncertainty as to whether they constituted actual substantive change or merely changes of wording. Secondly, the narrow time frame granted to the Constitutional Council for concentrating on the tasks specifically assigned to it became even narrower. The Council had a maximum of four months in which to complete tasks which had already been of sizeable proportions, but the overall workload grew considerably and became a more complex challenge with the addition of a comprehensive revision of the human rights section. The view taken here is therefore that these circumstances had a serious negative impact on the overall quality of the Proposal eventually submitted by the Constitutional Council to the Speaker of the Althing on 29 July 2011.

From the outset, there was much criticism of the quality of the Constitutional Council's Proposal, particularly with regard to the purpose and possible unforeseeable consequences of the suggested amendments. They bore the marks of having been prepared in a very short time, as a result of which not all issues could be

54 See: Chapter 10 by Ragnheiður Elfa Þorsteinsdóttir in this collection.

55 *Skýrsla Stjórnlaganefndar,* 1. bindi [Report of the Constitutional Commission, Vol. 1] 36.

56 Ibid. 36 and 43.

carefully considered and suffered from an obvious lack of harmonisation.[57] In June 2012, the Althing appointed four experts selected by the Constitutional and Supervisory Committee of the Althing to review the Council's Proposal for a New Constitution from the standpoint of legal technical issues, harmony with international human rights obligations, and comparison with existing constitutional provisions on the protection of rights. This expert group made various amendments, not all of them of a technical nature, which will not be discussed further here, and finalised its work on 12 November 2012.[58] After a Bill based on the Council's Proposal for a New Constitution (with the aforementioned amendments) was eventually presented to the Althing more than a year after the Council finalised its task, on 16 November 2012, the formal opinions of 55 experts and stakeholders on the Bill were sought.[59] Eventually, 179 individuals, NGOs, and institutions submitted comments and opinions on the Bill.[60] While many welcomed the proposals, particularly in view of the broad democratic participation in their preparation, most of the more detailed comments were highly critical, both of their substance and of the short time allowed for bringing the matter to a conclusion. In this connection, reference should be made to the comments made by the Venice Commission, which visited Iceland in January 2013 and met representatives of the Constitutional Council, MPs, academics, representatives of NGOs, etc. The Venice Commission's Opinion expressed grave doubts about the proposals, particularly about the human rights provisions, and concern over the lack of clarity in the delineation of rights.[61] The Commission's Opinion was discussed in the Althing and widely publicly debated. It raised even stronger doubts with respect to the quality of the document and whether it was more likely to create confusion and instability in the constitutional and political system rather than improving it.[62] Other serious

57 Björg Thorarensen, 'The Constitutional Council. Objectives and Shortcomings of an Innovative Process' in Valur Ingimundarson, Philippe Urfalino, and Irma Erlingsdóttir (eds), *Iceland's Financial Crisis: The Politics of Blame, Protest and Reconstruction* (Routledge 2016) 243. See also Chapter 8 by Skúli Magnússon in this collection.

58 These experts were Oddný Mjöll Arnardóttir and Hafsteinn Thor Hauksson from the University of Iceland, Páll Þórhallsson from the Prime Minister's Office and Guðmundur Alfreðsson, expert in international and human rights law. See: Bill on a Constitutional Act on a Constitution for the Rebublic of Iceland [Frumvarp til stjórnarskipunarlaga um stjórnarskrá lýðveldisins Íslands] 28. www.althingi.is/altext/pdf/141/s/0510.pdf

59 The list of stakeholders' opinions that were formally sought can be seen on the Althing website: www.althingi.is/thingstorf/thingmalin/umsagnabeidnir/?ltg=141&mnr=415

60 The list of opinions and comments from individuals, experts, institutions, associations, and other bodies is accessible on the Althing website: www.althingi.is/thingstorf/thingmalin/erindi/?ltg=141&mnr=415

61 Venice Commission, *Opinion on the Draft New Constitution of Iceland*, 11 March 2013, CDL-AD (2013) 010 paras. 179–182, para. 32 and 184: www.althingi.is/pdf/Feneyjanefnd_skyrsla_e_11_03_2013.pdf

62 'Venice Commission's Opinion on Iceland's Constitution', *Iceland Review*,' posted 12 February 2013: www.icelandreview.com/news/venice-commission%E2%80%99s-opinion-iceland%E2%80%99s-constitution/

and argued criticism came from academics in political science and constitutional law (including the author of this chapter), as well as a detailed and argued opinion from the Althing's Ombudsman, to mention some examples.[63]

Concluding reflections

This chapter has described how the decision to appoint a seven-person Constitutional Commission was taken only in the final stages of parliamentary discussion of the 90/2010 Act on a Constitutional Assembly; the idea had not been mooted previously. The Commission's task was neither explained in much detail in the Act itself nor in the accompanying Explanatory Notes. Thus, in fact, rather little thought lay behind the decision to establish the Commission and how it was expected to contribute to the process of the constitutional revision. Indeed, the main motive for calling the Commission into existence seems to have been a desire to compensate for the short time allowed to the Constitutional Assembly (later the Constitutional Council) in which to revise the Constitution of Iceland. This time was shortened from 11 months (as originally proposed in draft legislation) to only four. Moreover, the idea behind the National Forum was intended to highlight the involvement of more of the general public in the process than would have been apparent through the election of 25 representatives to do the work.

In addition, the Constitutional Commission was given very little time to complete its threefold mission, namely: (1) to organise the National Forum, (2) to assemble all relevant materials, and (3) to prepare its own ideas for a new Constitution: only eight months. It employed this time well, but there is no doubt that far more time would have been needed to construct a better methodological approach to the question of what was to be obtained from the National Forum. In this, more attention should have been given to how the general indications arising out of the Forum could, or should, have been used in designing or revising the Constitution. Under Act 90/2010, the National Forum was to endeavour to call for the principal viewpoints and priorities of the public concerning the organisation of the country's government and constitution. However, the National Forum was provided with no substantive framework of the type laid down in Article 3 of the 90/2010 Act regarding points that were specifically to be addressed by the Constitutional Assembly (Constitutional Council) in the revision of the Constitution. This meant that conflicting messages were given as to the path to be followed in amending the Constitution. When drawing up its proposals for constitutional change in the form of two full alternative comprehensive proposals for a constitution, the Constitutional Commission followed the provisions of Article 3 in all main respects. However, when the Commission submitted its Report to the Constitutional Council, the Council took a new direction in its work on proposals for constitutional amendment, emphasising human rights as one of its main tasks, citing a powerful undertow from the National Forum.

63 Umsögn Umboðsmanns Alþingis frá 21. janúar 2013: www.althingi.is/altext/erindi/141/141-1276.pdf

In the light of this shift of focus, the value of the Constitutional Commission's Report in facilitating the work of the Constitutional Council proved to be somewhat less than had been expected. Accordingly, what in fact became the centrepiece of the Council's Proposal, namely to include a completely new chapter on human rights, had not been prepared at all by the Commission. This impacted the quality of the Council's proposals, which were much discussed and criticised due, amongst other things, to the evident lack of necessary preparation and assessment of their objectives and consequences. At the same time, valuable time was lost for more elaborate work on aspects of Iceland's constitutional system, which the Council was intended and expected to address specifically, such as the political institutions.

There is still an urgent need for some of the amendments that were originally intended for the Icelandic Constitution, such as rewriting provisions regarding the structure of the legislative and executive branches and the limits of their respective powers, the role and independence of the judiciary, public participation in the democratic process, utilisation of natural resources, and the transfer of sovereign powers to international organisations and the conduct of foreign affairs. However, it seems unlikely that any revision, be it of limited scope, will be made in the near future without a fundamental change of heart among the politicians elected by the people.

6 The work of the 2011 Constitutional Council[1]

A democratic experiment in constitution-making

Salvör Nordal

Introduction

The main focus of this chapter is the role of the Constitutional Council which drafted the Proposal for a New Constitution in 2011. Set up by Act 90/2010 as an elected Constitutional Assembly, it was meant to revise Iceland's Constitution and was given less than four months to do so. In addition, the chapter highlights a number of issues which were never clarified throughout the process and complications which arose once the Council had finished its task.

In the first part, I discuss the framework set up by the parliament in Act 90/2010 on the Constitutional Assembly adopted on 16 June 2010. Then I describe, in a loose chronological order, the issues faced by the Constitutional Council from the election of the Constitutional Assembly until the Proposal for a New Constitution was finalised in July 2011. Thirdly, I give a brief description of what happened to the Proposal after it was presented to the parliament on 29 July 2011. Finally, I reflect on some of the issues raised in this chapter.

A weak framework for the Constitutional Council's work: Act 90/2010

One can argue that Iceland's constitutional procedure did not get off to a good start. A first bill to change the Constitution was introduced in the wake of the financial crisis by a minority government, which took over on 1 February 2009, composed of the Social Democratic Alliance and the Left-Greens, and supported by the Progressive Party.[2] After a long and contentious debate, several attempts to pass the bill, and profound changes to its text, parliament accepted the bill to establish a directly elected Constitutional Assembly. As I have argued elsewhere, Act 90/2010 did not provide a strong framework for some of the key issues of the constitutional

1 This chapter is dedicated to the memory of my friend Ágúst Þór Árnason.

2 Bill to change the Constitution (Frumvarp til stjórnarskipunarlaga), 136. löggjafarþing 2008–2009, Þskj. 512–286. Mál: introduced on 4 March 2009: https://www.althingi.is/altext/136/s/0648.html. All webpages last accessed 1 June 2020.

revision procedure, such as the main task of the Constitutional Assembly and the interplay between the public and the parliament.[3] As a result, these issues remained unclear throughout the revision process. In particular, things did not get any easier for parliament after the Supreme Court invalidated the election of the Constitutional Assembly held on 27 November 2010. After some debate, Parliament reluctantly decided to appoint to a Constitutional Council (replacing the Constitutional Assembly) the originally elected members.

Before the April 2009 election: the constitutional bill of 4 March 2009

On 4 March 2009, the minority government of 2009 introduced a bill to change Iceland's Constitution.[4] It consisted of four amendments: the first one introduced a new article on natural resources; the second proposed to change the way in which the Constitution is amended, requiring a referendum as a part of the procedure; the third proposed a new article on public initiatives to hold a referendum on laws that have been passed through Parliament; and the fourth proposed to insert a temporary clause into the Constitution to elect a Constitutional Assembly to revise the Constitution.

According to Article 79 of the Constitution, amendments to the Constitution need to be approved by two successive parliaments, with a parliamentary election in between.[5] This means that parliamentary debates on this topic tend to be late in the term with the final decision being made just before the election. However, since the constitutional bill was introduced on 4 March, and parliament was dissolved on 17 April with the election due on 25 April, there was not much time for debating the proposal in parliament. Furthermore, there was a deep disagreement among the political parties on the project of constitutional reform at a time of serious crisis for Icelandic society. The constitutional bill was therefore not adopted before the election, making it impossible for it to become an amendment to the Constitution after the election.

Although the 4 March 2009 bill was rather short, it contained some interesting features concerning the Constitutional Assembly. The President of Iceland was to convene the first meeting of the Assembly established *to revise* (*endurskoða*) the Constitution, and the Assembly was supposed to work for 18 months, from 1 December 2009 to 17 June 2011, with a possibility of a six-month extension.

3 Salvör Nordal, 'Constitutional Revision: A Weak Legislative Framework Compounded by Political Disputes' in Valur Ingimundarson, Philippe Urfalino, and Irma Erlingsdottir (eds), *Iceland's Financial Crisis: The Politics of Blame, Protest, and Reconstruction* (Routledge 2016) 220–229. See also: Salvör Nordal, 'Þátttaka borgara í ákvarðanatöku og ábyrgð stjórnvalda. Lærdómar af stjórnarskrármáli' [Public Participation in Decision-Making and Responsibility of Government. Lessons from the Constitutional Making in Iceland] (2015) 189 *Skírnir* 119–141.

4 See n 2.

5 The text of the 1944 Constitution is available at: www.althingi.is/lagas/nuna/1944033.html

Before the Constitutional Assembly would approve its *Proposal for a new constitution'* (*frumvarp að nýrri stjórnarskrá*), it was to be sent to parliament for comments to be made within two months. Parliament could then send it back to the Assembly with comments; then, after a final vote of the Constitutional Assembly, a binding public referendum would be held for a final approval.[6]

As indicated in italics, when the bill was first introduced in March 2009, it was not clear whether the task was (simply) to revise the Constitution or to write a new one. Both phrases were used in the text of the bill, as well as in the parliamentary debates, and this continued to be so throughout the procedure and long after the adoption of Act 90/2010.[7] Other interesting features were the length of time for the Constitutional Assembly, the interplay between the Constitutional Assembly and the parliament, and the binding referendum.

After the April 2009 election

After the election, parliament convened for a short period, and once a majority was settled, it introduced a new bill on a Constitutional Assembly first on 24 July 2009[8] and again on 4 November[9] the same year. This time around, it was an ordinary bill instead of a constitutional bill designed to revise the Constitution, which meant that it could be adopted through the ordinary law-making process.

This bill on the Constitutional Assembly consisted of 29 articles and as such spelled out in more detail the role, the election process, and tasks of the Constitutional Assembly.[10] The President of the Republic still had the role of convening the Assembly, and again it was stated in the first article that the task was 'to *revise* (*endurskoða*) the constitution.' However, some fundamental changes had been made. First of all, the duration of the Assembly's work had been shortened to eight months instead of the 18 months originally intended. Moreover, there was no mention of a binding referendum (*lagt undir atkvæði allra kosningarbærra manna*). This issue had been highly controversial because under Article 79 of the 1944 Constitution, the power to change the Constitution lies with Parliament and not directly with voters. In the bill, it was recognised that a binding referendum represented a violation of the Constitution.[11]

When the bill was passed by parliament, after long and contentious debates, the working time of the Constitutional Assembly had been reduced further to two months with the possibility of a two-month extension. Moreover, the Speaker of

6 Constitutional Bill (n 2), Article 4.
7 Nordal (n 3).
8 www.althingi.is/altext/137/s/0302.html
9 www.althingi.is/altext/138/s/0168.html
10 Ibid.
11 Explanatory Notes to the bill on the Constitutional Assembly p. 9: www.althingi.is/altext/138/s/0168.html

the Parliament was to convene the Constitutional Assembly instead of the President of the Republic, as originally envisaged. According to the law, a Preparatory Committee (*undirbúningsnefnd stjórnlagaþings*) would be set up to take care of all the practical matters of the Constitutional Assembly, such as hiring staff and making housing arrangements.[12] The final version of the law also included other important features such as the creation of a Constitutional Commission (*Stjórnlaganefnd*) to organise and convene a National Forum (*Þjóðfundur*), and to prepare the work of the Constitutional Assembly.[13]

However, it was not clear how Parliament and the Assembly would interact. The March 2009 bill allowed for the possibility of some interplay between the two. This was later taken out, thus creating more distance between the Assembly and Parliament. Furthermore, the omission of the binding referendum meant that Parliament would take full control of the constitutional changes (in compliance with Article 79 of the 1944 Constitution) after the Constitutional Assembly finished its task. How Parliament would debate the Constitutional Assembly's Proposal was never spelled out; in particular, no decision was made on whether the majority would like to prioritise some issues or whether it would want to hold a referendum at some point.

The election of the Constitutional Assembly and its invalidation

The election of the Constitutional Assembly was unusual for Iceland, with the procedure set out in detail under Act 90/2010. There was a low threshold for eligibility, with each candidate needing only 30 referees or signatures.[14] Every Icelandic citizen over 18 and certified as having no criminal record could run for election. However, it was stated that the President of Iceland, Supreme Court judges, ministers, members of Parliament, their deputies, members of the Constitutional Commission, and members of the Preparatory Committee were not eligible.

Prior to the nomination deadline for candidacy, there had been some fear of limited interest among the public, but once the time was up, the total number of candidates was 522. This large number came as a surprise and caused some practical difficulties both for the candidates and for the organisers of the election. For general elections, Iceland is divided into six constituencies where each voter chooses one political party; by contrast, for the Assembly's election, there was only one constituency (similar to the presidential election). No candidate was provided with resources to travel around the country or prepare a serious campaign. Before the election, the government (the Ministry of Justice) published a brochure, in a newspaper format, distributed to all homes, with a short presentation

12 For further discussion, see: Chapter 5 by Björg Thorarensen in this collection.

13 See: The 'interim provision' at the very end of Act 90/2010.

14 In comparison, candidates to the presidential election need a minimum of 1,500 signatures each. In general election, the number of signatures depends on the number of parliamentarians in each constituency. If, for instance, the total number is 10, then each list needs 300 signatures.

of all the candidates.[15] However, the media did not want to discriminate amongst all the candidates and therefore more or less abstained from presenting individual candidates. An exception was made a few days prior to the election, when Icelandic National Broadcasting Service invited each candidate to give a pre-recorded statement on Radio One about his or her main issues in the election. These broadcasts took place between 23 and 26 November 2010, for around six to 11 hours a day, with a total of 35 hours in the last week before the election, thus giving three to four minutes to each candidate. Apart from this, the candidates were on their own, using their own social networks or social media to introduce themselves and to campaign. Moreover and importantly, the voting system itself was new and unfamiliar to voters. Namely, for the first time a single transferable voting system was used, meaning that each candidate was given a number and voters had to choose 25 individuals from a list, ranking them in order of preference from one to 25. The turnout at the election was 35.95%, considerably lower than in general elections.[16]

Complaints about how the election had been conducted were filed with the Supreme Court as it was argued that the manner in which the election was conducted deviated in important ways from the law on elections (Act 24/2000) on issues such as the design of the ballot papers, the use of screens at the polling stations instead of traditional polling booths, and of unlocked ballot boxes. Moreover, the fact that representatives of the candidates were not allowed to be present during the voting and the counting of votes was challenged. Although there were no complaints of fraud or wrong results, the Supreme Court invalidated the election on 25 January 2011. The ruling of the Supreme Court was heavily criticised, especially because it was argued that even if there had been some discrepancies between the electoral law and the election of the Constitutional Assembly, this was not serious enough to invalidate its election.[17]

The most logical reaction to invalidation of an election would be to repeat it. However, on 24 March 2011, parliament decided to offer the 25 people elected to the Assembly a seat on the Constitutional Council, thus formally appointing them instead.[18] The main reason was efficiency as it would save time and money because preparation for the Assembly had already been completed both by the Preparatory Committee and by the Constitutional Commission, which had finalised its two-volume Report on 24 February 2011.[19] Furthermore, it was argued that as the Constitutional Assembly was only supposed to be consultative and that, as nothing

15 www.stjornarradid.is/efst-a-baugi/frettir/stok-frett/2010/11/16/Kynningarbladi-um-frambjodendur-og-synishorni-af-kjorsedli-dreift/

16 Birgir Guðmundsson, 'Stjórnlagaþing, fjölmiðlar og frambjóðendur', [The Constitutional Assembly, Media and Candidates] 6 (2010) *Stjórnmál og stjórnsýsla*, 25 at https://skemman.is/bitstream/1946/9027/1/b.2010.6.2.2.pdf

17 Reynir Axelsson, 'Athugasemdir við ákvörðun Hæstaréttar um ógildingu kosningar við stjórnlagaþings' [Questions Regarding the Decision of the Supreme Court to Invalidate the Constitutional Assembly Elections]. His paper was published on the web, and he gave a presentation at a public meeting at the University of Iceland on 2 February 2011, where the invalidation was discussed.

18 Parliament sent each of them an invitation letter on the same date.

19 Chapter 5 by Björg Thorarensen in this collection.

suggested that the election issues had affected its result, it could be assumed that the public's trust in those who were elected had not been diminished.[20]

The decision to appoint the Constitutional Council on the basis of the Constitutional Assembly's election was criticised by many. One legal scholar stated that, although it was not against the law to appoint a Constitutional Council, it was 'inappropriate.'[21] According to another, this decision of parliament did in fact invalidate the Supreme Court ruling and was a clear sign of disrespect for the separation between legislative and judicial powers.[22]

After the invalidation of the election, the Prime Minister appointed an ad hoc committee (*Samráðshóp*)[23] representing all the political parties in parliament and chaired by the director general at the Prime Minister's office, to review the situation and come up with a proposal. Based on the opinion of this committee, the majority of the Parliamentary Constitutional and Supervisory Committee proposed to parliament to appoint the Constitutional Council.[24] This departed from the normal procedure, whereby the Prime Minister had introduced the bill on the Constitutional Assembly in parliament in 2009. Furthermore, the final decision to appoint the Constitutional Council was approved by 30 parliamentarians out of 63: 21 were against, 7 abstained, and 5 members of parliament were absent when the vote took place on 24 March 2011. There were critics in almost all the political parties. Among those who abstained were the Speaker of the Parliament (a Social Democrat), two ministers from the Left-Green Party, one being the Justice Minister, in charge of the judiciary. The detachment of the members of parliament was also visible in the invitation letter to take a seat at the Constitutional Council, which was signed by the Preparatory Committee and not by the Speaker of the Parliament, as would normally have been expected.[25] All this can be, and indeed has been, interpreted as weak political support and as undermining the mandate of the Constitutional Council even before it began working.

The work of the Constitutional Council

The Constitutional Assembly was supposed to start work on 15 February 2011 and finish two months later with the possibility of a two-month extension. Arrangements had already been made by the Preparatory Committee, which had hired a

20 See the majority opinion of the consultative group concerning the ruling of the Supreme Court on the invalidation of the election for Constitutional Assembly: www.althingi.is/altext/139/s/0930.html

21 Interview with Ragnhildi Helgadóttur in the newspaper *Morgunblaðið* 25 February 2011.

22 Sigurður Líndal, 'Stjórnlagaráð – til upprifjunar' *Fréttablaðið*, 17 March 2011.

23 The Committee, including Ágúst Geir Ágústsson (from the Prime Minister's Office), Álfheiður Ingadóttir (Left-Green), Birgitta Jónsdóttir (The Movement), Höskuldur Þórhallsson (Progressive Party), Valgerður Bjarnadóttir (Social Democrats), signed the proposal except the representative of the Independence Party, Birgir Ármannsson.

24 Álfheiður Ingadóttir (Left-Green), Birgitta Jónsdóttir (The Movement), and Valgerður Bjarnadóttir (Social Democrats).

25 The members of the Preparatory Committee were Þorsteinn Magnússon, Páll Þórhallsson, and Sigrún Benediktsdóttir.

General Manager, Þorsteinn Fr. Sigurðsson, and other support staff, and rented working space for meetings and offices. In addition, the newly elected Assembly had already held preparatory meetings, the first being on 4 December 2010. Moreover many of the members had asked for a leave of absence from their employer, since participating in the Constitutional Assembly was regarded as a full-time job to be paid in the same way as a regular MP's position.[26] After the election's invalidation, however, there was a brief period of limbo pending further decisions by parliament. Eventually, the Constitutional Council formally convened on 6 April 2011, having until the end of June to complete its task, with the possibility of a one-month extension which was granted by Parliament. The Council's work ended on 29 July, when the Proposal for a New Constitution was presented to the President of Parliament.

The members of the Constitutional Council

All those who had been elected to the Constitutional Assembly were offered a seat on the Constitutional Council. They included the following people, listed in order of votes received (first preference votes): Þorvaldur Gylfason, Professor of Economics, had previously been writing weekly op eds in one of the newspapers *Fréttablaðið*, circulated free to most homes, and took part in the discussion after the financial crisis. He received 7,192 as first preference votes.[27] I was the director of the Centre for Ethics at the University of Iceland and a lecturer in philosophy there. I had also been a member of the Working Group on Ethics, which published a report on the special investigation into the banks in 2010 (2,482 votes).[28] Ómar Ragnarsson is a well-known media presenter, journalist, and comedian (2,440 votes). Andrés Magnússon, physician, had been active in writing about the financial crisis (2,175 votes). Pétur Gunnlaugsson, lawyer and radio presenter secured 1989 votes. Þorkell Helgason (1930 votes), mathematician, and former professor, had for decades been the main advisor to parliament on the voting system used both for general elections and for the election of the Constitutional Assembly. Ari Teitsson was a farmer and former leader of the Farmer's Association (1,686

26 Article 19 of Act 90/2010.

27 The result of the elections can be found at www.stjornlagarad.is/frettir/lesa/item32937/ and also https://en.wikipedia.org/wiki/2010%E2%80%9313_Icelandic_constitutional_reform. The total number of votes for Þorvaldur Gylfason was 28,807, and the numbers of votes of elected candidates varied between 5,000 and almost 29,000. In a paper by Þorkell Helgason, who had advised the Parliament on the electoral system and was later elected to the Constitutional Assembly, the order of the elected members is slightly different. See: Þorkell Helgason, 'Greining á úrslitum kosningar til stjórnlagaþings 27. November 2010' [Analysis of the Constitutional Assembly's election 27 November 2010] (2011) 7 *Stjórnmál og stjórnsýsla* 40–71.

28 Vilhjálmur Árnason, Salvör Nordal, and Kristín Ástgeirsdóttir, 'Sidferdi og starfshættir í tengslum vid fall íslensku bankanna 2008' [Morality and Working Practices in Relation to the Collapse of the Icelandic Banks 2008], in Páll Hreinsson, Sigrídur Benediktsdóttir, and Tryggvi Gunnarsson (eds), *Report of the Special Investigation Commission* (Althingi 2010), vol. 8, 54 (in Icelandic).

votes). Illugi Jökulsson, journalist and writer, was active in Iceland's debate on political issues (1,593 votes). Freyja Haraldsdóttir was a manager and activist for disabled people in Iceland (1,089 votes). Silja Bára Ómarsdóttir, a university teacher in international politics at the University of Iceland, obtained 1,054 votes. The members with fewer than 1,000 votes included Örn Bárður Jónsson, pastor in Reykjavik (806 votes); Eiríkur Bergmann Einarsson, associate professor in political science (753 votes); Dögg Harðardóttir, a nurse (674 votes); Vilhjálmur Þorsteinsson, investor and chair of CCP games (a popular interactive entertainment), a company which specialises in interactive online entertainment (672 votes); Þórhildur Þorleifsdóttir, theatre director and former parliamentarian for the Women's alliance 1987–1991 (584 votes); Pawel Bartoszek, mathematician and lecturer in mathematics (584 votes); Arnfríður Guðmundsdóttir, professor of theology at the University of Iceland (531 votes); Erlingur Sigurðsson, historian and former high school teacher (526 votes); Inga Lind Karlsdóttir, media presenter and a university student (493 votes); Katrín Oddsdóttir, lawyer and an activist in the financial crisis (479 votes); Guðmundur Gunnarsson, trade union chair (432 votes); Katrín Fjeldsted, a physician and former parliamentarian for the Independence Party (418 votes); Ástrós Gunnlaugsdóttir, political scientist and university student (396 votes); Gísli Tryggvason, consumer spokesperson (348 votes); Lýður Árnason, physician and filmmaker (347 votes).

Overall, there were 10 women and 15 men; thus the election reached the required quota of 40% women specified by Parliament. Three members lived outside the Reykjavik area, although many had strong links with rural areas as is often the case with Icelanders. Many professionals were among the elected, and five of us had academic positions. There was one farmer and a former leader of a trade union. Some had taken part in political parties, and two had been members of parliament. However, political parties did not, at least not openly, participate in the election.

All those originally elected eventually accepted their positions on the Constitutional Council, except Inga Lind Karlsdóttir. As a result, the one who had been number 26 in the election, Íris Lind Sæmundsdóttir, was offered the seat, which she accepted. Íris Lind is a lawyer and worked at the time at the Ministry of Foreign Affairs. Personally, I must admit that I found it difficult to accept a seat at the Constitutional Council. Prior to the election, I had been a member of the Working Group on Ethics which collaborated with the Special Investigation Commission on the fall of Iceland's banking system, and we had written one volume of the nine-volume report issued in April 2010.[29] Our report contained harsh criticism of the Icelandic financial system, administration, and related political decisions. I was therefore faced with a dilemma and a credibility issue since I felt that the decision to appoint the Constitutional Council was problematic,

29 Árnason, Nordal, and Ástgeirsdóttir (n 28).

being badly prepared and with a weak mandate. At the same time, I felt responsibility towards those who had elected me to the Assembly and to the whole process, and I feared that withdrawing might jeopardise important revision of the constitution.[30]

Organising our work[31]

Act 90/2010 on the Constitutional Assembly specified that it should elect its own chairperson and work in three separate committees with three members of the Assembly in each committee, and it provided further detail about organisational issues.[32] Further details about special working rules were approved by the Speaker's Committee (*Forsætisnefnd*) in parliament shortly after the Act was adopted.[33] This framework gave the chairperson of the Assembly and the three committee chairpersons a greater role than other members. After the appointment of the Council, we decided to simplify the rules of procedure provided by Parliament and to involve more members of the Council in active roles by creating vice-chairpersons of the committees. The Council was not bound by Act 90/2010 anymore as the election had been invalidated, and we were informed by the Preparatory Committee that the Act 90/2010 would be invalidated, which happened on 12 April 2011.[34]

During the first weeks, the new rules of procedure were debated, a chairperson and a vice-chairperson for the Council elected, committees formed, and chairpersons and vice-chairpersons elected. Therefore, out of the 16 weeks allocated to the Constitutional Council for its work, the first three weeks were used for sorting out practical issues and getting started. This was followed by 11 weeks, which were used to debate issues within committees. Finally, two weeks were used for finalising the Proposal for a New Constitution.

At the first meeting of the Constitutional Council (on 6 April 2011), chaired by the oldest member of the Council, Ómar Ragnarsson (who was 70 at the time), the chair of the Constitutional Commission, Guðrún Pétursdóttir, presented its Report.[35] Thereafter a committee of five members was chosen to examine and finalise the rules of procedures of the Council.[36] The following day,

30 I did voice my criticism in 'A letter to Althingi' [Bréf til Alþingis], published in *Fréttablaðið*, 30 March 2011.

31 The official webpage of the Constitutional Council contains further information, such as minutes and transcripts of the full member meetings, board meetings, and the committees: http://stjornlagarad.is/

32 Act 90/2010, article 17.

33 The Speaker's Committee consists of the Speaker of the Parliament and Deputy Speakers, one from each party in Parliament. At its meeting of 29 November 2010, the Committee approved the working rules for the Constitutional Assembly: https://www.althingi.is/pdf/Starfsreglur_1des.pdf

34 Act 31/2011 invalidating Act 90/2010 with immediate effect: www.althingi.is/altext/139/s/1280.html

35 See Chapter 5 by Björg Thorarensen in this collection.

36 http://stjornlagarad.is/english/rules-of-procedure/

the Council held its second meeting where the main issue was to choose a chair and a vice-chair. The General Manager had asked the members of the Council for an expression of interest to become the chairperson, and eight members came forward. These were then voted on. In the first round, the Council members selected two possible candidates, and in a second round, the Council chose between the two who obtained the most votes, namely Þorvaldur Gylfason and me. I obtained the most votes and was elected the chair with a 15-to-9 split. A similar process was followed for the vice-chairperson: in the first round, five members were selected by Council members for this position, and Ari Teitsson was elected in the second round against Þorvaldur Gylfason (13 to 10). The third meeting of the Constitutional Council was held a week later, on the 13 April 2011, and it primarily focussed on discussing the structure of the work and working rules. At that meeting, a group was appointed to come up with a proposal about working committees. This group eventually suggested three committees, A, B, and C.

Committee A discussed the structure of the constitution and its division into chapters, natural resources and environmental issues and human rights, including the national Church. Silja Bára Ómarsdóttir was elected as its chair, and Örn Bárður Jónsson as its vice-chair. Committee B discussed the foundations of the Icelandic constitution, the role and position of the President of Iceland, the role and responsibilities of Parliament, the government, the responsibilities of the President and the ministers, the obligations of the executive power, and the status of the municipalities. Katrín Fjeldsted, was elected as its chair and Vilhjálmur Þorsteinsson as its vice-chair. Committee C discussed the public's participation in decision-making (including possible changes of Article 79), the amendments to the Constitution), the independence of courts, judicial oversight of other branches of power, parliamentary elections, the constituency system and members of Parliament, international contracts and foreign affairs. Pawel Bartoszek was elected chair and Íris Lind Sæmundsdóttir, vice-chair. Each committee had a secretary from the support (or administrative) staff, one of whom was a lawyer and two were political scientists. A senior lawyer, Sif Guðjónsdóttir, supervised the support staff. Each committee included eight members. As the chair of the Constitutional Council, I was the only one who was not a member of any of the committees; instead, my role was to organise the overall work and to have oversight of the whole process. I sometimes attended the committees' meetings to discuss individual issues or to follow the debates.

The board of the Constitutional Council consisted of the chair, vice-chair, and the committees' chairpersons; the vice-chairpersons also attended board meetings, along with the General Manager and the senior lawyer. The board held regular meetings every week, a total of 28 meetings. At the beginning of our work, some complaints were made regarding formalities which had been arranged before we started working. We were seated in a similar way as a parliament, where the chair, the vice-chair, and the General Manager of the Council faced the members of the Council and directed the meeting. To some extent we were also constrained by the nature of the premises in which we were housed.

The task of the Constitutional Council

The work of the Constitutional Council started with reading and discussing the Report of the Constitutional Commission, which had been made public and distributed among the members at the first Council meeting. The task of the Constitutional Commission had been to analyse selected constitutional issues and the outcome of the National Forum of 6 November 2010[37] and to prepare the work of the Constitutional Assembly (Council). Their Report, which consisted of 700 pages in two volumes, was very useful for the Council members, and it became an important reference point in its work.[38] On many issues, the Constitutional Council followed the Report when putting together its own proposals.

One of the first issues that the Council had to decide was how it should present the Proposal, in particular on its specially created webpage. The question was whether the document should be presented as a number of amendments to Iceland's Constitution or as a separate and self-contained document. Underlying this issue was the uncertainty as to whether, as previously discussed, the Constitutional Council's task was to revise Iceland's Constitution or to draft a new one. This issue had remained unclear even though the first article of Act 90/2010 stated that the task was 'to revise Iceland's Constitution.' Similarly, parliament's letter inviting us to take a seat in the Constitutional Council stated that the Council was expected to discuss the Constitutional Commission's Report and to 'make changes to the Constitution.'[39] This ambiguity had not been discussed by the Constitutional Commission; instead, it presented two different versions, A and B, in their Report, introduced under the heading 'An Idea for a New Constitution' (*Hugmynd a nýrri stjórnarskrá*).[40] The differences between these two versions are not explained specifically, although every reader can see them. It is fair to ask whether the Constitutional Commission went beyond its mandate in presenting these two versions for a *new constitution* in this way and whether it had thereby invited the interpretation that the task was to write a new constitution rather than focus on revising the specific issues listed under Article 3 of Act 90/2010.[41] In any event, the Constitutional Council followed this signal in the document, which gradually took shape; however, our final document was entitled 'Bill for a constitutional law' (*Frumvarp*

37 www.thjodfundur2010.is

38 The two volume Report is available at: www.stjornlagarad.is/other_files/stjornlagarad/skyrsla-stjornlaganefndar/skyrsla_stjornlaganefndar_fyrra_bindi.pdf

39 In the invitation letter, we were offered a seat in the Constitutional Council, 'with the task to discuss Constitutional Commission's report and propose changes to the Constitution of Iceland's Republic.'

40 Report of the Constitutional Committee, Volume 1, 182–214. www.stjornlagarad.is/other_files/stjornlagarad/skyrsla-stjornlaganefndar/skyrsla_stjornlaganefndar_fyrra_bindi.pdf

41 The members of the Constitutional Commission most likely believed that they were presenting a *revision* of the Constitution as their changes were marked in bold within the text of the 1944 Constitution. My point here is that their heading was 'A New Constitution,' which indicated that this was the task.

til stjórnarskipunarlaga).[42] During the work of the Constitutional Council, the proposals for change were usually presented in a document with three columns, namely one including the new proposal, the second one the proposal of the Constitutional Commission, version A or B or both, and the third Iceland's Constitution. With this method, the aim was to keep all these options in focus.

Another issue that perhaps was not specifically discussed within the Council was the extent of the changes to be made. In parliament's Resolution 19/139 of 24 March 2011 to appoint the elected members, the Council's tasks was to discuss the same issues as stated in Article 3 of Act 90/2010.[43] These included the foundations of the Icelandic constitution and its fundamental concepts; the organisation of the legislative and executive branches and the limits of their powers; the role and position of the President of the Republic; the independence of the judiciary and their supervision of other holders of governmental powers; provisions on elections and electoral districts; public participation in decision-making, including the timing and organisation of a referendum, including a referendum on a legislative bill for a constitutional statute; transfer of sovereign powers to international organisations and the conduct of foreign affairs; environmental matters, including the ownership and utilisation of natural resources. In addition, it was said that more issues could be taken on.

This list is long and challenging enough. In its Report, the Constitutional Commission did, however, add issues such as the status of municipalities, the role of Parliament, as well as a brief discussion of human rights, following which the human rights chapter had been moved to the beginning of the Constitution.[44] The Constitutional Council followed this lead and took it further. There was, for instance, a considerable interest among the Constitutional Council's members to revise the human rights chapter[45], although the list of issues (under Article 3 above) did not include it as it had been extensively revised in 1995. Moreover, when the Council members were invited to choose between Committees A, B, and C to participate in, there was more interest in the seats on Committee A on human rights and natural resources and less interest in taking part in Committee B on the structure of the state.

Weekly working schedule and work

At the fifth meeting of the Constitutional Council on 19 April 2011, all chairs of the Committees were elected, and each member chose his or her Committee. Once the

42 The 2011 Proposal for a New Constitution with a Commentary is available on the official webpage of the Constitutional Council: http://stjornlagarad.is/other_files//stjornlagarad/Frumvarp-til-stjornarskipunarlaga.pdf. However, on the Council's webpage this was translated as 'A Proposal for a New Constitution for the Republic of Iceland' (http://stjornlagarad.is/other_files/stjornlagarad/Frumvarp-enska.pdf). Therefore, the confusion between revising and adopting a new constitution continued in the titles of the document drafted by the Council and in their translations.

43 The Resolution 19/139 is available at: www.althingi.is/altext/139/s/1120.html

44 Discussion in the Report, volume 1 (n 40), chapter 5, 82–89.

45 In *Fréttablaðið*, 4 December 2011, all the elected members of the Constitutional Assembly were asked to name their main interests. Nine out of 25 mentioned human rights, and several others, discussed the importance of natural resources. There was also considerable interest in human rights and the natural resources among participants at the National Forum meeting.

Committees had been formed, the work on the Constitution could start. The weekly schedule was organised in such a way that on Mondays and Tuesdays the Committees worked separately on their respective topics. On Wednesdays, the Council as a whole came together informally in meetings where each Committee presented their proposals to the other Council members. This was to prepare for a weekly open Council meeting on Thursdays, where all Council members were present. The Thursday meetings, which sometimes extended to Friday, were streamed online. Before the Thursday meeting, all recommendations were also published on the Council's webpage. After the discussion at these formal Council meetings, either the relevant Committee would take recommendations and comments from other Council members and from the public to revise the recommendations further, or, if the meeting accepted the changes, they were recorded in the Constitutional Council's Progress Document (*áfangaskjal*). Even if a text had been noted in that Document, it could still be taken up again and changed subsequently. In this way, the public could follow the Council's drafting process for making a recommendation for change. The Progress Document was not final until it was voted on at the end of the Council's work.

The main work took place within the Committees where compromises were made. These meetings were not streamed online, and the minutes of these meetings give only an outline of what was being discussed.[46] In addition to the informal meetings on Wednesdays, the Council held numerous other informal meetings which were not minuted in any way. There was a strong feeling among the members of the Council that the Committees worked towards consensus, endeavouring to draft a proposal that most of the members could accept. At the same time, it was clear that most of the Council members focussed on the work of their own Committee as time was short and it was difficult to follow closely the work done in all three Committees.

At some point, it was suggested by one member of the Constitutional Council's Board that the Committees should rotate halfway through the Council's work, so as to involve more members in broader subjects and to minimise tendencies to claim ownership of certain articles or issues. However, given that the actual committee work only took ten weeks, it was quite hectic to change halfway through, and nothing in our working rules permitted such a change.

The drafting of the Proposal for a New Constitution

The first issues to be discussed were presented at the sixth weekly meeting of the full Council, on 28 April 2011. Committee C proposed a chapter on the judicial system. Committee A proposed the structure of the Progress Document, which only included headings of the chapters but no actual text. It was also suggested to add a preamble to the revised/new constitution (as the 1944 Constitution does not

46 The minutes of the Committees are available at: http://stjornlagarad.is/starfid/

contain one) and to move the human rights chapter to the beginning of the (new/revised) constitution. At the eighth weekly meeting of the full Council, on 12 May 2011, the first articles of the human rights chapter were introduced, as well as the first proposals from Committee B for strengthening the legislative power.

From then on, issues and proposals were introduced from one week to the next to be debated at the Council's full meetings. As was to be expected, some matters were discussed longer, and in more depth, than others. Proposals presented early went through several phases of discussion at Council meetings, other issues – and perhaps the most complex ones – were presented later, and there was less time for discussion and analysis. In addition, the Committees had different workloads, as is represented in the number of meetings they held and the number of articles introduced in the final proposal. Committee A held 43 meetings and presented 31 articles, Committee B held 42 meetings and presented 61 articles, and Committee C held 48 meetings and proposed 23 articles.[47] Committees A and C had almost finished going through their tasks by early July when Committee B was still wrestling with complex issues, such as the role and position of the President of Iceland, as well as the powers of Parliament and of the government and ministers. Proposals on these issues came late, which gave everyone little time to evaluate them.

The final version and the last two weeks

After about 11 weeks of committee work on individual chapters and articles, it was time to debate the Progress Document as a whole if we were to finish before the end of July. We were running out of time. According to our working rules, individual members could at that point present formal amendments to the Progress Document. The deadline to present such amendments was 18 July 2011, i.e. before the formal discussion of the whole draft was due to take place on 20 July 2011. At that point, a simple majority vote was used to decide whether the changes should be approved or not. Fortunately, an electronic voting system had been set up for us in the Council. When the deadline was up, more than 100 proposals had been handed in by individual Council members. Some of these proposals had already been discussed earlier in the process and rejected; others were new and were introduced on 18 July. At the 20 July meeting, around 60 proposals were approved. It is obvious that so many changes at this rather late stage did frustrate the work on the whole document and our consensual approach.

Between the first (20 July 2011) and the second (26 July 2011) round of discussion, some informal discussion took place to settle some of the disagreements, for

47 2011 Proposal for a New Constitution with a Commentary (n 42) p. 28–29.

instance, on the article on natural resources. In the second round of discussion, each article was voted on, followed by the Document as a whole. Not all articles were approved by all the members, but the final vote approving the Document was unanimous.

Outstanding was the issue of the preamble. Committee A had proposed early in the process to add a preamble to the new/revised constitution. It was clear from that point that there were mixed views on this idea, but it had been set aside during the 11 weeks. Towards the end, a few members of the Council took up the topic again, and they presented their version at the final Council meeting. Again this was received with mixed views among the members: some did not want to have a preamble at all, others wanted the proposed text to be revised, and the third group wanted the text to be put forward as it was. At the final meeting on 26 July, when the final vote took place, the majority decided to postpone the discussion on the preamble to the very last day of our work, i.e. when we were scheduled to meet informally to finalise the cover letter presenting the overall Proposal. For this reason the preamble was not part of the overall document when it was finally voted on. At the informal meeting on the last day, 28 July, the preamble was discussed and voted on with 13 votes in favour and 11 abstentions.

The final vote and the final statement

At the final vote on the document as a whole, each of the members of the Constitutional Council probably had her or his own understanding of the Proposal for a New Constitution and what his or her vote meant. I explained my own voting in the following way:

> Our work has been an important step in changing our Constitution. The time we had was short and to my knowledge, some issues need more analysis and better explanation and, as some have argued among us, our Proposal needs a stress-test. The document has been changing until the very last minute. On these grounds and with this in mind, I give my vote to the Proposal.[48]

In my mind, we had worked hard during the time we had been allocated to complete our task and had reached the end; however, our Proposal was not to be regarded as a final document which was not to be developed further. This has been my view ever since.

After that final formal meeting where all members gave their votes to the document as a whole, the Council met on 28 July for its last meeting to discuss

48 *Transcript of the Council's Meetings* available at, volume 2, p. 732: http://stjornlagarad.is/other_files/stjornlagarad/stjornlagaradstidindi2b.pdf

the cover letter and to finalise the preamble. After some discussion of the content of the cover letter, it was finalised and signed. In particular it clearly stated:

> The Constitutional Council expects that the open dialogue on constitutional matters will continue. In our Proposal, amendments to the Constitution are supposed to be voted on by the public. The Council members believe that the members of the public should be given an opportunity to vote on a new constitution (i.e. a referendum) before the Parliament gives its final vote. If some changes to the Council's Proposal are to be done by Parliament, the Council members are willing to convene again before such a referendum [þjóðaratkvæðagreiðsla] is held.[49]

Outsourced or crowdsourced?

According to many members of parliament, electing members of the public to revise the Constitution or to write a new one was regarded as an important step to build a bridge between the political system and the public.[50] In so doing, parliament outsourced its role to amend the Constitution as provided under Article 79 of the 1944 Constitution. In addition and as discussed above, the Constitutional Council adopted an open and transparent approach to the drafting process. Two questions have been greatly debated since, namely: the extent to which the Proposal for a New Constitution was drafted by the public outside the Constitutional Council, and what the role of experts was in the whole process.

The Constitutional Council worked to a large extent in an open environment, consulted experts, received formal and informal proposals and suggestions from the public, not unlike the work of Parliament, or from members of parliament. The Commentary, published shortly after the final draft was presented to the Speaker of Parliament, provides an explanation of the main arguments within each Committee and how the conclusion was reached. The Commentary also contains references to experts, to formal proposals, to the Constitutional Commission, and to the National Forum of 950 participants, but few if any direct references to the Council's discussion on possible reliance on social media as part of the drafting process.[51] There are also considerable differences in this respect between the Committees: Committee A referred much more to public consultation such as formal comments and suggestions from the public than did Committees B and C.[52] It is therefore understandable that members of the Council experienced the consultation differently, some being

49 *Proposal for a New Constitution* with Commentary, in Icelandic, (n 42) p. 5.

50 For my analysis of the debate in Parliament, see: Nordal (n 3).

51 *Proposal for a New Constitution* (in Icelandic) n 42.

52 Ibid.

more active than others in consulting with experts or in engaging in a debate on social media.

The role of experts

As the chair of the Constitutional Council, and like the Committees and individual members, I did consult with various experts, both formally and informally, along the way. There are numerous references to experts in the Commentary, as well as elsewhere in the Council's documents such as the transcripts from the Council's meetings. Nevertheless, it is difficult to give an overview, let alone complete references, of all the experts who were consulted by the Council. In the Commentary, some references to experts are very general, such as 'according to experts consulted,' while in other cases individual experts are named. It is possible to separate several levels of expert consultation.

Firstly, there was varied expertise among the Council members and staff members. In Committee A, which discussed the human rights chapter and the article on natural resources, was a professor of economics, a political scientist, a human rights lawyer, and a human rights activist. In addition, a professor of theology and a pastor sat in Committee A, where the articles on religious freedom and the national Church were discussed. In Committee B, which discussed the role of Parliament and the government, there were two former MPs, two lawyers, and a political scientist. In Committee C, which discussed electoral systems, there were various experts too, including one of the main specialists on Iceland's electoral system. In the Commentary on the Proposal, one can see how expertise within the Council is reflected in the amount of discussion about particular articles. For instance, there are long and detailed discussions about the articles on religious freedom, the national Church, nature and natural resources, as well as the electoral system, the discussion of which is one of the most detailed in the Commentary.[53]

Secondly, the work of the Constitutional Council relied on many topics on the work of the Constitutional Commission, which itself included some of the main experts in Icelandic constitution law. This is particularly apparent, for instance, in the chapters on Parliament, the President of Iceland, ministers, and the government, where the explanations for each article often refer to the Constitutional Commission and its Report. These parts also refer a lot to the constitutions of other Nordic countries or Germany.

Thirdly, each Committee reached out to experts at various stages of its work. For instance, Aðalheiður Jóhannsdóttir (law professor) gave an expert opinion on nature and natural resources; Birgir Hermannsson (political scientist) gave an expert opinion on Parliament; Páll Þórhallsson (legal specialist at the Prime Minister's Office) and Björg Thorarensen (law professor) met or gave expert opinions to Committees B and C. Late in the Council's drafting process, there was an informal meeting between the Council and professor in political science

53 Ibid.

Ólafur Þ. Harðarsson about the electoral system. In addition, towards the end, we consulted several experts on the document as a whole. In my own archive of the Council work, I have a copy of a critical comment from Ragnhildur Helgadóttir, law professor, on the full draft dated from 24 July where she argued that the draft was considerably less coherent after all the changes that had been made following the votes on 20 July. Another professor of law, Eiríkur Tómasson, gave an expert opinion dated 25 July, in which he urged us to make at least two important changes before the final vote on 26 July.

Fourthly, there was some attempt to seek feedback and assessment on the whole document from relevant ministries. At the very end, the Proposal was sent out to several ministries, including to the Ministry of Culture and Education for comments on the human rights chapter and to the Prime Minister's office for a comment on the different branches of power. The Ministry of Education and Culture sent us a ten-page comment on freedom of speech, freedom of information, freedom of the press, and the right to education, dated 15 July 2011. The Prime Minister's Office's comments on seven pages were dated 18 July 2011. However, in July, time was running out, and it was not possible for the Council to respond or evaluate to all the comments or suggestions made.[54]

The Constitutional Council's interaction with the public

It has been stated that the Proposal for a New Constitution was 'the world's first 'crowdsourced' constitution'[55] and that it 'made extensive use of crowdsourcing.'[56] I understand that crowdsourcing aims at getting people together on a web-based platform for problem-solving; however, this concept was not well understood at the time of the constitutional drafting.[57] In this section, I am not going to debate whether or to what extent crowdsourcing describes the work of the Constitutional Council, although I tend to side with those who argue that the participation of the public can be defined as 'weak public.'[58] Rather, I am going to outline how consultation with the public is represented in the Council's Commentary on its Proposal for a

54 All these are on file with the author but not available on the Council's official website. Committee A also received comments from the Ministry of Fisheries and Agriculture and Ministry of Foreign Affairs. Committee C received comments from the Ministry of Interior. I do not have a copy of these comments. www.stjornlagarad.is/other_files/stjornlagarad/Frumvarp_med_skyringum.pdf (pp. 28–30)

55 Harvey Morris, 'Crowdsourcing Iceland's Constitution' *The New York Times*, October 24, 2012: https://rendezvous.blogs.nytimes.com/2012/10/24/crowdsourcing-icelands-constitution/

56 Anne Meuwese, 'Popular Constitution-Making: The Case of Iceland' in Dennis J Galligan and Mila Versteeg (eds), *The Social and Political Foundations of Constitutions* (CUP 2013) 469, 472.

57 Daren C. Brabham, *Crowdsourcing* (MIT Press 2013) xix.

58 Bjarki Valtysson, 'Democracy in Disguise: The Use of Social Media in Reviewing the Icelandic Constitution' (2014) 36 *Media, Culture and Society* 52–68.

New Constitution.[59] Again, I am certain that individual members of the Council experienced this differently. In the Act 90/2010, there is an emphasis on open environment, and during our work media advertisement was used to encourage the public to get acquainted with what we were doing and to send in suggestions. I myself did not take part in any social media discussion on our work.

As previously mentioned, the Constitutional Council was committed to holding its meetings as openly as possible, and one weekly meeting was streamed online and open to the public.[60] In addition, proposals were published on the Council's webpage where people could comment through Facebook or other social media; members of the public could also send in ideas, suggestions, or proposals by other means, such as by e-mail or regular mail. In this way, people could follow how each proposal changed and developed from one week to the next.

The Constitutional Council received 395 formal suggestions from individuals, groups, and NGOs, and some sent in several suggestions.[61] The Council's Committees discussed these suggestions: 167 for Committee A, 121 for Committee B, and 107 for Committee C.[62] In the Commentary, one can find some discussion of Committees A and C on these formal suggestions but hardly any from Committee B. It has been claimed that the Constitutional Council received around 3,600 comments on social media.[63] The difficulty with this is that these comments on social media (Facebook) cannot be analysed since they are not openly available anymore, and there is hardly any reference to these comments in the final Commentary.[64] Some readers might find the numbers of comments and suggestions rather low. However, we must bear in mind that the most important work of the Constitutional Council took place during the summer holidays in June and July.

Last but not least, the public influenced the work of the Constitutional Council through the National Forum, where around 1,000 randomly chosen participants discussed constitutional issues on 6 November 2010. Although the National Forum considered numerous issues, it did not come up with particular proposals in any detail. Rather, the discussion showed what the public was most interested in.[65] The Constitutional Commission analysed the outcome of the National Forum, and its outcome did influence the work of the Constitutional Council in many ways.

From this discussion, one can see that similarly to the work of any parliament, the Constitutional Council consulted various experts and members of the public during its work. Nevertheless, the Council did debate all these issues and was

59 *Proposal for a New Constitution* (in Icelandic), n 42.

60 Act 90/2010, Article 18.

61 They are accessible on the website: http://stjornlagarad.is/erindi/

62 *Proposal for a New Constitution* (in Icelandic), n 42, pp. 28–30.

63 Alexander Hudson argues that almost 10% of the final text comes from crowdsourcing or from members of the public outside the Constitutional Council. See: Alexander Hudson, 'When Does Public Participation Make a Difference? Evidence from Iceland's Crowdsourced Constitution' (2017) *Policy and Internet* 185–217.

64 *Proposal for a New Constitution* (in Icelandic), n 42.

65 Official website of National Forum (in English): http://www.thjodfundur2010.is/english/

responsible for the final outcome. My conclusion is therefore that the Council's Proposal was written neither by experts nor by the public. Instead, I would argue that the final text of our Proposal for a New Constitution was written by us – the Council members – and influenced by a wide range of people, including experts and members of the public.

The debate in Parliament

Once our work was over, I had the modest expectation that the Proposal would at least be seriously debated within Parliament. I also hoped that the democratic aspect of the procedure, namely its consultation with the public, would continue, for instance with civic meetings in different parts of the country to discuss the Proposal, keeping the openness of the process alive. At the same time, I also believed that there was a need for expert analysis both of individual parts of the Proposal, as well as of the Proposal as a whole. However, the lack of clarity that had characterised the process from its start became more evident once the Constitutional Council had finished its work and Parliament regained control of the constitutional revision process.

The Parliamentary Constitutional and Supervisory Committee (*Stjórnskipunar- og eftirlitsnefnd*) was given the role of preparing a formal bill on the basis of our Proposal for Parliamentary debate, but there was no general strategy on how the Committee should proceed, e.g. what were to be its main tasks or priorities, whether a referendum should be held, and, if so, at what point or whether the government wanted to go ahead with full revision or pursue only the route of partial amendments. Therefore, the steps taken in the following months from August 2011 to March 2013 were often hesitant and inconsistent.

The debate in the Parliamentary Constitutional and Supervisory Committee

Several months after the Council had finished its work, the Parliamentary Constitutional and Supervisory Committee convened meetings in Parliament to discuss the Council's Proposal. The meetings were held in several sessions on 4 November 2011. Firstly, the chair of the Constitutional Commission, Guðrún Pétursdóttir, described the Commission's work and the National Forum. Secondly, Ari Teitsson, the vice-chair of the Constitutional Council, and I described our work in general terms.[66] Thirdly, representatives from each of the Council's Committees met with the Parliamentary Constitutional and Supervisory Committee in three sessions. The first two stages of this discussion were open and streamed online.

66 www.althingi.is/thingnefndir/fastanefndir/stjornskipunar-og-eftirlitsnefnd/fundargerdir?faerslunr=5432

In the following months, there was further discussion within the Parliamentary Constitutional and Supervisory Committee.[67] As the chair of the Constitutional Council, I took part in some formal and informal meetings, and I was repeatedly asked whether the Council would accept some particular changes to specific provisions. In my view, however, no one could speak for the Council after it was dissolved at the end of July, it was now up to parliament to take decisions. I went back to academia and became more interested in following the philosophical questions that had risen during my work with the Constitutional Council and analysing the procedure from that standpoint rather than becoming engaged in the politics that followed.[68]

However, we had stated in our final letter that we would be willing to take part in further discussion if parliament asked us formally, which they did. Therefore, the Constitutional Council convened again for four days between 8 and 11 March 2012. Apart from me, Andrés Magnússon, Pawel Bartoszek, and Örn Bárður Jónsson, all of whom were unable to attend this meeting for different reasons – I was scheduled to take part in a workshop abroad and due to the short notice we were given, it was difficult for me to make alternative arrangements – all other members of the Constitutional Council took part in the meeting. At that meeting, the Council was given questions and comments from the Parliamentary Constitutional and Supervisory Committee and asked if the Council would accept specific changes to the Proposal.

The 2012 advisory referendum and legal evaluation

Parliament decided in May, after some previous discussion, to hold a referendum on the Constitutional Council's Proposal no later than 20 October 2012. Although the referendum would strengthen the legitimacy of the whole procedure after the invalidation of the Constitutional Assembly election, it also added to the confusion – not only because it was advisory and its six questions were unclear but also because it took place in the middle of parliament's evaluation of the Council's Proposal. Not only had the Parliamentary Constitutional and Supervisory Committee already been discussing various changes to the Proposal, as the questions to the Constitutional Council in March reflect, but it had also decided in June to ask five legal experts to analyse 'legal technical issues.'[69] The legal experts' role was also to examine possible inconsistencies within the Council's Proposal, in particular the

67 www.althingi.is/thingnefndir/fastanefndir/stjornskipunar-og-eftirlitsnefnd/fundargerdir/?lthing=140

68 In addition my sister Ólöf Nordal was at the time a member of the Parliament for the Independent Party and she was a member of the Constitutional and Supervisory Committee of the Parliament.

69 This was a group of five legal experts: Guðmundur Alfreðsson, Hafsteinn Þór Hauksson, Oddný Mjöll Arnardóttir, Páll Þórhallsson, and Ragnhildur Helgadóttir: www.althingi.is/thingnefndir/fastanefndir/stjornskipunar-og-eftirlitsnefnd/fundargerdir/?faerslunr=5967

human rights chapter in relation to international treaties. The legal experts were also asked to examine and write Explanatory Notes. No deadline for completing this task was mentioned.

When deciding to hold a referendum, parliament had explicitly declared the need for extensively communicating with the public about the issues at stake, as well as about what would happen following the referendum. A brochure, which presented the original 2011 Council Proposal, was sent to all homes. However, politicians abstained from political debate, leaving it instead to people interested in the issues, such as members of the Constitutional Society[70] and former members of the Constitutional Council, to explain the content of the Proposal. To be sure, their views were important. However, they could not explain to voters how the referendum result would be interpreted by parliament, what would follow, let alone what changes had already been made by the Constitutional and Supervisory Committee.

Once the referendum was over, the lack of a plan and the confused nature of the process became even more obvious. Only around three weeks after the referendum, on 12 November 2012, the legal experts presented their comments including numerous revisions to the Proposal for a new Constitution.[71] Thereafter, the Constitutional and Supervisory Committee formally introduced the constitutional bill at the first parliamentary debate on 20 November 2012, a month after the referendum. The bill included changes made by the legal experts, as well as changes made by the Parliamentary Constitutional and Supervisory Committee approved by the Constitutional Council at the March 2012 meeting; it was therefore quite different from the one that had been presented to the voters at the referendum. Moreover, as if that was not enough, in January 2013, the Constitutional and Supervisory Committee asked the Venice Commission to evaluate the 2011 Proposal, and it delivered its (draft) Opinion on 11 February.[72] Still more changes were made to the constitutional bill by parliament in the following weeks.

Parliament was dissolved on 28 March 2013 to prepare for the general election, which took place on 27 April. The constitutional bill was debated towards the very end of the parliamentary session. There was some attempt to take out a few issues and to get parliament to approve some articles on e.g. natural resources and public referendums – but without success. Strong voices still argued for the whole document and were not willing to compromise on only limited parts.

Whose proposal? Which document?

Many have argued for the need to accept the Proposal for a New Constitution as a whole. This has, for instance, been the view of the Social Democrats and the Pirate

70 Official website of the Constitutional Society: https://stjornarskrarfelagid.is; and in English: https://stjornarskrarfelagid.is/?page_id=2598

71 Legal experts' letter to Althingi. They presented quite extensive documents and listed around 80 changes to be made to the proposal: www.althingi.is/pdf/skilabref_undirritad.pdf

72 Opinion of the Venice Commission: www.venice.coe.int/webforms/documents/default.aspx?pdffile=CDL-AD(2013)010-e

Party, but these parties also supported its revised version in March 2013.[73] Therefore it is interesting to ask which document they had in mind. The Proposal as originally presented by the Constitutional Council to Parliament on 29 July 2011? Or the Proposal with the changes the Constitutional Council accepted at the three-day meeting in March 2012? Or were they referring to the bill that was debated in parliament in March 2013, which included the legal experts' comments and those of the Venice Commission, together with the changes made by the majority of the Parliamentary Constitutional and Supervisory Committee, led by a member of the Social Democrats and the Left-Greens, with the support of the Pirate Party?

I mainly ask these questions to highlight the complexities we are dealing with when discussing this issue. In 2018, the Constitutional Society published the original Proposal of the Constitutional Council in a book with a preface by a former President of the Republic where it is argued that the 2011 Proposal must be approved by parliament.[74] This, however, overlooks all the work of the majority of parliament, which had initiated the constitutional procedure on the Proposal, as well as the changes made to the 2011 Council's Proposal between August 2011 and March 2013, and takes the discussion back to square one.

Concluding remarks

Although the constitutional reform process in Iceland faced many complications from the start, it also raised fascinating issues and questions about how constitutions should be changed, about interactions between different branches of state power, about public participation and interaction between politics and the public, to name but a few. On the basis of the outline given in this chapter, during the four years between 2009 and 2013, it is safe to say that it was a complex and sometimes rather chaotic process. In my view, the main reason for this is related to the weaknesses in the framework set out by Act 90/2010, which suggested that Parliament could somehow be bypassed by this new constitutional revision procedure, or at least that its role could be minimised. At the beginning of this chapter, I highlighted the ways in which Iceland's 1944 Constitution is amended according to Article 79, namely that amendments must be approved by two successive parliaments, with a parliamentary election in between. Therefore, it was inevitable that Parliament would have to play a leading role from the beginning to the end of the constitutional revision process. Therefore, it would have helped to have a clear plan on how parliament was to handle the text to be drafted by the Constitutional Council and to set this out from the beginning in Act 90/2010

Not only does Parliament have the leading role in changing Iceland's Constitution, but this process also requires a broad consensus, as two parliaments need to

73 Birgitta Jónsdóttir became a member of the Pirate Party after the 2013 election.

74 *The New Iceland's Constitution*. Preface by Vigdís Finnbogadóttir and introduction by Thorvaldur Gylfason (Constitutional Society 2018).

accept the proposed constitutional revision. The debate within parliament reflected deep disagreements amongst members of parliament, and one of the biggest parties (the Independence Party) was against the whole reform process as a matter of principle and from the beginning. In light of this, it should not have come as a surprise that the constitutional bill was not even voted on in parliament before its dissolution in March 2013 ahead of the general election.

The first constitutional bill (March 2009) on electing a Constitutional Assembly was introduced by the Prime Minister, which represents clear leadership on such an important issue. However, the distance between the government and parliament grew during the process, and once the Proposal was being debated in Parliament, the revision procedure was led by the chair of the Constitutional and Supervisory Committee rather than by the Prime Minister.

Revising a constitution, let alone writing a new one, is an enormous task. In the original bill, the Constitutional Assembly was supposed to work in sessions, which would have given time for discussion in between with both Parliament and the public. Even if considerable time was used in parliamentary debate, such as whether to have a Constitutional Assembly, how to respond to the election's invalidation, and whether to have a referendum, little time was in fact allocated to writing the Proposal for a New Constitution – less than four months during these four years.

Iceland's constitutional reform procedure, with its openness and involvement of the public, has been described as a democratic experiment.[75] It engaged the public on different levels, such as attending a National Forum, electing members of the Constitutional Assembly, voting in the 2012 referendum, and involvement in the general debate on constitutional issues. It has been argued that democratic experiments are vital for the development of democracy. With a better educated public and easier access to information and new technology, it is important to look for new ways in which we can develop democracy with more involvement of the public in decision-making.[76]

The word 'experiment' has many different meanings and can be used to describe everything from activities that follow strict scientific or academic methods to be repeated in different settings, to artistic performances or happening which depend on the performer and the atmosphere at the time of the performance. The experiment which took place in Iceland did not follow any given model, and those who were involved needed to do their best along the way. For instance, the Committees which worked within the Constitutional Council all found their own way to complete their tasks under a lot of pressure. Nor is it a model that other countries can use unless the weaknesses discussed in this chapter are acknowledged.

75 Jon Elster, *Securities Against Misrule: Juries, Assemblies, Elections* (CUP 2013), and Hélène Landemore, 'Inclusive Constitution-Making: The Icelandic Experiment' (2015) 23 *Journal of Political Philosophy* 166.

76 Jón Ólafsson, *Lýðræðistilraunir. Ísland í hruni og endurreisn [Democratic Experiments: Iceland in Collapse and Renaissance]* (Háskólaútgáfan 2014).

Analysis of parliament's debates on the 2012 constitutional bill shows that some MPs saw the Constitutional Assembly as an opportunity for rebuilding trust with the public which had been diminished by the financial crisis.[77] This could have been an important step in a healing process, which was much needed after the nation's shock generated a deep distrust of the government, administration, and business sector in Iceland. The revision process took place at a historical moment in Iceland shortly after the financial crisis and gave hopes for change, but instead it became part of a harsh political battle in Icelandic society at the time. It was an experiment in public engagement and raised crucial questions and issues. As such it was thus important for the development of democracy in Iceland. However due to the design failure, the experiment did not provide us with resources or methods to solve the issues and close the debate. This is the main reason why the issues are still unsettled.[78]

77 Nordal (n 3).

78 I am grateful to Þorsteinn Fr. Sigurðsson, the General Manager of the Constitutional Council, for commenting on earlier drafts. I am deeply indebted to Catherine Dupré, editor of this book. While writing this chapter, I have had numerous discussions with her on various issues which she has helped me clarify. I would like to thank her for her enormous help, dedication, and patience during this time.

7 Crowdsourcing the 2011 Proposal for a New Constitution

When experts and the crowd disagree

Jón Ólafsson

Introduction

The Icelandic constitutional reform process has received worldwide attention, and this chapter focusses on the period between July 2009, when the newly elected leftist government (a coalition of two parties, Social Democrats and the Left-Green Movement) first proposed a bill on the Constitutional Assembly, and the end of that electoral term, in April 2013. The Icelandic reform process has been described as the first of a kind and as iconic for new practices of open government, especially for the Constitutional Council's unprecedented engagement with the general public, which has been widely seen as one of the best examples of democratic crowdsourcing and on which this chapter reflects.[1]

Experts – legal experts in particular – were involved in the process in various ways during the time the Constitutional Council was working on its Proposal for a New Constitution, as well as after the Council submitted its Proposal to the Althingi (the Icelandic Parliament) on 29 July 2011. The Council worked both with experts consulted individually and with government officials who were asked to report on various legal issues that arose during the drafting discussion on the Proposal for a new Constitution. Moreover, the Althingi asked for various expert views on some of the aspects of the Proposal, and a group of legal specialists were appointed to assess the document in a technical manner, i.e. look at whether it was likely to achieve what the Constitutional Council intended, and to suggest changes needed to this end.[2] Finally, on 16 November 2012, the Commission of Democracy

1 Hélène Landemore and Tanja Aitamurto, 'Five Design Principles for Crowdsourced Policymaking: Assessing the Case of Crowdsourced Off-Road Traffic Law in Finland' (2015) 2 *Journal of Social Media Organizations* 2.

2 See: List of expert reports and opinions received by the Constitutional Council on the Council's website (www.stjornlagarad.is/starfid/alit/); an overview of expert opinions received by Althingi during the discussion of the Proposal for a New Constitution can be accessed on Althingi's website (www.althingi.is/thingstorf/thingmalin/erindi/?ltg=141&mnr=415); Althingi's group of legal specialists was appointed by the Constitutional and Supervisory Committee on 13 June 2012 (www.althingi.is/thingnefndir/fastanefndir/stjornskipunar-og-eftirlitsnefnd/fundargerdir/?faerslunr=5967). It submitted its report to Parliament on 12 November (www.althingi.is/pdf/skilabref_fylgiskjol.pdf). All sites in this chapter were last accessed 22 August 2019.

through Law, also called the Venice Commission, was invited to evaluate the 2011 Proposal, and it submitted its final Opinion to the Althingi on 11 March 2013.[3]

Yet the critical reaction to the Proposal by some prominent scholars and legal professionals was quite hostile to the effect that a conflict between experts[4] and activist supporters of the Proposal emerged after it was submitted to the Althingi. A central target of this criticism was the lay character of the Proposal and the Constitutional Council's failure to meet the expectations of the academic community. While a conflict of this kind may be unavoidable when non-experts take part in the production of legislative (including constitutional) texts, it also reflects an inability to accept the epistemic contribution of ordinary citizens in political processes. Experts will often have difficulty in distinguishing innovation from error, and they arguably tend to interpret deviation from tradition as the result of the public's ignorance. In my view, an examination of the choices faced by supporters of the constitutional reform process shows that there are good reasons to conclude that some expert criticism of the Proposal for a new Constitution stems from a failure to understand the innovative aspects of public engagement. I will therefore argue in this chapter that, in failing first to provide clear guidance to the Constitutional Council and subsequently in failing to provide a path in Parliament for adopting or rejecting it, the Althingi was unable to counter or utilise such criticisms.

Engaging the public in the constitutional drafting process

The Icelandic constitutional reform process was designed to be fully open and transparent with the possibility of active participation by the public at all stages of the creation of the draft constitution.[5] A Constitutional Commission was appointed by the Althingi and asked to produce materials in preparation for the Constitutional Assembly elected on 27 November 2010.[6] It was also given the task to convene a National Forum, a one-day meeting of around 950 randomly selected citizens, on 6 November 2010, who selected guiding values and visions

3 Commission for Democracy through Law, 'Opinion on the Draft New Constitution of Iceland' (94th Plenary Session March 2013): www.althingi.is/pdf/Feneyjanefnd_skyrsla_e_11_03_2013.pdf

4 In this chapter, I use the word 'expert' in a broad sense to refer to academics, professionals, and other specialists in the field of law, political science, and philosophy.

5 Hélène Landemore has emphasised this aspect of the constitutional process, arguing that transparency was perhaps its greatest novelty. See her 'Inclusive Constitution-Making: The Icelandic Experiment' (2015) 23 *The Journal of Political Philosophy* 166, 180–181.

6 Act 90/2010 and Parliament Announcement 2 July 2010 ('Undirbúningur stjórnlagaþings og þjóðfundar'): www.althingi.is/tilkynningar/nr/18. The Constitutional Commission played an important supportive role in the process. It edited a two-volume Report, which provided the Council with legal and historical analyses of Icelandic constitutional debates after 1944 and even included two different draft constitutions which the Constitutional Council consulted in preparing its Proposal. Guðrún Pétursdóttir and Guðbjörg Eva H. Baldursdóttir (eds), *Skýrsla Stjórnlaganefndar 2011: þjóð til þings* (Stjórnlaganefnd 2011). This is further discussed by Björg Thorarensen (Chapter 5) in this collection.

for a new constitution.[7] Efforts to include the public in the process were continued with the so-called crowdsourcing by the Constitutional Council in the summer of 2011 and, finally, with the advisory referendum held on 20 October 2012.

The Constitutional Council convened its plenary sessions in public, the sessions were streamed on the Internet, and verbatim transcripts of proceedings were made available.[8] Under the Act 90/2010 (explicitly Article 20), the public was encouraged to send formal proposals which were then considered by the appropriate Committee – i.e. at least one of the three Committees of the Council, among which the topics of the emerging draft were divided. Moreover, through social media, anyone could participate in an ongoing discussion of successive drafts, make critical comments and suggestions, and engage in discussion with Constitutional Council members.[9]

Although the term 'crowdsourcing' was employed neither by organisers nor by the Council members to begin with, the unusual openness of the process caught international attention, and before the Constitutional Council had completed its work, the Proposal for a New Constitution was widely known internationally as the 'crowdsourced Icelandic Constitution.'[10] Many organisers and Council members happily accepted this label. It caught their imagination to the extent of becoming one of the main ambitions of the Council to connect with the public. The Council's initial commitment to seek public engagement with the writing process itself, strengthened by international recognition of the process as a unique crowdsourcing experiment, had paradoxical effects. Whereas initially public support was seen as the main source of justification for the Council's work, now public engagement increasingly became the measure of its success. Critics claimed that was in fact less than sufficient to justify the exercise, sometimes making unrealistic demands about participation.[11] It is fair to assume that even though fewer than 2% of Icelanders either participated in the Council's work by sending in comments or by directly observing the discussions taking place on its site, public engagement before and after the Council began its work significantly influenced the Proposal for a New Constitution.[12] Opinion polls have consistently shown around two-thirds support

7 Information on the work and conclusions of the National Forum are available on its website: www.thjodfundur2010.is/english/

8 All this material is still available on the Constitutional Council's website. www.stjornlagarad.is/gagnasafn. See also: Chapter 6 by Salvör Nordal in this collection.

9 Alexander E. Hudson, 'When Does Public Participation Make a Difference? Evidence from Iceland's Crowdsourced Constitution' (2018) 10 *Policy and Internet* 185, 195–196.

10 Eiríkur Bergmann, *Iceland and the International Financial Crisis: Boom, Bust and Recovery* (Palgrave Macmillan 2014) 179.

11 James Fiskhin, 'Rökræðulýðræði og lýðvistaða stjórnarskráin' in Jón Ólafsson (ed), *Lýðræðistilraunir. Ísland í hruni og endurreisn* [*Democratic Experiments: Iceland in Collapse and Renaissanc*] (Háskólaútgáfan 2014) 23, 28–29; Hudson (n 9) 198–199.

12 Hudson (n 9) 201. The paper shows that at least 10% of what the public proposed impacted the Proposal.

for this Proposal, which also suggests that the public did not feel alienated from the project.[13]

A bewildered parliament

When the Althingi received the Constitutional Council's Proposal for a New Constitution in August 2011, it quickly became clear to the general public that MPs had no strategy on how to work with it. This failure is, in my view, the result of three interrelated mistakes which rendered the process extremely vulnerable to attacks from experts. Firstly, when the Constitutional Council submitted its Proposal for a New Constitution to Parliament in 2011, it was not only unclear what was to be done with it. It also seemed unclear what kind of obligations it conferred on the Althingi: the question remained open about what kind of work MPs were supposed or allowed to do on the document. This made it difficult for the Althingi, irrespective of disagreements about the constitutional process, to come to terms with the document itself. Secondly, it will be recalled that the Constitutional Council was not the originally planned Constitutional Assembly (CA) which was elected on 27 November 2010. Since the Icelandic Supreme Court annulled the CA elections on 25 January 2011 because of technical faults, the Althingi, instead of calling new elections, simply appointed the elected Assembly members to form a Constitutional Council.[14] The Council, however, saw its mandate as unchanged, thereby emphasising its independence from the Althingi. Parliament never clarified whether it regarded the Constitutional Council as simply a parliamentary commission or an extra institutional body with a special public role. The lack of clarity made its relation to the Althingi conflicted and damaged the reception of the Proposal for a New Constitution. Thirdly, while the Althingi decided on 24 May 2012 to put the CC Proposal and five additional questions about the constitution to a consultative referendum, it failed to determine in advance how the results should be understood. Since some of the questions put to the people yielded conclusions that were open to interpretation, such as the principal question, which asked whether voters were in favour of making the Proposal for a New Constitution 'a *basis* for a new draft constitution,'[15] this made it difficult to work with the results of the referendum. I will now discuss each of these points in more detail.

13 MMR (Market and Media Research) conducted an opinion poll in the spring of 2012 which showed 66.1% support of making the Constitutional Council's constitutional proposal a 'basis' for a new draft constitution: https://mmr.is/frettir/birtar-nieurstoeeur/249-tveir-trieju-styeja-tilloegur-stjornlaga-raes. A similar survey made in 2017 showed 56% support in getting a new constitution within the next four years: https://mmr.is/frettir/birtar-nieurstoeeur/249-tveir-trieju-styeja-tilloegur-stjornlagaraes

14 Resolution 19/139 of 24 March 2011 (Um skipan Stjórnlagaráðs): www.althingi.is/altext/139/s/1120.htm. Twenty-four of 25 elected Constitutional Assembly members accepted the appointment. The person who had received the 26th place in the elections was therefore appointed to the Constitutional Council.

15 Icelandic: 'Vilt þú að tillögur stjórnlagaráðs verði lagðar til grundvallar frumvarpi að nýrri stjórnarskrá?'

Coming to terms with the 2011 Proposal for a New Constitution

There was some confusion at all stages of the constitutional process, but the confusion in how the Althingi reacted to actually receiving the Constitutional Council's Proposal for a New Constitution was perhaps most consequential. Immediately after the Proposal was submitted to the parliament, a debate began in the media as well as within the political establishment about its completeness and how the parliament should continue working with it. This debate was based partly on trust in institutions, especially the Althingi.[16] One of the reasons of how the work of the Constitutional Council had evolved in 2011 was the low level of public trust in government after the 2008 financial crisis, which had devastating consequences for the Icelandic banking sector and which brought unprecedented financial hardship on a considerable part of the population.[17]

The lack of trust in public institutions, however, had also been used to argue against convening a Constitutional Assembly in the first place since it was claimed that when trust in institutions was limited, constitutional revision ought to reflect that situation rather than help increase trust.[18] Some people felt that this view was given a bold expression in the Supreme Court decision of 25 January 2011 when the Court determined that the results of the elections should be annulled. The Court found several technical flaws that could have made the election vulnerable to attempts to falsify the results, although it was never alleged that fraud had actually been perpetrated.[19] The Supreme Court could easily have justified a decision not to invalidate the elections and recommend that a stricter standard be employed in future. Critics suggested that the technical flaws were used as a pretext by the judges to sabotage a democratic process of which they had little understanding and which they may have seen as a threat to political stability.[20]

Once it started operating, the Constitutional Council consistently ignored other public institutions in its work, such as the Althingi, insisting that this was necessary

16 Annual trust survey by Gallup: www.gallup.is/nidurstodur/thjodarpuls/traust-til-stofnana/

17 Stefanía Óskarsdóttir, 'People versus Politicians: The Political Aftermath of the Financial Crisis in Iceland' (2013) 4 *Open Citizenship*. An open access web version of this article is accessible without page numers: https://oc.citizensforeurope.org/ojs/people-versus-politicians-the-political-aftermath-of-the-financial-crisis-in-iceland/. Concerns about public trust were also expressed in various ways in the parliamentary debates when the original bill on the Constitutional Assembly was proposed to Althingi in 2009. See: Stjórnlagaþing, 1. umr. 12 November 2009 at www.althingi.is/altext/138/11/l12170658.sgml. See especially remarks of Valgerður Bjarnadóttir, chairperson of the Constitutional and Supervisory Committee: www.althingi.is/altext/138/11/r12182341. For further discussion in this collection by Kristrún Heimisdóttir (Chapter 4).

18 See e.g.: Baldur Arnarson, 'Óljós róttækni stjórnlagaráðs' (Interview with Emeritus Professor Sigurður Líndal) *Morgunblaðið* 19 December 2012, 16.

19 Paul Fontaine 'Constitutional Assembly Elections Ruled Invalid' (2011) *Reykjavík Grapevine* 26 January: https://grapevine.is/news/2011/01/25/constitutional-assembly-elections-ruled-invalid/

20 Reynir Axelsson, 'Athugasemdir við ákvörðun Hæstaréttar um ógildingu kosningar til stjórnlagaþings'. A commentary which appeared on numerous blogsites but was never officially published. It can be accessed through the website of Iceland's Constitutional Society: http://stjornarskrarfelagid.is/wp-content/uploads/2011/07/Article_by_Reynir_Axelsson.pdf

in order for the Council to retain its integrity.[21] In addition, it was openly acknowledged by many Council members that they saw the Council's role as an attempt to recapture public trust, and MPs were in general seen as too dependent on protecting antiquated structures serving the common interests of political elites rather than the people.[22] Therefore they were also eager to consult with individuals independently of institutional affiliations.[23] Unfortunately, no common or dominating understanding of the Constitutional Council's role emerged, and this contributed to the confusion about how to understand and assess the Constitutional Council's Proposal. Two issues in particular were contentious. First was the question of whether the Proposal was morally binding, i.e. whether the parliament was morally required to adopt it as it had received it from the CC or whether it could decide not to do so. The second question was whether the Constitutional Council's Proposal for a New Constitution was to be seen as an incomplete text of a future constitution or whether it should be seen as a complete constitutional proposal, i.e. in the sense that it should not be subject to further changes.

Table 7.1 is an illustration of four different ways in which the 2011 Proposal can be understood. Some, though not all, CC members saw it as a complete proposal for a new constitution ready to be voted on immediately by the Althingi. For this group, any changes to the text made by the parliament amounted to an illegitimate

Table 7.1 Moral significance and completeness of the 2011 Proposal

	1 *Proposal morally binding*	*2* *Proposal not morally binding*
A Proposal as a more or less complete text	Only cosmetic changes in order	Take it or leave it (possibly create a counterproposal)
B Proposal as incomplete text	Some (technical) changes in order	Any changes that can be shown to be important in order

21 Jon Elster, 'Icelandic Constitution-Making in a Comparative Perspective' in Valur Ingimundarson, Philippe Urfalino, and Irma Erlingsdottir (eds), *Iceland's Financial Crisis The Politics of Blame, Protest, and Reconstruction* (Routledge 2016) 187; Pasquale Pasquino, 'Constituent Power and Authorization: Anatomy and Failure of a Constitution-Making Process' in Valur Ingimundarson, Philippe Urfalino, and Irma Erlingsdottir (ibid.) 230.

22 A good example of this sentiment is a blog piece by Eiríkur Bergmann, a Constitutional Council member: 'Stjórnlaga hvað?' *DV* (Reykjavík 8 August 2011), http://wayback.vefsafn.is/wayback/20111221081408/www.dv.is/blogg/eirikur-bergmann/2011/8/8/stjornlaga-hvad/. See also: Jón Ólafsson, 'The Icelandic Constituent Assembly: A Study in Failure' in Valur Ingimundarson, Philippe Urfalino, and Irma Erlingsdottir (n 21) 250, 254–255.

23 Eiríkur Bergmann, 'Participatory Constitutional Deliberation in the Wake of Crisis: The Case of Iceland' in Min Reuchamps and Jane Suiter (eds), *Constitutional Deliberative Democracy in Europe* (ESPR press 2016), 24. Jón Ólafsson, 'An Experiment in Iceland: Crowdsourcing a Constitution' (2011) www.academia.edu/1517443/Experiment_in_Iceland_Crowdsourcing_a_Constitution (not otherwise published).

interference, since they also argued that the parliament should be committed to complete the work of the CC by passing a constitutional bill with the text as the CC had prepared it without substantive changes, as well as putting it up for a national referendum (A1). But even if the Proposal was considered complete or final, some observers acknowledged the right of the parliament to reject it (A2).[24] Many supporters of the CC and of the constitutional process, however, thought that the CC's product should be seen as a draft which needed at least to go through some 'technical' evaluation – i.e. changes should be made to ensure that the text would be interpreted by the courts in the way intended by the Constitutional Council. Moreover, certain consequences should also be avoided such as overburdening the state with costs that could be incurred because of one or other provision in the constitution (B1).[25] Finally, there was the view that it was really up to the Althingi to determine what changes would have to be made to get the necessary political support for adoption of the Proposal as the new constitution (B2).[26]

The problem was that consensus or agreement between CC and parliament on either of these two key questions never emerged. Therefore, it remained contested whether the 2011 Constitutional Proposal should be considered morally binding and what that meant, or whether the consultative nature of the Constitutional Council meant that the Althingi could do with the draft what it saw fit.

What kind of institution was the Constitutional Council?

Not only was there no consensus on the constitutional and political status of the Proposal for a New Constitution submitted to the Althingi, but the status of the Constitutional Council itself also remained contested. As will be recalled, the election results were annulled by the Supreme Court, and all but one of the formerly elected Constitutional Assembly members were appointed by the Althingi to sit on a new Constitutional Council. How exactly should that be understood? Were the CC members justified in continuing to see themselves as representing the people? Was the CC just one political institution akin to Parliament, or was it a body that in some meaningful way stood outside of institutional structures? These questions were never answered conclusively, thus giving rise to a few interpretive possibilities represented in Table 7.2.

24 Thorvaldur Gylfason, 'Democracy on Ice: A Post-Mortem of the Icelandic Constitution' *Open Democracy* (19 June 2013): https://www.opendemocracy.net/en/can-europe-make-it/democracy-on-ice-post-mortem-of-icelandic-constitution/

25 Atli Þór Fanndal, 'Fínpússa tillögur stjórnlagaráðs' *DV* (Reykjavík, 14 May 2012) 3; Salvör Nordal, who chaired the CC, in repeated public statements said she had always expected the proposal to be modified in accordance with expert analysis and clarification. See also: Baldur Arnarson, 'Þingmenn skýri spurningarnar' *Morgunblaðið* (Reykjavík, 17 October 2012) 6; Pétur Blöndal, 'Er ný stjórnarskrá í kassanum?' *Morgunblaðið* 21 October 2012, 4.

26 See e.g.: 'Gerðu umtalsverðar breytingar' *Morgunblaðið*, 17 November 2012, 12. For a layperson's view to this effect, see: Óðinn Sigþórsson, 'Heimsmet í að teikna stjórnarskrá' *Morgunblaðið*, 1 March 2012, 23.

Table 7.2 Independence and representativeness of the Constitutional Council

	1 *CC representing the people*	*2* *CC parliament's creation*
A CC an independent forum	Althingi is morally required to continue and complete the CC's work.	Althingi must bring the CC's work to a formal conclusion.
B CC a one task commission	Althingi should work closely with the CC during its discussion of the Proposal.	Althingi has no obligations to CC after receiving Proposal.

In 2009, the perceived need to abandon established institutional structures in order to achieve what politicians could not achieve was one important reason for electing a Constitutional Assembly rather than following the revision procedure under Article 79 of the 1944 Constitution.[27] From this point of view, the CA – and the CC for the same reason – could be seen as an extra-institutional body or at least not simply a new political institution. This would then in fact be the source of its moral authority. The CC, however, was in some sense an institution in itself, even if created to accomplish only one task, and it is fair to say that the non-institutional activist character of the CC remained contested. Moreover, the question of representation remained unanswered. Supporters of the process were inclined to think of CC members as continuing to be elected representatives in spite of the Supreme Court decision to annul the elections. It is fair to point out, however, that the CC could just as well be seen as an appointed parliamentary commission since its formal role was determined by a parliamentary resolution, even if CC members had originally been elected. So, again, we have four interpretive possibilities which lead to different understandings of the political status and legitimacy of the CC.[28]

As can be seen in Table 7.2, clarifying the precise status of the CC is important for understanding the nature of cooperation to be expected between the CC and the parliament. A1 gives us a body which is both independent of institutional structures and representative. B1 gives us a body which should seek to work with the Althingi on an institutional level. A2 presents the case where the CC is importantly a parliamentary commission but still representing the public. B2 shows the case where the CC is simply a commission created by the Althingi and is not representative.

27 Explanatory Notes to Act 90/2010 on the Constitutional Assembly, Althingi 138th Session, 2009–2010: www.althingi.is/altext/138/s/0168.html

28 Resolution 19/139 (n 14). The Resolution states that the Constitutional Commission is to prepare for the work of the Constitutional Council in accordance with Act 90/2010 on the Constitutional Assembly. It did not explicitly say that the new Constitutional Council should be bound by that law. Instead it stated anew, albeit quite briefly, the tasks of the Council and therefore in fact gave it more independence to plan its work than Act 90/2010 had done.

Which option is the correct one? No single one is. The tragedy of the CC is precisely that this question remained unresolved and the status of the Council contested. The failure of the Althingi to clarify the Constitutional Council's status before appointing its members arguably increased the confusion around the constitutional reform process which, of course, did not facilitate any reconciliation with the project for those who positioned themselves against it. Moreover, because of the parliament's indecisiveness and the Supreme Court's intervention, the CC's Proposal for a New Constitution needed strong support to overcome political opposition, as well as to defend and justify its radically innovative approach to changing the Constitution. As repeated opinion polls have shown, this did not lead to rejection by the Icelandic public of the Proposal for a New Constitution itself, but it may have contributed to public apathy about the Proposal.[29] Foreign visitors observed that there seemed to be much more enthusiasm about the constitutional experiment abroad than within Iceland.[30] Finally, the Constitutional Council had two characteristics which affected its work in different ways. On the one hand, it was a deliberative forum in which the general content and spirit of the future Icelandic constitution was to be discussed, debated, and to some extent resolved. This was expected to happen in the four months that the CC was given to complete its work. On the other hand, it was a body that had been given the task of submitting a certain document, i.e. a constitutional proposal (or at least a text that would then be put forward in the form of a constitutional bill) to be adopted by the parliament. The first task certainly generated support and interest among the public. This, however, does not mean that the great majority also believed in the success of the project – i.e. that it would overcome legal and political hurdles and eventually produce a document that would replace the 1944 Constitution. It is therefore no paradox that the public could be at the same time supportive of the project to revise the Constitution and yet sceptical about its success in terms of delivering a new constitution.[31]

29 Results of opinion polls by Market and Media Research (MMR) from 12–17 April 2012 (summary in Icelandic): https://mmr.is/images/stories/PDF/1204_mmr_tilkynning_stjornarskra.pdf. These results showed similar support of the CC Proposal for a new Constitution as the national referendum on 20 October 2012. Surveys made by MMR in September 2017 and October 2018 showed 56% and 52% support for a new constitution, not specifying whether it should be based on the CC Proposal. See main results: https://mmr.is/frettir/birtar-nieurstoeeur/640-meirihluti-vill-nyja-stjornarskra and https://mmr.is/leitarnidurstodur?searchword=stjórnarskrá&searchphrase=al. Other surveys, e.g. on support of political parties, clearly indicate a continuing majority support. See: MMR survey from January 2015 where 60% of respondents trust the parties that supported the Proposal to 'lead a revision effort of the constitution'; results available at: https://mmr.is/frettir/birtar-nieurstoeeur/453-theim-faekkar-sem-treysta-sjalfstaedhisflokknum-fyrir-innflytjendamalum

30 I am referring here to more than one personal conversation during the 2011 drafting process. Among my interlocutors was Tom Ginsburg who later co-authored an assessment of the 2011 Proposal for a New Constitution; see: Zachary Elkins, Tom Ginsburg, and James Melton, 'A Review of Iceland's Draft Constitution' (2012) Comparative Constitutions Project: https://comparativeconstitutionsproject.org/wp-content/uploads/CCP-Iceland-Report.pdf?6c8912

31 Jón Ólafsson, 'Þekkingarmiðað lýðræði – þegar þekking lýðsins ræður' (2016) 12 *Icelandic Review of Politics and Administration* 511, 528–531; Jón Ólafsson and Katrín Oddsdóttir, 'Fer biðinni að ljúka?' *Kjarninn* (Reykjavík, 20 June 2017).

Due to weaknesses caused by these ambiguities, the Proposal for a New Constitution was particularly vulnerable to attacks once it had been submitted. The Althingi was unable to present its vision for bringing the CC's work to completion, and, instead of celebrating the innovative aspects of the document and the strengths of the CC's work, including its somewhat revolutionary vision of what the new constitution should look like, scholarly scepticism prevailed about most aspects of the Constitutional Council work.[32]

Furthermore, the CC's independence arguably increased the vulnerability of the project. The Constitutional Council, as will be recalled, started working in April 2011 and spent the first few weeks debating how to proceed. During this initial phase, the Althingi gave no further guidance to the CC's members, apart from what Act 90/2010 on the Constitutional Assembly and Resolution 19/139 on the Constitutional Council stated. It was therefore up to the CC itself to decide whether and to what extent it would base its work on the Report provided by the Constitutional Commission, which certainly contained a lot of material sanctioned by legal experts, including the two possible versions of a new constitution produced by the Constitutional Commission. Full freedom to determine its task and course of action, in my view, undermined the work of the CC and partly explains the difficulty for the Althingi to work with it.[33]

Normative implications of the 2012 referendum

On 20 October 2012, more than one year after the Constitutional Council submitted its Proposal for a New Constitution to the Icelandic parliament, an advisory referendum was held on the Proposal. The principal question of the referendum was: 'Do you wish the Constitutional Council's Proposal to form the basis of a new draft constitution?'. Some 67% of the voters supported a new Icelandic constitution 'based on' the 2011 Proposal for a New Constitution, and a majority did agree with the Constitutional Council's Proposal on four out of five additional key issues, on which voters were asked to express their opinion. These included a provision on public ownership of natural resources and on the right of a certain percentage of the electorate to demand referendum on legislation passed by the Althingi.[34] The Althingi had passed a resolution on the referendum on 24 May 2012 after lengthy debates on what to ask and how to formulate the questions. Given experts'

32 A fairly complete and thorough philosophical criticism of the Constitutional Council can be found in Vilhjálmur Árnason, 'Valdið fært til fólksins? Veikleikar og verkefni íslensks lýðræðis í aðdraganda og eftirmála hrunsins' (2013) 187 *Skírnir* 11. A milder tone is struck in Vilhjálmur Árnason, 'Icelandic Politics in Light of Normative Models of Democracy' (2018) 14 *Icelandic Review of Politics and Administration. Special Issue on Power and Democracy in Iceland* 35, 53–54.

33 Jón Ólafsson (n 22) 252–272.

34 An informational website was created by the Institute for Legal Studies at the University of Iceland at the Althingi's request, to help voters become oriented in the various questions about the constitution and the work of the Constitutional Council. An English version of it was also made available: www.thjodaratkvaedi.is/2012/en/index.html

misgivings, as well as the hotly contested status of the Proposal, it was a logical step to try to renew the legitimacy of the project and to clarify the status of the Proposal for a New Constitution by holding a referendum. This, however, proved an elusive goal as the referendum questions, including the principal question, arguably raised more questions than they settled.[35]

Immediately after the referendum, some MPs, mostly from the Independence Party, voiced their opinion that the results of the referendum were not to be taken seriously. Two arguments were made to justify this. First was that, with participation at 48.9%, the referendum could not be taken as a reliable measure of public support for the Proposal for a New Constitution.[36] Second, for many observers, criticism of the Council's Proposal by philosophers, political scientists, and legal experts was serious enough to raise doubts about the wisdom of enacting it at all. Since repeated surveys suggest that the referendum does reflect public opinion in Iceland, I will not dwell on the first point. The second point, however, did expose real vulnerabilities. Given the expert criticism, so forcefully presented in the weeks and months after the referendum, it was not totally unreasonable for some MPs to feel justified in arguing that there were strong reasons not to abide by the result of the referendum. If elected representatives have a choice between one option which enjoys public support but may create considerable uncertainty in public administration, and another option which is supported by specialists that can convincingly be shown to be for the better – how should they proceed?[37]

To make things even more difficult, the results arguably allowed for more than one interpretations. Although they reflected a general support of the CC's work as surveys had always indicated, it was not obvious what the majority meant by voting for 'basing a new draft constitution' on the 2011 Proposal. Starting a few weeks after the referendum and, as many thought, in reaction to it, four Icelandic universities jointly organised a series of public meetings where political scientists and legal specialists presented their critical assessments of the Constitutional Council's Proposal.[38] At these meetings, strong doubts were voiced about the

35 Resolution proposal and the debates in the Althingi: www.althingi.is/thingstorf/thingmalalistar-eftir-thingum/ferill/?ltg=140&mnr=636

36 This argument has mainly come from observers and politicians associated with the Independence Party. See e.g.: Birgir Ármannsson, 'Allt eða ekkert í stjórnarskrármáli' *Morgunblaðið* 28 October 2016, 23.

37 Birgir Ármannsson, an MP for the conservative Independence Party, in an opinion piece, presses this point, arguing that in an unstable political environment, radical constitutional changes will simply cause chaos and rhetorically asks: 'Is chaos the answer to instability? ['Er upplausn svarið við óstöðugleika?'] *Morgunblaðið* 5 October 2017, 43.

38 Speakers were selected Icelandic scholars, including law professors Ragnhildur Helgadóttir, Björg Thorarensen, Skúli Magnússon, and Hafsteinn Þór Hauksson; political science professors Indriði Indriðason, Gunnar Helgi Kristinsson, Ólafur Þ. Harðarson, Stefanía Óskarsdóttir, and Ómar H. Kristmundsson. The Institute of Public Administration and Politics at the University of Iceland posted information about the meetings as well as the slides used and recordings of talks on its website (http://stjornsyslustofnun.hi.i). The meetings were well attended by the public and by MPs. The recordings, unfortunately, have been lost by the Institute.

Proposal, which considerably increased insecurity among MPs who had previously supported it.[39] This situation created an epistemic challenge for MPs who must, on the one hand, take care to act in accordance with the express will of their constituencies rather than seek justifications not to do so or, in the case of MPs, find reasons to put the legitimacy of the democratic process in doubt. On the other hand, MPs should also be committed to finding the best solutions and form policies that they sincerely believe are for the common good. It is the classic dilemma of representative politics: to do both what the public wants and what is for the best.[40] Since the parliamentary majority had already allowed a broader debate on the wisdom of revising the Constitution to take place and failed to use the public support of the project to insist on finding a way to move the project forward, this dilemma, together with the interpretive difficulty, had disastrous consequences.[41]

The referendum results could have provoked various kinds of action by the Althingi. However, its advisory nature meant that its results did not bind the parliament to any specific action. In spite of this, the results might have been expected to stimulate some action, such as a clear declaration by majority leaders that they would make sure that the parliament would now act in accordance with the referendum results. And, what is worse, real discussion on how to interpret the results and act hardly took place. The main interpretive question was how the term 'basis' (*grundvöllur*) is properly understood and further what kind of discussion this required, since voters overwhelmingly were in favour of making the Proposal a 'basis' for a new draft constitution – i.e. a constitutional bill to be further discussed by the Althingi. For instance, what limitations should be put on possible changes, and how should the fundamental issues in the Proposal be identified? This important discussion unfortunately was never taken up by the Althingi.

The referendum, it can be argued, instead of renewing the legitimacy of the Constitutional Council and reopening an opportunity for the Althingi to bring the project to conclusion, did the opposite. Namely, weak and failed mechanisms for directing the work of the CC, as well as unclarity about its status contributed to a deadlock whereby leaders of the political parties who had supported the constitutional revision process lost confidence in pursuing the matter within the parliament. My conclusion is that the Althingi failed in its democratic obligations by neglecting to clearly define the task and character of the Constitutional Council

39 Majority opinion by the Althingi's Constitutional and Supervisory Committee, 26 January 2013: www.althingi.is/altext/141/s/0947.html

40 Some supporters of the Constitutional Council and especially former Council members experienced these conferences as staged – a deliberate attempt to undermine the project after its success in the referendum. See e.g.: Vilhjálmur Þorsteinsson, 'Vondur fundur um stjórnarskrána' (Personal blog, 9 November 2012, https://blog.dv.is/vthorsteinsson/2012/11/09/vondur-fundur-um-stjornarskrana/), Þorvaldur Gylfason, 'Fræðasamfélagið og frumvarpið' *DV* (Reykjavík, 11 January 2013).

41 See e.g.: Ragnheiður Elín Árnadóttir 'Vöndum okkur – það er hægt að ná sátt' *Morgunblaðið* 23 October 2012, 19; Birgitta Jónsdóttir 'Skyggnilýsingarfundir í Valhöll' *DV* (Reykjavík, 24 October 2012) 15; 'Ber að fylgja þjóðaratkvæðagreiðslu um ekki neitt?' Editorial, *Morgunblaðið* 25 October 2012, 20.

to begin with, and by not presenting a clear and practical strategy to work with the Proposal for a new Constitution (as demonstrated in Table 7.2). These failings might have been reverted by fully respecting the referendum results. As I have suggested, however, it is not unreasonable from a democratic point of view for MPs to be swayed by strong experts' criticisms of a proposal or a policy. I will now discuss the character of that criticism, audible from the very beginning of the process in 2009 but presented in a forceful manner after the referendum. I will then move on to a discussion of why expert criticism should not have been as consequential as it was.[42]

Enter the wise: expert criticism of the 2011 Proposal for a New Constitution

The 90/2010 Act on the Constitutional Assembly was created with the explicit intention of engaging the public in discussing and thinking about constitutional matters during the constitutional revision process. The instructions on how to achieve this were, however, rather vague. The Explanatory Notes to the 90/2010 Act only contain references to historical social contract theories, suggesting a certain idealisation of the philosophical background without relation to contemporary democratic theory.[43]

The Constitutional Council used its own ad hoc online archive which contained a lot of material related to its task. While rather incomplete, this selection was designed to be helpful for anyone wanting to start some explorations in addition to taking part in online or face-to-face discussions on the emerging constitutional Proposal.[44] Some scholars specialising in this field found the archive too limited to be taken seriously. In particular, Indriði H. Indriðason, a professor of political science at University of California Riverside, who followed the process closely and offered scholarly and practical comments, made a mockery of it.[45] Indriðason

42 Newly elected leaders of the governing coalition parties, Katrín Jakobsdóttir (Left-Green Movement) and Árni Páll Árnason (Social Democrats), together with the leader of one of the opposition parties Guðmundur Steingrímsson (Bright Future), reached a compromise with the other parties in the parliament to put the issue on hold but to simplify the procedure for changing the Constitution. Technically, this amendment simplified a revision of the Constitution, but since an enlarged majority would be needed to pass a constitutional bill, it was not politically realistic to expect that the Constitutional Council's Proposal for a new Constitution would be revived (see Bill on Constitutional amendment, 1139–641, 6 March 2013: www.althingi.is/altext/141/s/1139.htm). The bill was passed on 28 March 2013. It was adopted a second time after the elections as Constitutional Act 91/2013, whereby the Constitution was temporarily amended: www.althingi.is/altext/142/s/0088.html

43 Explanatory Notes to Act 90/2010: www.althingi.is/altext/138/s/0168.html. See especially Parts 4 and 5 of the commentary that follows the proposed articles, where historical examples of Constituent Assemblies are discussed, and references are made to seventeenth- and eighteenth-century political theory.

44 The archive is available at the Constitutional Council's website, http://stjornlagarad.is/gagnasafn/

45 Indriði H. Indriðason, The Constitutional Council, a personal website: www.constitutionalassembly.politicaldata.org. The first entry was posted 15 November 2010, and the last one just before the parliamentary elections on 26 April 2013.

offered his own list, 'by no means complete,' of 80 books and articles that should be 'required' for those who had volunteered to write a new constitution.[46] In a talk given at one of the previously mentioned conferences at the University of Iceland after the 2012 referendum, he pointed out that only a very small part of sources listed on the Constitutional Council's website were from political science, that none of the specialist memos used by the Council were drafted by political scientists, and that only one of the specialists who actually met with the Council was a political scientist:

> [T]he fact that the Council has almost completely ignored the work of political scientists – the very people that actually study these issues – is puzzling and the only explanation that I can think of is that its members were simply unaware of what political science is.[47]

Another political scientist, Gunnar Helgi Kristinsson, professor at the University of Iceland and an experienced advisor to the government on administrative reform, equally severely criticised the Constitutional Council for having expanded its mandate and decided to write a new constitution instead of focussing on the parts of the 1944 Constitution that really needed revision. Kristinsson argued that since the Constitutional Council had in fact no democratic mandate, this was not politically viable. He also argued that it was intellectually unsound due to the lack of adequate knowledge resources and research. According to him, the 2011 Proposal for a New Constitution can be understood as a 'wish list' rather than as a complete proposal for a whole new constitution.[48]

It should be pointed out that while the original statute on the Constitutional Assembly was quite detailed about the Assembly's work, the 19/139 Resolution that created the Constitutional Council after the invalidation of the Constitutional Assembly elections only contained the list of topics that the Council was

46 Indriði H. Indriðason, The Constitutional Council, Required Readings: www.constitutionalassembly.politicaldata.org/Leslisti.pdf.

47 Indriðason gave his talk (which was not published) in Icelandic. He does have a summary of his remarks, however, on his Constitutional Council website. The quote is taken from there: www.constitutionalassembly.politicaldata.org/?p=41. As a specialist employed by a prestigious university abroad, Indriðason's reputation was quite strong and his comments biting. He later also accused supporters of the Constitutional Council and former Council's members of dishonesty for interpreting positive comments on the constitutional project made by Tom Ginsburg, Zachary Elkins, and James Melton as an endorsement of the Constitutional Council's work. These comments were made in a paper on the draft constitution that compared it to other constitutions using a methodology Ginsburg, Elkins, and Melton had developed as a part of the Comparative Constitutional Project (n 30). Indriðason further claimed in an interview with the daily newspaper *Morgunblaðið* that the Icelandic supporters of the constitution were trying deliberately to deceive the public (Baldur Arnarson, 'Kasta ryki í augu fólks' *Morgunblaðið* 12 January 2013, 14).

48 Gunnar Helgi Kristinsson 'Ráðskast með stjórnarskrá' (2012) 8 *International Review of Public Administration*, 565, 568. Indeed, one may argue that the Council's decision was unwise. See: Jón Ólafsson (n 22) 255.

specifically asked to consider. Although the task was the same, the Council was basically left free to decide how to proceed. Both the Act 90/2010 and the Resolution state that, in addition to the key issues listed, the Assembly/Council was authorised to consider other issues too.[49] Whether that meant that the Council was authorised to do what it did – i.e. not only consider other issues but in fact write a new constitution – was never conclusively answered.

Both Kristinsson and Indriðason submitted more detailed commentary on particular aspects of the Proposal to the Althingi's Constitutional and Supervisory Committee, as part of the parliamentary process, but since my interest here is in the general character of their remarks, I will not discuss their content as such. Kristinsson's commentary focusses on five topics in the Constitutional Council's 2011 Proposal for a New Constitution: on elections to Parliament, on the President of Iceland, on presidential elections, on the role of the President in forming government, and on national referendums. In all cases, his commentary rehearses general reservations about the Constitutional Council's Proposal and complaints that neither are those proposals clearly argued for nor is the need for them sufficiently well explained. Indriðason emphasised the reading list he felt constitution-makers needed to be familiar with.[50]

Legal specialists also criticised the Council's Proposal for a New Constitution from a related point of view, arguing that the lack of legal knowledge had resulted in a document difficult for the courts to interpret. The most scathing criticisms attacked the structure of the draft itself, pointing out that it was a mix, i.e. that the Proposal conflated legal traditions in a way that might create unsurmountable problems for legal interpretation which could in the worst case lead to a constitutional crisis.[51] Unlike political scientists, the legal specialists who criticised the Proposal did not directly attack the Constitutional Council itself for the technical ignorance of its members or for exceeding its mandate, but in the discussion that ensued after the Constitutional Council submitted its Proposal for a New Constitution to the Althingi, it became clear that many of them thought that the document needed to be substantially revised to avoid serious problems of interpretation in due course.[52]

49 Act 90/2010 (n 6); Resolution 19/139 (n 14).

50 Gunnar Helgi Kristinsson, 'Minnisblöð um stjórnarskrá' 20 August 2012; Indriði H. Indriðason, 'A Letter to Althingi's Constitutional and Supervisory Committee' 13 December 2012. Both are accessible on: www.althingi.is/thingstorf/thingmalin/erindi/?ltg=141&mnr=415. Kristinsson wrote his commentary at the request of the group of legal specialists, appointed on 13 June 2012.

51 Skúli Magnússon and Ágúst Þór Árnason: 'Erindi nr. Þ. 140/909' January 18, 2012 10. (Comments on the Constitutional Bill sent to Althingi's Constitutional and Supervisory Committee (www.althingi.is/altext/erindi/140/140-909.pdf). Björg Thorarensen, 'Constitutional Reform Process in Iceland – Involving the People in the Process', Oslo-Rome International Workshop on Democracy (Oslo, November 2011). Kristrún Heimisdóttir, a legal specialist with some expertise in constitutional law made a similar argument: 'Gerðu umtalsverðar breytingar' *Morgunblaðið* 17 November 2012, 12. For further discussion in this collection, see Chapter 8 by Skúli Magnússon.

52 Some comparative research on the proposed constitution gave it a passing grade, predicting that it would have a longer than average lifetime, if it were to be adopted. See: Elkins, Ginsburg, and Melton (n 30).

On a less forceful note, Ragnhildur Helgadóttir, pointed out that the mix of traditions should be seen as the result of extensive borrowing from other various other constitutions (27 were identified all in all), which was not bad in itself. She argued that borrowings were mostly 'the result of considered, well-supported choices.' Yet the problems could not be ignored and clearly warranted an 'impact and workability assessment [. . .] before the enacting of the constitution.'[53]

Thus, political scientists and the legal specialists argued that the Constitutional Council had made decisions without the necessary foresight and that the actual consequences of adopting the Constitutional Council Proposal without major changes might be very different from what its authors had intended. This criticism, when taken as a whole, implies that only specialists could effectively foresee and thus prevent such disasters.[54]

Limits of expert wisdom and the contribution of the ignorant

While it is difficult to disagree with the claim that consulting specialist literature and research in the relevant field has beneficial effects when revising an existing constitution or adopting a new one, there is a deeper question at stake which goes right to the heart of democracy itself: if the creation, revision, and competent criticism of political institutions must be based exclusively on expert knowledge, which only few people can claim to possess, should we not also have strict conditions limiting participation of the public in policy and decision-making?

This argument, taken to extremes, might lead one to favour 'epistocracy' over democracy. In a weaker form, it leads to the weaker claim that some minimal expertise must be acquired by those who assume roles to revise or adopt constitutions or indeed ordinary legislation. We can call this 'the argument of necessary expertise,' whereby expertise need not mean more than having knowledge of relevant literature, familiarity with key concepts in the field, historical knowledge of past efforts, and some skill in acquiring new knowledge in the field. This view, however, ignores key characteristics of the collective efforts and co-creation processes, the strength of which mainly lies in how different and even contradictory pieces of experience and knowledge are meaningfully gathered in such a cooperative endeavour. In the case of the Constitutional Council, the fact that there were three political scientists among Council members should suffice to dismiss

53 Ragnhildur Helgadóttir, 'Lessons Concerning Constitutional Borrowing from the Icelandic Draft Constitution' (2011), www.academia.edu/8244150/Lessons_Concerning_Constitutional_Borrowing_from_the_Icelandic_Draft_Constitution_2011?auto=download. Not otherwise published.

54 The group of legal specialists appointed by the Althingi on 13 June 2012 was asked to make suggestions of a 'technical' nature about improvements to the draft constitution, where the goal was to adjust the legal language of the document to avoid interpretive deadlocks; see: Skúli Hansen. 'Sérfræðingahópur gerði fjölda breytinga' *Morgunblaðið* 14 November 2012, 16. Interestingly when the Venice Commission later published its Opinion on the draft (n 3), it criticised some of the changes made by the legal specialists, apparently unaware of the team's work.

Indriðason's remark, quoted earlier, that its members were 'unaware of what political science is.'[55] This remark implies that the Council should work not as a facilitator of public engagement, but rather as a kind of expert group, with its effort to harness views, experiences, and pieces of knowledge by public engagement not being considered to have any independent value.[56]

The argument of necessary expertise is important in the discussion of participatory processes since it concerns the way in which they are or can be knowledge driven. Clearly, if we take this argument seriously, we would expect everyone who is selected or who volunteers to participate in a decision-making process to make an effort to increase his or her theoretical knowledge about the task at hand, just as we don't want people who volunteer in disaster relief or peacekeeping to be complete novices or send them to the field without the training necessary to be useful. The problem with this view is in the nature of the task. While public choices must be informed by the best available knowledge, such knowledge is arguably not exhausted by the point of view that the expert provides by proposing solutions to narrowly defined problems. To demand that someone acquire a certain amount of specialised knowledge before he or she actually qualifies for participation in decision-making processes ignores the incomplete and discontinuous parts of relevant knowledge and experience that any individual brings to a decision-making process. It therefore imposes a standard of knowledge designed to exclude what is assumed to be ignorance rather than to include knowledge in its diversity. Since the ignorance is ignorance on a narrow range of things, knowledge on a wide range of potentially (but not always or necessarily) important things is excluded. However, thereby the potential for finding the best solutions and decisions is seriously reduced: the specialist filter limits the range of options to the specialist's horizon.[57]

As a result, the argument of necessary expertise (a constraint on inclusion to a policy-making project) must be countered by an 'argument of necessary diversity.' According to this argument, it is certainly important that findings of political science are considered in a constitution-making or -revising process. However, it

55 These members are Eiríkur Bergmann, professor at Bifröst University; Silja Bára Ómarsdóttir, lecturer at the University of Iceland; and Ástrós Gunnarsdóttir, who finished an undergraduate degree in political science in 2010. It might be added that four members of the Council had a degree in law, which also suggests that at least some specialist knowledge was available within the Council in that field. There were also three medical doctors – in fact, the Council's educational background was strong. Nineteen out of 25 Council members had university degrees. See: 'Fulltrúar í Stjórnlagaráði.' at http://stjornlagarad.is/fulltruar.

56 Vilhjálmur Árnason (2013) (n 32).

57 The argument here rests on old and new literature: we can see John Dewey arguing in this way in his well known *The Public and Its Problems* (1927). Scott Page makes a similar argument in *The Difference* (2007). An impressive illustration of it, however, is made in Sidney Lumet's film *12 Angry men* (1957), where a jury discussion reveals a number of relevant considerations which together make it obvious that a murder defendant cannot be guilty. Each jury member has knowledge or experience relevant to reaching this conclusion, but only the discussion that brings them together can make use of the various bits and pieces.

would not be less important to have a broad range of other insights, experiences, lessons, knowledge, and perspectives. This argument further implies that not only does political equality demand inclusion without qualification, i.e. inclusion regardless of epistemic background; it also demands epistemic diversity in order to provide access to knowledge otherwise excluded from the deliberation process. In other words, the seemingly irrelevant experiences of participants may turn out to be not only major sources of knowledge providing valuable insights in policy-making processes, but in fact furnish pieces of information whose value depends on that particular context and that can be identified and judged by a non-expert, problem-solving collective.

There is a strong tendency in political theory to worry about the participation of the (presumed) ignorant.[58] In contemporary democratic society, however, the flow of information should arguably neither be controlled nor to any significant degree restricted. Ignorance of some things is not necessarily due to deprivation but to social orientation, cultural background, education, etc. Every citizen is to some extent specialised as well as being ignorant of various things. Therefore, the ignorant have a place and function in participatory processes that aim at eliciting the people's experience and insights, regardless of particular cognitive skills or specialised knowledge.[59] This, it goes without saying, does not suggest that specialised knowledge is unimportant. It simply shows that citizens coming from different parts of society, with different information, quantitatively and qualitatively, are collectively well equipped to engage in planning and policy-making for a society they commonly belong to. The role of experts, although important, must be demarcated very clearly. In an open and inclusive society, political knowledge, knowledge about how public processes work, and an understanding of what kind of problems should be addressed by public institutions are in most cases gained by participation rather than primarily by academic study. Specialists, professionals, and scholars alike, who are trained in well-defined and often quite narrow subjects, may lack the experience, insights, and overview that non-specialists have.

This is not to say that laws should be passed, or policy planned, without consulting specialists, rather only that the power of making decisions should not be given over to experts. Moreover, if public consultation and engagement should be considered a necessary part of policy-making, it is because among the public there will be more relevant, fine-tuned, and diverse experiences and insights to deal with many different cases than among either elected officials or experts. Yet the idea of empowerment through public engagement seems to evoke doubts and resistance,

58 Ilya Somin, 'Why Political Ignorance Undermines the Wisdom of the Many' (2014) 26 *Critical Review* 151; Jason Brennan, 'How Smart Is Democracy? You Can't Answer That Question a Priori' (2014) 26 *Critical Review* 33.

59 For a discussion of the consequences of ignorance see e.g.: Simon T. Kaye, 'Democracy despite Ignorance: Questioning the Veneration of Knowledge in Politics' (2015) 27 *Critical Review*, 316, 332–335; Hélène Landemore, 'Deliberation, Cognitive Diversity, and Democratic Inclusiveness: An Epistemic Argument for the Random Selection of Representatives' (2014) 190 *Synthese* 1209, 1224–1228.

within governmental administrations – where such efforts are frequently seen as either mere pretence or just a waste of time – and among those theorists who claim that general ignorance, as well as the lack of political knowledge, makes empowerment through participation undesirable.[60]

Conclusion

One of the central issues of contemporary democracy is how political decision-making is streamlined to concur with best current knowledge and experience. Wide public engagement in policy-making and decision-making (such as attempted by the Constitutional Council) is an effort to channel the public's knowledge (or 'the wisdom of the crowd') into political processes. Such attempts are vulnerable to many kinds of criticism and attacks from powerful interest groups, from conservative parties and movements, and, significantly, from scholars and experts who feel that state–of-the-art knowledge will go amiss if the ignorant public is given a determining role.

In this chapter, I have discussed the Icelandic constitutional process 2009–2013 as a successful experiment in public engagement. Its success makes it particularly important to explain why the Constitutional Council ultimately still failed in the sense that a new constitution was not adopted. I have explored some of the main reasons here, which I claim are:

- The project lacked necessary institutional support.
- The Constitutional Council was given too much independence to choose its own approach and strategy.
- Parliament neglected to prepare the ground, politically and conceptually, for receiving the 2011 Proposal for a New Constitution and bringing it to an acceptable conclusion in the parliament (i.e. by passing or rejecting it).
- The attempt to clarify the status of the Proposal by conducting a national referendum failed to give a clear message to MPs.
- The expert community put up formidable resistance against the project in a series of academic conferences, held at a crucial stage in the process.

We can also look at the Constitutional Council's failure from the point of view of its principal rationale: engaging the public. Public engagement in legislative and constitutional efforts should achieve two objectives. First, it must empower. It must truly give the public a voice that it previously lacked. Engagement cannot

60 Vilhjálmur Árnason, 'Democratic Practices, Governance and the Financial Crash' in Valur Ingimundarson, Philippe Urfalino, and Irma Erlingsdottir (n 21) 121, 131–133. For the discussion on epistocracy see: Catherine Holst, 'What is Epistocracy? Dimensions of Knowledge-based Rule' in Simen Andersen Øyen, Tone Lund-Olsen, and Nora Sørensen Vaage (eds), *Sacred Science: On Science and Its Interrelations with Religious Worldviews* (Wageningen Publishers 2012) 41–54. On consulting the crowd, see: James Surowiecki, *The Wisdom of Crowds: Why the Many Are Smarter Than the Few* (Abacus 2004) 262.

be successful unless it creates a visible public role. Second, it must be effective. If great efforts and fanfare around a public engagement project do not lead to substantive change in policy, cynicism should not come as a surprise.

The Constitutional Council achieved the first objective quite well. Not only did it present a force that the public by and large recognised as legitimate (this, at least, can be concluded by the public support shown in opinion polls); its visibility has extended far beyond its lifetime, both in Iceland and internationally where it continues to attract interest among media, practitioners, and academics. The second objective, however, it did not achieve. Its work has, so far, not resulted in any constitutional change, and its Proposal is not likely ever to become a basis of a new constitution, even though politicians do express willingness to take it into account in future revision efforts.

In order to understand the failure of the Constitutional Council to achieve the second objective, both the particular epistemic character of public engagement and the importance of clear institutional structures must be put in the foreground. This I have tried to do in the chapter. It is, I believe, fair to conclude that since the epistemic character of public engagement was poorly understood, it was simply difficult for politicians, scholars, the general public, and even practitioners to fully grasp what the Constitutional Council had done.

Part III

Constitutional proposals and bills